PROGRAMMING IN PASCAL

PROGRAMMING

Vladimir Zwass

in PASCAL

BARNES & NOBLE BOOKS
A DIVISION OF HARPER & ROW, PUBLISHERS
New York, Cambridge, Philadelphia, San Francisco,
London, Mexico City, São Paulo, Singapore, Sydney

FIRST EDITION

Designer: Charlotte Staub

Library of Congress Cataloging in Publication Data

Zwass, Vladimir.
 Programming in PASCAL.

 (College outline series; CO/201)
 Includes index.
 1. PASCAL (Computer program language) I. Title.
II. Series.
QA76.73.P2Z88 1984   001.64′24   84–47615
ISBN 0–06–460201–X (pbk.)

---

85 86 87 88 89 10 9 8 7 6 5 4 3 2 1

For Joshua Jonathan

CONTENTS

4. Boolean and Character Data 60

5. Control of Program Execution Flow: Fundamental Structures 74

6. Type Definition. New Ordinal Data Types 98

7. Supplementary Control Statements 108

Part Two. MODULAR PROGRAMMING

Introduction. Goals of Modular Programming 126

8. Procedures 129

PREFACE

This book teaches computer programming with the use of Pascal. It is designed for individual study, for direct classroom use, or as an aid to understanding concepts presented in the classroom. It is also meant to serve as a review book and a reference manual. Complete Pascal is discussed. At the same time, techniques are taught which should enable the student to transfer his or her skills to another programming language.

One does not become a programmer by learning a programming language construct by construct. One must learn to analyze the problem, to select or design an algorithm on which the program will be based, and then to use the programming language in a methodical fashion to express thoughts (rather than code in a helter-skelter manner). Only such a program, fully documented, may be expected to work reliably and be amenable to modifications (to which all practical programs are subject sooner or later).

Pascal is an excellent language with which to learn programming skills. It was designed in the late 1960s and early '70s by Professor Niklaus Wirth of the Swiss Federal Institute of Technology (ETH) in Zurich as:

- a higher-level language offering fundamental programming constructs in a natural and simple fashion, developed expressly for teaching and practicing programming as a systematic, design-oriented discipline; and
- a language efficient in its implementation, thanks to careful selection of control structures and data types.

It has since acquired wide popularity.

The language was named after Blaise Pascal, a seventeenth-century French philosopher, mathematician, pioneer of the scientific method, and inventor of the first mechanical digital calculator to reach the market. Called by its designer **la Pascaline,** this calculator was able to add and subtract (and thus perform multiplication and division indirectly by repeated additions or subtractions).

In the present book, emphasis is laid on methodical, structured design and structured programming. Students will learn how to design an algorithm via stepwise refinement of their original solution to the problem. Pseudocode is employed as the vehicle for this design. In the process of refinement, self-contained program units handling functionally separate subtasks are identified and later become program modules. Structured, top-down design and programming, relying on functional modules, leads to comprehensible and more easily maintained programs.

Instruction in programming technique is embedded throughout the book; certain important aspects are also brought together in separate *"Technique"* sections.

> Good programming practices, leading to reliable and modifiable programs, are presented often inside boxes, as shown here.

Crucial to the text are numerous examples, many of them programs. Programs and their output are reproduced from computer printout. Both batch and interactive programming techniques are discussed. The book's stress on interactive programming reflects its increasing popularity, both in time-sharing and personal computing environments.

The book is based on Standard Pascal, as defined by the referenced ISO and ANSI/IEEE standards. The use of standard language is very important: it furnishes students with a transferable skill and allows them to create programs that are portable from one computer to another.

▷ Language features which are implementation-dependent or additional features provided by commonly used versions (UCSD Pascal, for example) are discussed and set off with triangular markers as illustrated here. ◁

The design of the book allows for early discussion of procedures (following Chapter 5) and arrays (following Section 7–C), if desired. This is clearly shown in the text.

This volume may be used as a textbook in a one-semester programming course. It applies to the CS1 and CS2 courses of the Association for Computing Machinery Curriculum '78. A companion book in such courses, also in the Barnes & Noble Outline Series, is the author's **Introduction to Computer Science.** A source of additional problems with extensive commentaries is recommended at the end of the book.

I wish to thank my colleague Professor JoAnna Mitchell for her scrupulous scrutiny of the manuscript and the system manager extraordinary Peter Munzo, for his all-around assistance. My editor, Jeanne Flagg, has given me her expert aid; she and her associates have made the writing of this book a pleasure.

Vladimir Zwass

PROGRAMMING IN PASCAL

computers are general-purpose information processors → *need language to give commands to process*

binary code machine language process cpu

INTRODUCTION TO THE COMPUTER AND PASCAL

Computers as we know them today emerged in the 1940s. Since then they have entered most fields of human activity as tools for the processing and storage of information.

A computer is not an independent problem solver. Its operation is directed by a program made up of a sequence of instructions. If we change the program, the function of the computer also changes. Thus, computers are general-purpose information processors.

Basic components of a computer system are the central processing unit (CPU), main and secondary memories, and input/output devices. The central processor of a computer is only able to execute instructions expressed in a binary code called the machine language of the computer. However, thanks to systems software, users can program the computer in languages which reflect their thinking of the problem solution. Systems software also gives users convenient access to the computer system's resources.

Pascal is a prominent member of the family of higher-level programming languages. These permit the programmer to concentrate on the problem itself, without requiring familiarity with the details of computer organization. Before a program written in such a language is executed, it must be translated into machine language. This translation is performed by the computer itself under the control of a systems program, most often a compiler. A program written in Standard Pascal will run on any machine equipped with a compiler conforming to the standard; such a program is portable from one computer model to another.

translates program language into useful binary is compiler

A. WHAT A COMPUTER IS

A *computer* is a machine for the manipulation of symbols. These symbols represent information of various kinds, for example, a number or a name.

1

In its operation, the computer is directed by a *program*, that is, a sequence of *instructions* that determine the operations to be carried out by the machine. The program is the procedure for obtaining the desired results. To obtain the results, most programs require *data*.

EXAMPLE 1-1 *data can be numeric or character in form —*

(a) A program may be written to compute the square root of a nonnegative number.

The data item needed in this case is the number whose root is to be calculated. Thus, the program is general enough to compute the square root of *any* number greater than or equal to 0; the data make the program specific to the task at hand.

(b) A program may be written to prepare mail solicitation letters in which the name and address of the prospect are inserted into a standard text.

The file of names and addresses comprises the data for this program. These data are nonnumeric; they are text (character) data.

Computers are versatile: change the program, and instead of computing the square root of a number, for example, the computer will produce solicitation letters. Thus, the function of the computer at any moment is determined by the program it is executing. The data make the program specific. Therefore, a program applies to a class of problems: it may be computing the square root of 15 or of 155.

B. ORGANIZATION OF A COMPUTER

1. FLOW OF INFORMATION IN A COMPUTER

The capabilities (and cost) of computer systems vary widely. Their basic organization is, however, the same. Thus, a computer system includes a number of functionally separate devices that constitute its *hardware*. These comprise the *central processing unit (CPU)*, at which the program instructions are directed, the memory subsystem, where the instructions and data are stored, and *input* and *output devices* for communication with the environment of the system.

The flow of information in a computer system is shown in Fig. 1-1.

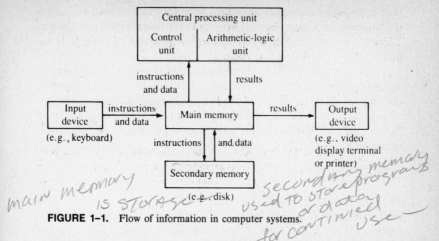

FIGURE 1-1. Flow of information in computer systems.

[handwritten annotations: "main memory IS STORAGE", "secondary memory used to store programs or data for continued use"]

An input device receives the information and places it in the *main memory* (memory is often called *storage*). The CPU of the computer actually executes the instructions by applying them to data (with the use of its arithmetic-logic unit) and by directing the operation of other system units.

The intermediate and final results are stored in the main memory. As the execution of the program progresses, the results may be communicated to the outside world via an output device. They may also be stored in memory until the program has been fully executed, to be presented all at once.

Users often want to store programs or data for extensive periods of time in order to avoid introducing them repeatedly from an input device. Slower *secondary memory* devices of large capacity are used for this purpose. Before the information stored there is brought to the attention of the CPU, it has to be transferred to the main memory. In microcomputer systems, secondary memory (such as floppy disks) also serves to enter packaged, that is, commercially prepared, programs into the system.

For technological reasons, all the information handled by a computer is encoded internally as a string of 0's and 1's, i.e., in binary representation.

All the system components are electronic, with the exception of most of the input/output and secondary memory devices. (These usually have mechanical elements.)

The following sections describe the components of a computer system in sufficient detail for programming in a higher-level language such as Pascal.

2. CENTRAL PROCESSING UNIT

The central processing unit (CPU) of the computer is designed to "comprehend" elementary instructions expressed in binary code. Three examples of such instructions are: add two numbers, compare two numbers and indicate the larger one, carry out the next instruction from the given memory location. This instruction code constitutes the *machine language* of the given computer.

A CPU consists of two functionally distinct parts: the control unit and the arithmetic-logic unit. The *control unit* directs the action of the system by carrying out the instructions and establishing their sequence according to the program. The *arithmetic-logic unit (ALU)* contains the circuitry needed to perform the basic arithmetic operations and the logical ones (for example, a comparison).

3. MEMORY

The main memory of a con uter consists of a number of *locations,* called *words,* which contain instructions or data items. Every word consists of a uniform number of *bits* (holding 0 or 1) and has a unique *address,* its number in memory. The CPU identifies (addresses) a given word in order either to *write* into this location, storing new contents in it, or to *read* from it, fetching the contents of the word without erasing them. In this manner, the CPU can obtain the instructions and data for the program and subsequently store the results in memory. Word length, fixed for the given computer, is typically 16, 32, or up to 64 bits. Most computers recognize also a smaller unit of information, called a *byte.* A byte, 8 bits long, stores the binary representation of a single character.

From the programmer's viewpoint, the main memory has the structure shown in Fig. 1–2.

Address	Contents
0	0110 . . . 111
1	1100 . . . 010
⋮	⋮
W	0100 . . . 001

Word length
(*n* bits)

FIGURE 1–2.   Programmer's view of the main memory.

In order to extend the capacity of the main memory at a reasonable cost and to provide long-term memory, computer systems usually have secondary (auxiliary) memories, selected from cheaper and slower types of storage than the main memory. Programs and data that are not expected to be needed soon by the CPU are stored there. A user's program held in the main memory may be replaced by another program loaded in its place; also, in most main-memory designs used today, the information held in this memory is lost when the computer is switched off (or the power supply is momentarily interrupted). In secondary memory, information may be held permanently. The items contained in secondary storage are accessible to the CPU only following their transfer to the main memory. A named unit of information stored in secondary memory—for example, a program or an organized collection of data—is called a *file.*

A typical secondary memory device is a magnetic disk. In microcomputers, floppy disks are widely used. Magnetic tape units, often used in addition to disks, are much slower.

4. INPUT/OUTPUT DEVICES

A number of various input/output (I/O) devices may be employed to communicate with the computer system. The most widely used input devices are keyboards, often attached to a video display terminal (VDT) or a printer. Output is most often displayed on a video display such as a cathode ray tube (CRT) screen, or on a line printer, which prints one line (rather than a single character) at a time.

5. SYSTEMS SOFTWARE

The intermediary between computer users and hardware is *systems software,* a set of programs that facilitates the use of the computer system. Programs written to apply the computer to the task at hand are called *application software.*

A user of the computer, during the process of program design and implementation called *programming,* must specify the operations to be performed by the computer. Natural languages used for human communication, such as English, are not fit for programming because of their ambiguity and lack of precision. On the other hand, programming in machine language would be extremely tedious and would limit the applicability of programs, since they are not transferable to a different computer in this form.

Users, therefore, program in *programming languages* that must be translated into machine language. In entering the program from a terminal, the user is assisted by a *text editor,* a systems program that manages the entry and modification of files. The computer itself performs the translation of the application program under the control of another systems program, a *translator.* A *compiler* is a frequently employed type of translator.

A program submitted to a computer system constitutes a *job* to be performed and requires the use of system resources, both hardware and software. In order to assign the needed resources to a program and, in a shared system, to mediate between the demands made by various users, a special systems program is required. This program, which manages all of the system resources, including the users' programs, is called an *operating system.*

Extensive programs are required to manage data stored in the system, and to facilitate remote communication between a user's terminal and the system or between distantly located computers in a computer network.

The operating system, along with language translators, programs for data management and telecommunication, text editors, and various utility programs (sorting programs, for example) constitute systems software. User's programs can be simpler because of this software.

C. PASCAL AS A HIGHER-LEVEL LANGUAGE

As already explained, in order to perform a task, the computer follows the instructions of a program.

We also know that the hardware of the computer or, more precisely, its central processor, "understands" only the instructions expressed in the machine language of the given computer model. A machine language instruction looks like this:

$$1001000110111010$$
(a 16-bit word is assumed)

A part of the instruction specifies the operation to be performed (e.g., add, compare), and another part gives the addresses of the memory locations that hold the operands involved.

Programming in such binary code is extremely cumbersome; the programmer has to remember all the addresses of data and the binary codes of all of the operations. To modify such a program is an arduous chore.

To simplify the programmer's work, every computer model (or series) has its own *assembly language,* a low-level programming language that permits the programmer to refer to a data item with the use of a symbolic name (instead of a binary address) and to use mnemonic, easy to remember, operation codes.

For example, the instruction shown above may look, in the assembly language of this hypothetical machine, as follows:

ADD GROSS, SALES

An assembly language program is translated into machine language by a rather simple translator, called an assembler.

Skillful programming in assembly language leads to efficient use of computer resources. These languages, however, have two essential disadvantages that significantly limit their use. They are demanding of the programmer's time because of the very detailed work required. Moreover, an assembly language is specific to a computer model; a program written in such a language is not portable from one computer model to another, then.

For these reasons, programming is done predominantly in *higher-level languages*. These allow the programmer to present the program in a terse and machine-independent fashion. The form of program expression is also closer to the way we actually think about the problem solution, hence less effort goes into the programmer's encoding of the solution into the programming language. Also, little or no knowledge of the machine's organization is required. Programs written in a higher-level language are essentially portable (although minor modifications may be needed in certain cases, as discussed in Section D).

The higher-level programming language Pascal was developed in the early 1970s by Niklaus Wirth with the following goals:

- to support teaching and practicing of programming as a systematic discipline, that is, to foster good programming practices through a method called structured programming;
- to include only fundamental programming facilities, thus leading to efficient language implementation.

Since its development, Pascal has gained wide popularity, joining previously established higher-level languages in wide use, such as BASIC, COBOL, FORTRAN, and PL/I. It is rather simple to learn these languages when one knows Pascal.

D. HOW A PROGRAM IS PROCESSED: LANGUAGE IMPLEMENTATION

Since computers cannot directly execute the instructions of a higher-level language program, it has to be translated before execution. A Pascal program is usually translated completely before its execution begins; such translation is called compilation.[1] A *compiler* translates the *source program* (in a higher-

---

1. As an alternative, a higher-level language program may be interpreted: translated and executed statement by statement under the control of a translator called an *interpreter*. There are no Pascal interpreters in wide use.

level language) into an *object program* (in machine language). Thus, your Pascal program has to be submitted first to the computer for compilation, and only then executed (see Fig. 1–3).

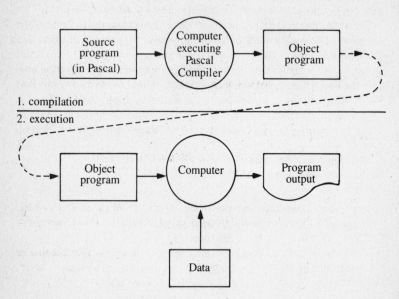

FIGURE 1–3. Processing of a Pascal program.

Actually, before the execution of a program begins, another systems program, called a *loader,* has to place the object code in the main memory locations assigned to it. The loaded object program is then executed. Loading is often transparent to the Pascal programmer.

As can be seen from the above discussion, what the computer does in response to a program written in a higher-level language depends to a degree on the compiler that is used to translate the program. The compiler, together with the hardware of the computer, constitutes the *implementation* of the language. It is desirable to limit the differences between implementations: ideally, a Pascal program should be executed identically in any implementation and thus be fully portable.

To promote portability of programs and programming skill, Standard Pascal has been defined; this standard form of the language is taught throughout the present text.[2] It is suggested that you avoid using nonstandard (implementation-dependent) features of the language unless important considerations prevail (and the Pascal manual for your installation is carefully consulted). A standard program is portable and easier to modify.

Important facilities offered by popular Pascal implementations are, however, pointed out in the text.[3] In particular, these include extensions to the language offered by UCSD Pascal (a version of the language developed at the University of California, San Diego), embedded in the p-system operating system.

The combination of hardware and software which translates and runs Pascal programs in a given system is often referred to as the *Pascal processor.*

E. HOW TO PREPARE AND RUN A PROGRAM

To prepare and run your program, you will have to follow rather rigid procedures. While the essence of these is similar in all systems of a given type, the details are specific to the system and should be observed scrupulously.

It is most likely that you will be preparing your program at a terminal or using a personal computer. In this case, you will employ a text editor to enter the program text and store it as a file. The program may then be run:

- in *interactive mode,* that is, accepting data from you (at the terminal) as it is running, and giving you the output on the terminal; or
- in *batch mode,* with the complete data for the program supplied along with the program itself, and the results obtained after the execution has been completed.

Certain programming differences between interactive and batch programs are discussed in Chapter 3–E–3.

If cards (or a similar medium) are used for input, the program will be run as a batch job and you will obtain a printout of the results.

---

2. The official Standard Pascal promulgated by the International Standards Organization (ISO dp7185) is equivalent to the approved U.S. standard ANSI/IEEE 770X3.97–1983, but ISO Pascal includes in addition (in the so-called Level 1) conformant array parameters, discussed in Chapter 13–H.

3. Implementation-dependent features are set off by triangular markers as illustrated here.

1. PROGRAM PREPARATION

a. On a Terminal or a Personal Computer

A program is most easily prepared on a personal computer or at a terminal connected to a computer system shared by you with other users. In both cases, a keyboard is your input device, and a screen (or, more rarely, a printer) your principal output device.

You will enter your program into the computer system under the control of a text editor. It will be entered as a file, so that you may retrieve it later under the name you have given to the file. Text editors are word processing programs designed for: *input data*

- creating a file, that is, accepting the contents of a new file from an input device; and
- editing a file, that is, changing the contents of an existing file.

Thus, editors have two modes of operation: input (entry of file contents) and edit. In the edit mode you can delete or insert specified lines or words, change characters, move text around, etc. You will enter this mode when you make a mistake during the input of your program or if you later want to modify your file.

Once your program is stored as a file, it may be submitted to the Pascal compiler. You will receive on your terminal either an indication of successful compilation or error messages. Note that any error messages received now concern only your use of the Pascal language (perhaps you have missed a semicolon?); they are not an indication of the correctness of your solution approach (this is further discussed in Chapter 2–I).

If you wish, you may now order that a copy of your program be printed so that you can determine needed corrections. To correct the errors, use the text editor (in the edit mode) on the file holding your program. When successful compilation occurs, the program is ready for execution.[4]

b. In a Punched-Card Environment

In some installations, punched cards are employed to enter programs and data. A keypunch is then used to prepare the card deck off-line (that is, the keypunch is not connected to the computer). Subsequently, the deck, containing the program, data, and control commands, is read into the computer memory via a card reader.

Punched cards are used to submit batch jobs only. After program execution in this mode has been completed (see Section E–2–b below), a printout is

---

4. In some systems you have to specify that the object program be loaded; in others this step occurs automatically.

obtained, showing the program listing and results (or, perhaps, error messages).

If errors have been discovered, one needs to replace the offending cards with newly punched ones. Then the job has to be resubmitted. In many systems it is possible to store the program in a file once the deck has been read in.

2. PROGRAM EXECUTION

Programs may be prepared for interactive or batch execution, depending on the problem and the nature of your computing environment. If you are working on a terminal or personal computer, you usually have a choice between the two modes. The interactive mode is increasingly popular due to its responsiveness, and it is uniquely suitable for certain applications requiring instantaneous response to user requests. If you are working in a punched-card environment, you will have prepared a batch job. In general, the batch mode of operation is more efficient in the use of shared computer resources; this is important in a production environment, when programs are repeatedly executed with different data.

Aspects of programming for the two modes of program execution are further discussed in Chapter 3–E–3.

a. Interactive Execution

A program prepared and compiled for interactive execution is run while the user remains at the terminal. As the program is running, the user is prompted to enter data required by it directly from the terminal. Under the program orders, output is also written out to the terminal as obtained. Thus, the user and the program interact.

Interactive program execution in a shared system is supported by a *time-sharing* operating system which enables a number of users to work simultaneously at their terminals, each having an illusion of working at a personal computer.

b. Batch Execution

Running your program in batch may be the only way possible in your system, or you may opt for it over the interactive mode due to the nature of the problem.

To run a program in batch mode, you will need to submit:

- the source program in Pascal;
- complete data;
- properly placed commands to the operating system, requesting appropriate actions and resources.

After program execution is completed, you will obtain printed output (if you are using a terminal, it is possible to direct the output to it).

When a program is run in batch mode we usually include source code in Pascal, so an initial command to the system must request compilation. Thus, we have the following general sequence of lines (or cards) in order to specify a batch job:

- commands identifying the user ◀——not needed on a terminal
- command requesting compilation

  Pascal program│

- command requesting execution

  complete data │   ◀—if the program requires data

- end-of-job delimiter

You need to obtain the specific command sequences for your system. Special commands may be included to request, for example, storing of your program in a file, obtaining data from a previously prepared data file, or other special handling.

Part One

FUNDAMENTALS OF PROGRAMMING IN PASCAL

Introduction to the basic facilities of Pascal is an excellent vehicle for learning the technique of programming. Pascal was developed as a language supporting *structured programming:* a disciplined programming style relying on a limited number of proper structures for controlling the flow of program execution.

Fundamental control structures are: sequence, selection, and repetition (loop). The extended complement of structures includes also the multiple selection and alternative looping constructs. These control structures are offered directly in Pascal as structured statements.

Statements of a program operate on data. In programming, all data items are characterized by their type. In particular, the type of a data item determines the kind of values it may take on and the operations applicable to it. Pascal offers four standard data types: *integer* and *real* for numerical computations, *Boolean,* whose value may be either true or false, and *char,* whose value is a single character. In addition, programmers may define their own types to match the problem; this is done through the type definition facility of Pascal. This is another significant strength of the language.

It is crucial to realize that the programming task is not limited to that of coding in Pascal. It is rather a sequence of tasks: problem analysis, program design, program implementation (coding and testing). The method of stepwise refinement (also called top-down design) is a powerful technique for gradual development of a program, from the most abstract statement to the actual Pascal code. Pseudocode is a fine tool for the method. To make the maintenance (modification and enhancement) of the program possible, it must be accompanied by well-prepared documentation.

2

A PASCAL PROGRAM: GENERAL FEATURES

A simple program is presented and discussed in detail. We will also explain the rules for forming identifiers (names) of program entities and the basic elements of Pascal syntax.

A very important section on programming technique explains the steps necessary to deliver a correct, readable, and well-documented program.

A. A SIMPLE PROGRAM

Consider this Pascal program:

begin

(program
block   *)*

EXAMPLE 2–1

```
program talkToMe (output);
        {greeting is produced}
begin
    writeln ('Hi, I am your computer!')
end.
```

end

Submitted to the computer, this program produces the following output:

Hi, I am your computer!

This simple program requires no data; the program instructions themselves suffice here to produce the fixed message.

Every Pascal program consists of a *program heading,* which names the program and identifies the source of its data (if any data are required) and the disposition of its results (output), and a program block. The *program block* describes the nature of the data to be manipulated and includes the statements (action commands to the computer) specifying the steps in this manipulation.

15

In our case, the single statement in the program block (delimited by **begin** and **end**) is *writeln,* ordering the computer to "write a line" with the stated text.

Comments, included in curly brackets { }, explain the program to its reader. They are ignored by the computer.

Computer programs are written according to the strict *syntax* of the programming language. Syntactic rules are the grammar of the language; they specify how various symbols (called *tokens*) of the language are to be used in a program. A program which violates these rules will not be executed as its writer intended.

B. PROGRAM HEADING

A program heading appears at the beginning of every program (it may be preceded only by a comment). It has the following general form:

LIST

    program identifier (program parameters)

Until further discussion of program parameters in Chapter 17, we will use the following general form of the program heading:

    program identifier *(input, output)*

                          present only if there are input data

For example,

    program *distance (input, output)*

Identifiers, discussed in the following section, are the names given to various entities in a program. Thus, a program heading provides the name for the entire program; in our case it is *distance.*

Program parameters serve to communicate with the program environment. They are usually the identifiers of files (collections) of data. Two "prenamed" files, *input* and *output,* are provided by Pascal systems. Any data you submit to the program will be in the input file (until you learn to define your own files in Chapter 17). Anything the program "writes" as a result of its execution goes into the output file. These results are presented to you as discussed in Chapter 1.

C. IDENTIFIERS

An identifier is a name of an entity used in a program (for example, the identifier of the program itself or of a variable, which will be discussed in the next chapter).

word symbols Reserve-words
command for Pascal language.

The programmer is free to choose the identifiers in the program. They should, however, be different from the thirty-five *word symbols* (often called *reserved words*) which are a part of the Pascal language itself, along with other special symbols such as punctuation marks and arithmetic operators. The word symbols of Pascal are listed in Appendix B; an example is the word **program** used above.

Thus, for example, you cannot name your program simply *program*. We named it *talkToMe*.

All identifiers within the program block should be unique (this limitation does not apply, as we will see in Part II, to other blocks that may be embedded in a given program block). In particular, all identifiers selected by the programmer must be different from the "system-declared" identifiers[1] such as, for example, *input*.

The rules for creating an identifier are:

(1) The first character must be a letter; other characters may be letters or digits only (no spaces or punctuation marks, for example).

▷ (2) In Standard Pascal, identifiers may be of any length, but various implementations may ignore all but the first 8 or 15 characters (make sure you know how many characters are considered in your implementation).

In an implementation that ignores all but the first eight characters, these identifiers:

$$talkToMe|Softly \text{ and } talkToMe|Loudly$$

would be considered identical and thus could not be used in the same block since all identifiers need to be unique. But you still could use identifiers longer than eight characters!   ◁

(3) An identifier should be different from the 35 word symbols.

---

(4) An identifier should describe the entity named. Inappropriately short and meaningless identifiers should be avoided; identifiers are the essential means for making programs readable. To make the meaning of an identifier more obvious, it is good to capitalize the first letter of its consecutive component words.

---

1. These identifiers may indeed be redeclared in the program; we will avoid such usage, desirable only in very limited situations.

EXAMPLE 2–2

These are valid identifiers:

mean, firstLetter, altitude, sales.

These are invalid:

5mean (the first character is a digit); •
begin (this is a Pascal word symbol);
count$ (contains a character other than letter or digit);
talk to me (contains spaces, which are, of course, not letters or digits).

Do not use:

v to mean *volume*, or
karen to mean *editText*.

*Begin
where program operates
end*

D. PROGRAM BLOCK

Our program block in Example 2–1 consists only of the *statement part*. A *statement* is an instruction to be executed by the computer. In our case, the only instruction is for the computer to "write a line" (*writeln*) with the stated message. Statements are executed one after another by the computer.

The statement part of a program is always delimited by **begin** and **end.** The closing **end** of a program must be followed by a period.

As we will see in the next chapter, in most programs the statement part is preceded by the description of data to be manipulated by the program.

E. CHARACTER STRINGS

Used to write out statements

Computers manipulate at least as much text as numerical data. To specify a fixed text, we use a *character string:* a sequence of characters enclosed in apostrophes (single quotes). Any character available in your implementation may be included in a string.

Thus, the program of Example 2–1 causes a character string to be displayed (or printed). The apostrophes are not part of the string; they simply delimit it. The string is reproduced exactly as included in the apostrophes, with all the spaces. If a string itself includes an apostrophe, this has to be represented by two apostrophes.

Most implementations prohibit character strings from occupying more than one line. In general, it is best to define a separate string for each line as needed.

Whenever available, upper- and lower-case letters will be displayed exactly as specified in the character string.

EXAMPLE 2–3

These are some examples of character strings:

'My name is Frankenstein.'
'ANNUAL EARNINGS   ANNUAL PROFITS'
'$10'
'Sweat of one''s brow'

The last string will be displayed as:

Sweat of one's brow

F. COMMENTS

Every program should include comments, which help to explain its purpose and algorithm. The amount of commenting that is necessary depends on the complexity of the program. Judicious choice of identifiers and overall careful layout can make a program to a large extent self-explanatory, thus reducing the need for comments. Comments have no influence on program execution; they are simply included in the program listing (or display).

A comment is any text of any length enclosed in a pair of curly brackets, { and }[2]; it may not itself contain a closing bracket }. Thus, a comment may span several lines or may follow Pascal code on the same line.

EXAMPLE 2–4

These are legal comments:

{Author: X. Q. Lemming
Date: October 11, 1985}
program reduce (input, output);   {reduced weight computed}

You should adopt a consistent commenting style for your programs. Comments should not duplicate the code; they should be problem-oriented and aim to explain the task of the program and the strategy of the solution.

At the same time, the code should be to a large degree self-commenting; meaningful identifiers are the mainstay of this.

Comments should not blend with the code: their text, which will be ignored by the computer, must be easy for a reader of the program to distinguish.

---

2. Some Standard Pascal processors employ, instead of curly brackets, these double symbols: (* and *) to enclose comments.

G. SEPARATORS

Syntactic units (tokens) need to be separated from one another by one or more Pascal separators: spaces, end-of-line markers, or comments. Thus, in Example 2–1 a space separates the word symbol **program** from the identifier *talk-ToMe*.

Pascal is a free-format language, which means that its code lines do not have to be laid out rigidly.

3 spaces indent —

> Spaces are freely used within a program line (but not within tokens themselves!) to make it easier to read. In particular, they are used to indent the components of syntactic constructs, as will be seen throughout the text. The customary indentation in Pascal is 3 spaces (observe the indentation of *writeln* from **begin** in Example 2–1). Blank lines may be employed to separate meaningful program fragments that are devoted to specific subtasks. Consistent use of spaces and blank lines enhances the readability of programs.

The program heading, definitions and declarations (discussed in the next chapter), and statements are separated by semicolons. Any of these may extend over more than one line if necessary, or, alternatively, be placed several to a line; only semicolons separate them.

EXAMPLE 2–5a
Here is another complete program:

```
program obeisance (output);
        {making the computer pay its respects}
begin
    writeln ('I am your computer.');
    writeln ('What is your order, o Master?')
end.
```

In the preceding program, the two *writeln* statements are separated by a semicolon. The **begin-end** pair delimits the statement part of the program. No semicolon needs to be placed before the word symbol **end.**

> For readability's sake, usually a single data definition or declaration (see the next chapter) or a single statement is placed on a line. Certain word symbols, such as **begin** and **end,** for example, are also customarily placed on their own line.

Every Pascal program is terminated by a period. Thus, we have the general template for Pascal programs of Fig. 2–1, which we will refine in future chapters as we learn about its definition and declaration part.

program identifier *(input, output)*;

          if needed
    definitions and declarations;
begin
  ⋮ } statement part
end.

FIGURE 2–1.   General template for Pascal programs.

H. TYPEFACE STYLE IN PASCAL PROGRAMMING

A Pascal processor draws no distinction between upper- and lower-case letters. Thus, for example, an identifier written as

Cummings, CUMMINGS or *cummings*

will be treated as the same entity. Similarly,

begin and **BEGIN**

signify the same word symbol.

In this text, a customary form of presentation is adopted for Pascal programs, with the word symbols presented in boldface, and the remaining code predominantly in lower case. When you write programs in longhand, simply underline the word symbols.

Some computer printers print only upper-case letters; few have boldface capability. The printouts included in this text are a typical example of what you may expect in your system.

The following is the computer listing of the program presented in Example 2–5a. Please note the correspondences between the presentation form and the printout format.

EXAMPLE 2–5b
The computer listing of the program of Example 2–5a:

```
program obeisance (output);
        {making the computer pay its respects}
begin
   writeln ('I am your computer.');
   writeln ('What is your order, o Master?')
end.
```

This output was produced:

```
I am your computer.
What is your order, o Master?
```

I. TECHNIQUE 1: HOW TO PROGRAM

Programming is more than simply writing a program. It is the more demanding task of designing a correct and documented solution to a properly understood problem, and only then coding this solution as a program and convincing oneself of the correctness of the program. Several stages thus make up the programmer's task (actually, teams of programmers produce large programs).

The steps of the programming process are described in the present section. You will do well by returning to read it a number of times, in particular when devising and running your first programs.

More advanced discussions on programming technique are placed in the book as appropriate to the progression of your learning. Development of larger, modular programs is discussed in Part II.

> Also, guidelines on reliable programming and programming style are interspersed throughout the book, many in boxes like this one.

These are the steps to follow during programming.

(1) Make sure that you are solving the correct problem. To do so, clearly define and analyze the problem before proceeding to solve it. Actually, a thorough analysis of the problem is a large part of its solution. (For complex programs, the analysis results in functional specifications of the program, a voluminous document.)

(2) For any but trivial programs, the coding of the program has to be preceded by an explicit design of the solution. We thus need to specify the *algorithm* of the solution: an unambiguous sequence of steps that, when carried out, will result in the solution to the problem being produced in finite time. The final specification of the algorithm will be the program presented to the computer. But the coding of a program involves details which are best ignored during the design stage. In other

words, during the design we need to provide a more abstract and concise specification of the algorithm.

As will be further discussed in Chapter 3–J, a convenient tool for the expression of algorithms is pseudocode, a rather informal notation, close to English, but with strict sequencing of computational steps. Several refinements of the algorithm description, incorporating progressively more detail, may be needed for more complex problems. It is an important advantage of Pascal that the pseudocode, which is used to specify the algorithm, is written in a similar fashion to the program it will ultimately become.

Together with the design of the algorithm, tne representation of the data to be manipulated by it is also designed.

(3) Code a correct and clear program, expressing the algorithm. Remember that every detail has to be spelled out to the computer exactly according to the rules of Pascal as presented in this book (in some cases, you may want to consult also the language manual for your implementation).

Program clarity is achieved through:

- the use of appropriate language features;
- selection of meaningful identifiers;
- judicious use of comments helping a reader to understand the program;
- avoiding tricky code (aim for clarity of thought expressed in the code, not for "cleverness" in coding);
- good program layout, including consistent indentation and use of blank lines and spaces.

Remember, your code should not only be correct; it ought to be also readable!

This text contains detailed stylistic remarks, set in boxes. Follow them to code reliable and legible programs.

Programs, particularly those designed for interactive use, should be user-friendly. An interactive program should guide its user toward obtaining valid results, presented in the best form possible. In addition, it should be a pleasure to run a program!

(4) Study and hand-check the program or its crucial fragments. (Hand-checking consists of "playing the computer" by simulating the program execution by hand, using sample input.) Convince yourself that your program will work correctly:

- for typical input value(s);
- under the boundary conditions: for example, if an input may range

between -10 and 10, make sure that the program works for these two values;

- in special cases of input values: for example, is division by zero avoided?

(5) Compile the program (in an interactive system) or try to compile and run the program with sample data (in a batch system).

It may turn out that your program contains *syntax errors* (also known as *compile-time errors*); that is, you have made mistakes using the Pascal language itself. These errors were discovered by the compiler and they have to be removed before the program can be executed.

Your compiler will generate diagnostic messages. Due to the nature of the compilation process (and, sometimes, to lack of care on the part of compiler writers), a single error may cause multiple and/or misleading messages. Identify the crucial ones and, with the help of this text (and, possibly, of the Pascal manual for your installation), correct the offending statement(s). Remember that the computer is unforgiving: you cannot take liberties with a mere semicolon.

Resubmit the program for compilation. It may happen that you will get some of the old messages again, but also a new error message or two: some errors may have been masked by others, or you may have made another mistake. Correct the errors until you achieve successful compilation.

The process of finding and correcting errors (bugs) is called *debugging;* you have only begun it now. Correct compilation does not mean that the program is correct. (After all, correct use of English does not ensure the soundness of the ideas expressed by the speaker.)

(6) When no syntax errors are present, the program may be executed (run). However, now *run-time errors* may show up, and you may get error messages during execution. For example, you may have attempted to use a value not yet computed or to divide by zero.

Even when no run-time errors are indicated by messages, the results of the run may be incorrect due to *logic errors:* mistakes in the solution algorithm or in its translation into Pascal.

If any execution errors occur, you need to find their source by continuing to debug. To begin with, your program should echo (display or print) all the input data. This provides an echo check: in beginners' programs inputs are often read in incorrectly. Input values are most often printed also as a part of program documentation.

If a bug is discovered (through an error message or an incorrect result), you will have to work backward through the program to find its source. Aside from hand-checking, the technique used most often is to insert temporarily output statements—*write* or *writeln*—to display values and messages that will help you to locate the source of the error. Several such statements can be inserted in strategic places in the program; they will be deleted following debugging.

If your installation provides special software tools for debugging—they are called, not unnaturally, *debuggers*—by all means use them.

Be careful correcting errors; otherwise, syntax errors may appear again.

(7) By now you have the results of a correct run with your selected input data value(s). Now you should test the program thoroughly to convince yourself that it operates correctly over the allowed range of input values. Again, you need to test for typical values of inputs, as well as for boundary conditions and special cases. In order to test your program, you will need to design several test cases, reflecting the combinations of input values that will bring out the full functionality of the program. A test case ought always to include the expected output values.

In "real-world" programs it is also required that the program reject (display an appropriate message and, if possible, continue, otherwise stop execution) any input values outside of the range defined in the problem. This is the essence of so-called defensive programming. Some test cases ought to be designed with such "incorrect" input values to see whether the program is able to "defend itself."

Testing is the planned, repeated execution of a program (or a part of one) with prepared test data, with the intention of discovering errors. It is very important to keep in mind that during testing you are not attempting to prove the correctness of your program; on the contrary, you are trying to find errors in it. Absence of these errors will give you confidence in the reliable performance of your program.[3]

After an error has been discovered during the testing process, you need to find its source by debugging the program; carefully think of the way to remove it, do so, and retest the program. Incremental testing of modular programs is further discussed in Chapter 10–E.

(8) The programmer's task is complete only when the documentation of the program has been completed. The *documentation* is a set of materials that explain the program and its operation, making the program a finished product. The necessary documentation includes:

- the design documentation, with the pseudocode of the algorithm(s);
- the listing of the appropriately commented program—a set of header comments needs to be provided, to identify the name of the program-

---

3. There exist formal methods of proving program correctness, but in their present form they are not applicable in a practical environment.

mer and the date of the program's completion, to explain what the
program does and briefly state (or refer to) the method employed;
- a set of sample inputs with their corresponding outputs.

At this point, so-called production programs (to be used repeatedly,
for an extended period of time) go into operation and maintenance.
Such programs may require more extensive documentation, including
functional specifications, users' guide, and maintenance documentation.

We need to remember that production programs are often used and
maintained for ten to twenty years. During this time, such a program
will have to be modified many times to adjust it to changing user
requirements, new hardware and software environments, and (unfortu-
nately) to correct mistakes in the original development. Since modification is a crucial concern in the overall life cycle of a program, it is
necessary to develop modifiable programs in the first place. Program
modifiability is enhanced by extensive problem analysis, proper design
(see, in particular, Part II of this book), clear code, well-planned testing, and appropriate documentation.

3
PROCESSING OF NUMERICAL DATA

Pascal works with Two data Types real & integer numbers

Program statements operate on data. The essential attribute of a data item is its type. In particular, the type of a data item determines the operations applicable to this item. A data item may assume only the values specific to its type. Along with the types discussed later in the book, Pascal provides two basic numerical data types: integer and real.

A data item may be a constant or a variable. Since certain data items remain by design constant during program execution, such constants may be named to describe their meaning in the program.

Computation takes place by assigning values to variables, that is, to data items which are declared as variable with a certain type. A rule for manipulation of values, and thus computing a new value, is specified as an expression. The value of an expression may be assigned to a variable or directly sent into the output stream. To simplify data manipulation, Pascal provides several standard (built-in) functions.

Input and output are performed in Pascal with one of four standard procedures. The layout of the data on the output medium may be specified by the programmer.

Programming techniques leading to understandable programs and output are discussed. Understandable programs are, in general, more reliable and easier to modify.

Program design by stepwise refinement using pseudocode is shown to be a technique for gradual introduction of detail during the programming process. Program development thus proceeds from the most general outline of the solution to the actual code.

A. DATA AND DATA TYPES

Program statements manipulate data that are supplied to the program. These input data are symbols employed by the program to obtain other data—

10. Herbert Kruse (Krutschkowski), interview, 18 December 1983.
11. Petersen, letter to author, 20 March 1988.

Chapter Seven

1. Lüth, "Problems."
2. Nicholas Monsarrat, introduction to Schaeffer, *U-Boat 977,* ii.
3. Lüth, *Boot Greift Wieder An,* 237.
4. Petersen, interview.
5. Ibid.
6. Petersen, letter to author, 1 March 1984.
7. Ibid.
8. Edward F. Oliver, "Overdue — Presumed Lost," U.S. Naval Institute Proceedings 3 (1961): 98–105.
9. Arthur Gordon, "The Day the Astral Vanished," U.S. Naval Institute Proceedings 10 (1965): 76–83.
10. Deck log of U-575, cited in ibid., 80.
11. Gordon, "The Day the Astral Vanished," 82.
12. Lüth, *Boot Greift Wieder An,* 281.
13. Petersen, letter to author, 2 December 1986.
14. Ibid., letter to author, 5 February 1988.
15. Lüth, *Boot Greift Wieder An,* 292.

Chapter Eight

1. Perhaps the best presentation of U-boat operations in the South Atlantic and Indian oceans can be found in L. C. F. Turner et al., *War in the Southern Oceans* (Cape Town: Oxford University Press, 1961). Among other things, Turner explains the events leading up to the decision by BdU to send his boats south, and he describes in detail the defenses those boats met when they got there.
2. Walter Schmidt, interview, 22 December 1983.
3. Ibid.
4. Engel, interview.
5. Ibid.
6. *Bordzeitung* (newspaper) of U-181, 1942–43. U-181's newspaper was typed on board by an unidentified crewman and distributed internally. Only some of the issues still exist.
7. Petersen, letter to author, 3 March 1988.
8. Josef Dick, letter to author, 3 February 1988.
9. Engel, interview.
10. Dick, letter to author, 23 September 1983.

[handwritten annotations at top: "Because The data & program are stored separately program can be run with different data sets —"]

representing the information derived from program execution. Thanks to a fundamental tenet of programming, the independence of a program from its input data, a program may be run repeatedly with different values of data.

The essential property of a data item is its *type*. The type of a data item determines the set of values which may be assumed by it, the representation of these values, and the operations applicable to these values. For example, a representation needed for character strings (the main object of word processing) must differ from that for integer numbers, subject to arithmetic operations. It is also clear that adding two strings makes no sense, just as various editing operations, desired for strings, are not applicable to integers.

Pascal requires that the types of all data used in a program be explicitly declared. The language thus belongs (with minor deviations) to the category of *strongly typed* programming languages. Such declarations make it possible for the compiler to check the consistency between data and their manipulation by the program statements. This prevents many run-time errors.

Aside from the standard (also called required) types, Pascal offers programmers an opportunity to define their own data types, as required by the problem which is addressed by the program. Data types supported by Pascal, along with the type definition facility (discussed in Chapter 6), are some of the strengths of the language.

[handwritten annotation: "data type determines what group of value you can assign —"]

B. INTEGER AND REAL CONSTANTS

A constant is a value that does not change during program execution. Such a constant may be used in the program as a ready value or be given a name via a constant definition. The two standard data types provided by Pascal for computations are the integer and real data types. The integer data type is represented exclusively by whole numbers; real data may have fractional parts. The representations of integer and real data are considered here.

1. INTEGER DATA

Data items of the integer type, which are whole numbers, are used to represent entities that cannot have fractional values.

EXAMPLE 3–1

An integer will be used to represent each of the following:

- an identification number;
- the number of entries in a fixed-size table;
- the number of players in a bridge game.

These are examples of integer constants:

$$3 \qquad 0 \qquad -77 \qquad +5151$$

Integer constants consist only of digits; they must not contain a decimal point or a comma. The plus sign is unnecessary for positive constants.

The range of integer values is limited in every computer system. With most minicomputers, the range is -32768 to 32767; some of the larger machines accommodate integers from -2147483648 to 2147483647. The available range suffices for most problems handled by the machine. If you need to use large integer values in your program, find out the integer range of your implementation. In case you need to exceed this range, you may resort to the use of the real data type, which offers a far wider range (but a limited precision) or you will have to include statements in the program to manipulate individual digits of the integer numbers.

Pascal provides a predefined constant *maxint,* whose value depends on the implementation; it defines the range of integer values available. Thus, your implementation offers integers in the range:

$$-maxint, \ldots, -1, 0, 1, \ldots, maxint$$

EXAMPLE 3-2

These are valid integer constants: 7; -7; $+7$
These are invalid integer constants: -3.15; 100,000; \$10
This constant may be invalid (possibly beyond the representational limit of your computer): 41589231112

2. REAL DATA

Data items of the real type may have a fractional part and are thus generally useful in computation, representing, for example, physical measurements or statistical data.

Real constants may be represented in one of two formats. The more customary positional notation is exemplified by these real constants:

$$2.51 \qquad -3.0 \qquad +7151.314$$

In Pascal, a real constant written in positional notation must have at least one digit on each side of the decimal point. Thus, these are invalid real constants: 3. and .51. Instead, they ought to be represented as 3.0 and 0.51.

A real constant in positional notation may consist only of a sign ("$+$" being optional), digits, and the decimal point; commas are not allowed.

To represent a very small or a very large number concisely, exponential notation (also known as scientific or floating-point notation) is often used. In this notation, a *scale factor* (*exponent*) specifies the position of the decimal point.

Thus, in longhand notation, we would write

3.11×10^6 instead of 3110000
or
-3.11×10^{-4} instead of -0.000311.

In Pascal, real constants are represented in exponential notation in this general form:

$$\mp \text{integer.integer} E \mp \text{integer}$$
optional   optional   optional

For example,

     3.11E6, $-3.11E-4$, $-2E-03$,   5E05

In this notation, the letter E stands for "times 10 to the power of," and what follows is the scale factor.

These are equivalent representations in Pascal:

     110.0   1.1E2   1.1E+02

(it depends on the implementation whether 2 or 02 is presented on output as the scale factor).

Note:

(1) if there is a decimal point, at least one digit must appear on each side of it;
(2) as usual in Pascal, "E" or "e" may be employed;
(3) the scale factor is, of course, always an integer;
(4) no commas are allowed.

As in the case of integer values, there is a limit on the number of digits which may be stored in a given computer to represent a real value. In the case of real values, this translates into two limits:

(1) The magnitude of representable real numbers is limited. This limit is, however, far larger than in the case of integers. A typical range is between -10^{38} and 10^{38}.
(2) The precision (accuracy) is also limited. Thus, depending on the computer, from 7 to 17 digits are representable.

Unlike integers, real values cannot, in general, be stored exactly in computers. In some implementations this is apparent immediately—for example, when a real value such as 1.2 is input but prints out as 1.199999E+00; in others it may show up only during more complex computations (see also Section F–3).

EXAMPLE 3–3

These are valid real constants:

$$25.0 \quad -22.0 \quad +337.55 \quad 0.1 \quad -3.22E-03 \quad 17E1$$

These constants are invalid:

.1 (no digit before the decimal point)
5. (no digit after the decimal point)
2,111.3 (no commas allowed)
1.E2   2.3E   2E1.3 $2.10 (note various errors)

This is not a real constant (it is an integer):

$$25$$

These real constants are most likely beyond the representational limits of your computer:

$$5.41E77 \quad -3.75E-45$$

C. CONSTANT DEFINITION

The programmer may present a constant directly as a ready value whenever it is needed in a statement. Pascal also provides a constant definition facility which should be used as a matter of good programming style to name the important constants and thus describe their meaning in the program.

A constant definition has the following general form:

const
    identifier = constant;
         ⋮   ⎫
                 ⎬ optional
    identifier = constant;⎭

where the constant on the right-hand side of "=" may be any of these:

- an integer value (thus, an integer constant is being defined);
- a real value (thus, a real constant is being defined);
- a character string;
- a previously defined constant identifier, possibly with a preceding sign (thus, the predefined constant *maxint* may be used anywhere).

For example, this is a definition of eight constants:

```
const
    weekdays  =  7;
    week  =  weekdays;
    most  =  10;
    least  =  −most;
    limit  =  maxint;
    pi  =  3.14159;
    message1  =  'SUCCESS';
    message2  =  'FAILURE';
```

Note that each of these definitions at the time it is encountered provides a ready value. No computations may be involved on the right-hand side of the equals sign "=", and any constant identifier appearing there has to have been defined previously (thus, *most* has to appear before *least*).

After an identifier for a constant has been defined, it may appear in place of the constant. For example, we may write

writeln (message1);

instead of

writeln ('SUCCESS');

The type of constant on the right-hand side of the definition determines the type of the identifier.

Once defined, the value of a constant cannot be changed by the program.

The use of the constant definition facility contributes to the design of self-explanatory and modifiable programs. A constant identifier explains the meaning of the constant (it is no longer a "magic number") and prevents the erroneous use of different constants where the same value is meant. By changing a constant definition we can modify the program, if required, without a need to change all the statements where the constant is used.

The constant definition should not be used in place of input data for the program. The constants are the data items which will not change from execution to execution. Input data, in conjunction with variables to be described later, are used for general computation.

D. VARIABLES AND VARIABLE DECLARATION

A programmer may assign an identifier to a memory location. Such a location may then contain any value of the type declared for the identifier. This value may be unknown to the programmer at the time the program is written; it may subsequently be supplied as an input datum or computed during the program execution. The value may then be referred to simply by using the identifier of the memory location that holds it. For example, instead of saying, "multiply the given value by 2," we are able to say, "multiply whatever is in the location with such-and-such name by 2." Thus, we do not have to know the actual value!

A data entity with an identifier, type, and value which may change during the program execution is called a variable. Declaring and using variables actually distinguishes programming from calculation. All program variables have to be declared in Pascal.

A variable declaration has the following general form:

var

optional

identifier, . . . , identifier: type;

⋮ } optional

identifier, . . . , identifier: type;

optional

For example:

var
>   *distance, weight: real;*
>   *count: integer;*

The above declaration declares two real variables: *distance* and *weight* and an integer variable *count*. (Other types will be discussed later in the book.)

Thus, a variable declaration declares the identifier and type of the variable. The value of a variable is undefined until it has been assigned as the result of the execution of an assignment or input statement.

Assuming that the variable *count* has been assigned the value 5, we may think of it as shown in Fig. 3–1.

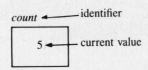

FIGURE 3–1. A variable.

Note that variables are declared (i.e., described) only in terms of their types, hence no equals sign appears in a declaration; constants, however, are defined by providing them with actual values through a constant definition. Note also that a variable declaration is necessary for all variables used in the program, while a constant definition is only of stylistic importance.

In the text of a Pascal program, variable declarations have to follow constant definitions. The template of a Pascal program including both is thus:

```
program heading;
const definitions;
var declarations;
begin ⎫
    ⋮  ⎬ statement part
end.  ⎭
```

E. BASICS OF INPUT AND OUTPUT

We need a way to read in the data required by the program and to write out the program output. The input to the program may be considered to come from the *input stream* and the output to be delivered to the *output stream*, both of which are related to the input/output devices used in the system. Both streams may be considered sequences of lines. We will, as is customary, refer to these streams also as the input and output files.

The fact that the program makes use of these streams is stated in the program heading, for example:

program *mean (input, output);*

Input and output are accomplished in Pascal by means of four standard procedures: *read* or *readln* for input, and *write* or *writeln* for output. These procedures are provided for direct use by the programmer as if the statements using them were primitive ones; thus we do not need to concern ourselves with the properties of procedures until Part II. Suffice it to say now that the lists of items to be read in or written out may be called parameter lists (data supplied to or by procedures are called parameters).

Input and output of integer and real data are discussed here; later we will learn to input and output data of other types and to control the input of data using loops (see Chapter 5–E). We will discuss general file input/output in Chapter 17.

1. INPUT

The general form of the statements reading data from the input stream is:

read (variable, . . . , variable)
        ⎵⎵⎵⎵⎵⎵⎵⎵⎵⎵⎵
              optional

or

readln (variable, . . . , variable)
          ⎵⎵⎵⎵⎵⎵⎵⎵⎵⎵⎵
                optional

When either of these statements is executed, values are obtained from the input stream and assigned to the variables on the above *input lists*. The positional correspondence rule applies: the next value (following the one previously read in by the program) is obtained and assigned to the first variable on the input list, the following value is assigned to the next variable, etc., until the input list has been satisfied. That means that all variables listed have been provided with values from the input stream. Thus, any number of values may be read in by an input statement. These statements are placed as required by the logic of the program. Typically, the input comes from a terminal keyboard or, ever more rarely, from cards.

EXAMPLE 3–4

The following declaration:

var
    count, position: integer;
    length, volume: real;

is given in the program containing this input statement:

read (count, length, position, volume);

If the corresponding input is:

        5   6.31   12   17.35

then, following the execution of the above read statement the value of *count* is 5, the value of *length* is 6.31, etc.

The same effect would have been obtained if the input data were presented as follows:

    5   6.31
        12
    17.35

Thus, only the order of the input data counts as long as there are no intervening separators other than blank spaces or ends of lines. We are free to lay out the input data in the fashion that suits us best.

These rules apply:

(1) Enough data must be provided to assign a value to every variable on the input list.

(2) The types of the variable and the input data must be the same; an exception (of which any use should be avoided as confusing) is that an integer value may be provided for a real variable.

(3) Data values are represented as discussed in Section B of this chapter.

(4) Numerical data items must be separated from one another by at least one space or end of line (as many of these as desired may be provided, however), but no other symbols; also, no separators may be embedded within a data value.

(5) Input lists may be broken up and allotted to consecutive input statements. Thus, there is no difference between the effect of the *read* statement in Example 3–4 and that of the following sequence:

read (count, length);
read (position, volume);

(6) No data value in the input stream may be read more than once! Once read, the value has "passed."

(7) If not enough data are provided to satisfy an input list, an execution error ensues. A batch program will "crash," that is, terminate without giving the desired results; an interactive program will "hang," waiting for data to come from the terminal.

The *read* statement does not terminate the current line of the input stream; a subsequent input statement may continue reading from it. On the other hand, the *readln* ("read a line") statement will read the values needed by its input list and then skip the remainder of the current line of the input stream. Thus, after this statement is executed, the data available for reading are those on the next line of the input stream.

A *readln* without parameters serves to discard the current input line. Note that these are equivalent:

readln (x, y, z);

and

read (x, y, z);
readln;

EXAMPLE 3–5
The following explains the actions of the *read* and *readln* procedures. In practice, we should strive for a regular layout of input data, however.
The following declaration:

```
var
    number, issue, id: integer;
    price, density: real;
```

is given in the program containing these input statements:

```
readln (id, price);
read (issue);
readln;
readln;
readln (density);
```

The following lines of the input stream are presented:

```
13751    12.35    111    222
15
        13
    0.15
```

After the input statements have been executed, these values are acquired by the variables:

id has the value 13751;
price has the value 12.35;
(111 and 222 are skipped by *readln*);
issue has the value 15;
(the next line is skipped by the second parameterless *readln*);
density has the value 0.15;
no value has been assigned to *number* by these statements.

The programmer should carefully present input data to ensure that every variable on an input list is given the desired value of the appropriate type.

---

2. OUTPUT

The general form of the statements writing data into the output stream is:

write (output list)

or

writeln (output list)

where *output list* may include variables, constants, expressions in general (see the next section), and character strings, all separated by commas. For example, we may use the statement:

    writeln ('Area of the triangle number ', triangleNo, ' is ', area);

assuming that the two variables have been declared (e.g., the first as integer and the second as real).

The values from the output list are placed in the output stream in the sequence in which they are listed. Any expressions listed are first evaluated, and the value is written out. Typically, the output goes to a terminal screen or a printer.

Character strings placed on the output list are reproduced exactly as specified within their enclosing apostrophes; thus the programmer should provide any desired leading or trailing spaces there.

Unless the programmer specifies the layout of numerical data (as described in Section H of this chapter), they are presented in a rigid format defined by the implementation. Namely, every implementation provides default values[1] for the total width of the fields in which integer and real numbers are presented or displayed. Also by default, real values are presented in exponential notation.

Thus, for example, a system which allots by default 10 columns to an integer number and 16 to a real value may print in response to the above *writeln* statement this line:

Area of the triangle number $\underbrace{\qquad\qquad 3}_{\text{10 columns}}$ is $\underbrace{\text{3.24000000E}+01}_{\text{16 columns}}$

This rigid output format has been provided in Pascal to simplify the output of columns of numbers and is frequently undesirable in other situations. In such a case the programmer may explicitly state the desired field width as discussed in Section H of this chapter.

In the default output format, integers are printed right-justified (with leading spaces) in the field provided by the system. Real numbers are automatically extended with zeroes to fill the field, as shown above, even though the precision of the number may not warrant the zeroes. Many implementations leave the first column blank, and the next column is reserved for the sign of the real number.

A *write* statement does not terminate the current line. The data to be written out as ordered by consecutive *write* statements is collected and written out when a *writeln* statement is executed. A *writeln* ("write line") statement forces writing of any pending output lists from the preceding *write* statements and then writes its own output list (if any). Subsequently, *writeln* starts a new line, ready for the data from the next output statement. In particular,

writeln;   {*no parameters*}

simply starts a new line.

---

1. Default value (or action) in computing is the one assumed (or taken) by the system in the absence of an explicit specification by the programmer.

EXAMPLE 3-6

These output statements are executed:

write (partial, increment);
writeln;
writeln;
write (count);
writeln (total);

Assuming the appropriate types and values of the variables, these outputs will be obtained:

$$\underbrace{-5.14120000E-02}_{16} \quad \underbrace{-1.23120000E-05}_{16}$$

$$\underbrace{17 \quad \underbrace{8.43100000E+03}_{16}}_{10}$$

In general, the programmer should ensure that the last output statement executed by the program is *writeln,* in order to write out any pending output (although in many implementations all pending output lists from *write* statements are written out before the next input statement is executed or before the program terminates). *Writeln* statements are more commonly used in Pascal programming than *write* statements.

When specifying an output list or a sequence of write statements, the programmer needs to consider the line width of the output device. This is typically 132 columns (characters) for a line printer and 80 columns for a terminal display (other values occur, though).

3. INTERACTIVE VS. BATCH PROGRAMS

The programmer will probably encounter both interactive and batch systems.

All the data required by a batch program are supplied with the program. A batch job submitted for execution includes, along with the program and data, the commands to the system identifying the resources required to execute the program.

The special features of interactive programming stem from the fact that data come from the user of the program, who is present at the terminal while the program is running. The program should request and identify specific data items with the appropriate *writeln* (or, more rarely, *write*) statements; this is called *prompting.* Unless a prompt is issued to identify the data requested of the user, the program will simply wait for data, and appear to be "hanging."

For reliability's sake, in many cases the entered data are redisplayed to the user. In practical programs, the validity of data entered is checked and the user is asked to reenter any item found invalid by the program.

As we will see in Chapter 17, both interactive and batch programs may also use data contained in files stored in secondary memory.

The following example illustrates interactive input; Example 3–12 will show in more detail the distinctions between interactive and batch programs.

EXAMPLE 3–7

This is a complete exercise program written for an interactive session:

```
program echo (input, output);
      {output all the input data presented}

var
   phoneNo, time, areaCode: integer;

begin
   writeln ('Phone call information is entered.');
   writeln;
   writeln ('Please enter the area code called:');
   readln (areaCode);
   writeln ('Please enter the number called (digits only):');
   readln (phoneNo);
   writeln ('Number called was: ', areaCode, phoneNo);
   writeln ('Please enter length of call in whole minutes, ',
            'and your area code:');
   readln (time, areaCode);
   writeln ('Length of call was', time, ' minutes, from area code',
            areaCode);
   writeln;
   writeln ('Thank you.')
end.
```

Note the prompts to the user of the program to enter the appropriate data, and the program "echoing" (displaying back) all the data for error detection. In a practical program, a similar segment would serve to enter the data to be processed by the program.

This is the protocol of a user session with the program (data entered by the user are underlined):

```
Phone call information is entered.

Please enter the area code called:
212
Please enter the number called (digits only):
5553000
Number called was:        212    5553000
Please enter length of call in whole minutes, and your area code:
3 201
Length of call was          3 minutes, from area code          201

Thank you.
   |
```

F. ASSIGNMENT STATEMENT AND EXPRESSIONS

Data manipulation is performed by computing the value of an expression. This value may be assigned to a variable by means of an assignment statement and subsequently used in further computations. In particular, calculations are done using assignment statements with integer or real data.

An assignment statement causes an expression to be evaluated and the result to be assigned to a variable. The order of evaluation of an expression is determined by the relative precedence of its operators and by the use of parentheses.

1. ASSIGNMENT

The general form of an assignment statement is:

$$\text{variable} := \text{expression}$$

where the double symbol ":=" is the assignment operator which may be read as "is set to." Thus, the new value of the variable is set to the value of the expression.

An expression (discussed in detail further in this section) consists of constants and variables of appropriate type, joined by operators. Parentheses may be used to impose precedence of evaluation.

During the execution of an assignment statement the following sequence of events occurs:

(1) The expression is evaluated according to the rules of precedence.
(2) The value obtained is assigned to the variable whose name appears on the left-hand side of the statement (i.e., the value is placed in the memory location named by the variable identifier).

EXAMPLE 3–8
These are three valid independent assignment statements:

(a) *total* := *10;*
(b) *newRate* := *oldRate* + *increase;*
(c) *volume* := *volume* + *1;*

Note that the last assignment statement is meaningful: it causes the value of the variable *volume* to be increased by 1.

Note the following:

(1) All variables whose identifiers appear in an expression must have been given a value earlier in the program.

> Undefined variable values are common beginner's errors!

(2) The values of the variables referenced only by the right-hand side of an assignment statement remain unchanged by it; the previous value of the variable on the left-hand side is replaced by the new one.

Since an assignment provides a new value for the variable on its left-hand side, that variable does not require a previously defined value (unless it also appears in the expression on the right-hand side, as *volume* does in assignment statement (c) of Example 3–8).

The action of assignment statement (b) of Example 3–8 is illustrated in Fig. 3–2.

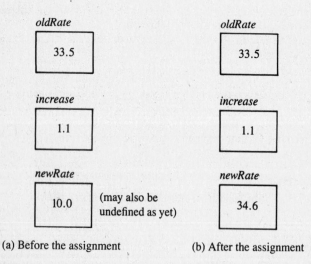

(a) Before the assignment   (b) After the assignment

FIGURE 3–2. Effect of an assignment statement (from Example 3–8–b).

In an assignment statement, the expression has to be "assignment-compatible" with the variable. Assignment compatibility means that, in general, the type of the variable on the left-hand side of an assignment statement and the type of the value defined by the expression must be the same (this rule is further discussed in Chapter 6–E).

The exception to this rule is that a real variable may be assigned an integer value. This exception is justified by the fact that for every integer there is an equal real value, and only a change of internal representation is involved in such an assignment.

Thus, these are legal assignment statements for numerical computations:

integer variable := integer expression

$$\text{real variable} := \begin{cases} \text{real expression} \\ \quad \text{or} \\ \text{integer expression} \end{cases}$$

2. ARITHMETIC EXPRESSIONS

An expression combines constants and variables[2] of appropriate type with compatible operators in order to compute a value.

We have already encountered the use of expressions in assignment statements. They may also appear in output statements, where the value computed is sent directly into the output stream.

Arithmetic expressions combine integer and real constants and variables with the operators for addition, subtraction, multiplication, and division. These expressions are written like formulas of ordinary algebra. The operators are specified in Table 3–1.

TABLE 3–1. Arithmetic Operators

Operator	Operation	Type of Operands	Type of Result
+ — *	addition subtraction multiplication	integer or real integer or real integer or real	integer, if both operands are of integer type, otherwise real
/	division	integer or real; second operand $\neq 0$	real
div	division with truncation	both integer; second operand $\neq 0$	integer
mod	modulo	both integer; second operand > 0	integer

2. As we will see in Section G, and in more general terms in Chapter 11, function designators may be included as well.

Note:

(1) The four basic operators $(+, -, *, /)$ apply to both integer and real operands. Moreover, one of the operands may be integer while the other is real; in this case the result is real.

> Mixing integer and real operands requires additional care and should be limited. Remember that the value of the expression is real in this case.

(2) The division of two integer values with the "/" operator gives a real result; if the fractional part is to be automatically discarded, the **div** operator should be used as described below.
(3) Division by zero is, of course, not allowed.
(4) The "$-$" sign may be also used preceding the first variable or constant identifier, or the first parenthesis, in an expression.
(5) There is no exponentiation operator in Pascal; one method of raising a value to a power is a repeated multiplication by itself.
(6) All operators must appear explicitly in an arithmetic expression ("*" may not be omitted, for example), and no two operators may abut.

EXAMPLE 3–9

These are some encodings of algebraic formulas as Pascal assignment statements (assuming that a, b, c, d are integer or real variables and constants, and x is a real variable):

algebraic notation	Pascal
$x = \dfrac{a + b}{c + d}$	$x := (a + b)/(c + d)$
$x = \dfrac{a + b}{c} + d$	$x := (a + b)/c + d$
$x = -5a + \dfrac{a}{b + c}[a - b(7 - c)]$	$x := -5 * a + a * (a - b * (7 - c))/(b + c)$

But do not forget about meaningful identifiers!

Of interest are the two operators **div** and **mod,** applicable only to integer values:

(a) i **div** j
integer division of i by j, which causes division with truncation (discarding) of the fractional part of the quotient; thus:

5 **div** 2 equals 2
−5 **div** 2 equals −2
2 **div** 5 equals 0

(b) i **mod** j (where j > 0)

for nonnegative i (the common case), computes the remainder of the integer division of i by j; thus:

5 **mod** 2 equals 1
2 **mod** 5 equals 2
4 **mod** 2 equals 0

If the value i is negative, the result is the smallest nonnegative integer which, if subtracted from i, produces an integral multiple of j; thus:

−5 **mod** 3 equals 1
−7 **mod** 4 equals 1

EXAMPLE 3–10

If the constant *pageSize* is the total number of lines per page of our output medium, and the program keeps a running count of output lines in a variable *lineCount,* then the expression

$$(lineCount\ −\ 1)\ \textbf{mod}\ pageSize\ +\ 1$$

computes the line number on the current page, and

$$(lineCount\ −\ 1)\ \textbf{div}\ pageSize\ +\ 1$$

computes the current page number.

The order in which an expression is evaluated is determined by the relative precedence of the operators that appear in it, unless this order is changed by the use of parentheses—similar to such usage in algebra.

The usual algebraic order of precedence among operators applies. This means that the operators joining two operands,

*, /, div, mod

take precedence over

+, −.

In order to modify this order of evaluation, parentheses are used. Only round parentheses are allowed. Parentheses must be matched, that is, every left parenthesis must have a matching right parenthesis.

It is sometimes wise to use parentheses to clarify the meaning of an expression, even though they are not necessary to impose an order of precedence. Also, when you are in doubt about the order of precedence, parenthesize!

The overall order of evaluation for arithmetic expressions is defined by these rules:

(1) If parentheses are present, the contents of the innermost parentheses are evaluated first. Then the contents of the next enclosing parentheses are evaluated, and so on.
(2) If there are no parentheses, or within a matching pair of parentheses, the operations are performed in the following order of precedence:

*, /, div, mod;
+, −

(3) Operations of the same level of precedence are performed from left to right.
(4) The order of evaluation of the two operands joined by an operator depends on the implementation.

EXAMPLE 3–11
When, for example, this expression:

$$(a - b) * (c + d)$$

is being evaluated,

$$a - b \text{ and } c + d$$

may be computed in either order (or even in parallel). Then, the multiplication will be performed.

This advice will help in legible coding.

(1) When in doubt, use parentheses.
(2) If a complex arithmetic expression has to be coded, breaking it up into several assignment statements may increase the readability of your program.
(3) Use blank spaces to increase the readability of a statement. In particular, you may place a blank on each side of every operator.

EXAMPLE 3-12

Here is a complete program, presented in batch and interactive versions.
Note the differences of approach.

(1) Batch version

```
program circle (input, output);     {batch version}
        {compute circumference and area of a circle}

const
   pi = 3.14159;
var
   radius: real;

begin
   readln (radius);
   writeln ('For a circle with the radius of ', radius,
            ', circumference is ', 2 * pi * radius);
   writeln (' and area is ', pi * radius * radius)
end.
```

With this input:

5.3719

the following output was produced:

```
For a circle with the radius of  5.37190E+00, circumference is  3.37526E+01
  and area is  9.06578E+01
```

(2) Interactive version

In this second version of the program, we will provide variables to hold
the values of expressions instead of placing the expressions directly into
the output list. Note that this makes the program somewhat more readable
but longer. This policy is not a feature of interactive programming!

Prompting the programmer (or user of the program), sitting at the
terminal, for data by describing the data is, on the other hand, necessary
for the successful operation of an interactive program.

```
program circle (input, output);     {interactive}
        {computes circumference and area of circle}

const
   pi = 3.14159;
var
   radius, circumference, area: real;

begin
   writeln ('Please input the radius of the circle:');
   readln (radius);
   writeln ('The radius is ', radius);
   circumference := 2 * pi * radius;
   area := pi * radius * radius;
   writeln ('The circumference of the circle is ', circumference);
   writeln ('The area of the circle is ', area)
end.
```

This is a sample session (the user's input is underlined):

```
Please input the radius of the circle:
3.0
The radius is   3.00000E+00
The circumference of the circle is   1.88495E+01
The area of the circle is   2.82743E+01
```

3. LIMITATIONS ON THE VALUE OF EXPRESSIONS

The value of an expression must not be larger (in absolute terms) than the limit imposed by the computer implementation, otherwise an *overflow* results.

For integer values, the limit is given by the constant *maxint,* as discussed in Section B–1 of this chapter.

In the case of real values, both the magnitude and the precision of the representable values are limited, as discussed in Section B–2. Since a real value cannot, in general, be represented exactly in a binary code used by computers, the results of real arithmetic are not entirely exact. Although in the majority of situations the programmer does not have to consider this fact, one should be aware of this limitation and act accordingly. Thus:

- Do not count with real variables instead of integers (obviously, this is always an integer value).
- Do not test for equality of two real values if at least one of them was obtained through a computation, since 10.0/100.0 in computer arithmetic may not equal 0.1, although in some implementations it may be printed as such. Instead, check whether the difference between the two values is as small as desired (see Example 4–3b).

G. STANDARD ARITHMETIC AND TRANSFER FUNCTIONS

Certain programming tasks, such as computing a square root or a power of a number, frequently recur. In order to simplify programmers' work, sequences of statements that perform these tasks are available in every Pascal system as required by the Pascal standard. These so-called standard (or required) functions are predeclared, that is, built into the Pascal system, and thus may be directly used by the programmer (as will be seen in Part II, programmers may also declare, i.e., write, their own functions).

Each of the standard arithmetic functions is presented with a single value, and computes the appropriate function of it also as a single value. The value to which a function is to be applied is supplied to the function in general as an expression (although in many cases it is simply a variable), and is called the *parameter* of the function.

A function is used by placing the function designator in the expression where its value is needed, in a manner similar to the use of a variable.

A *function designator* for a standard function[3] has the following general form:

$$\text{function-identifier (expression)}$$

For example, this statement uses the function *sqr* to compute the square of its parameter *radius:*

area := pi * sqr (radius);

The standard arithmetic functions are listed in Table 3–2.

Since the parameter of a function may be an expression, it may itself contain a function designator, as in:

writeln (sqrt (sqr (b) — 4 * a * c));

When a function designator appears, its parameter is first evaluated, if necessary, and then the function result is computed.

TABLE 3–2. Standard (Required) Arithmetic Functions

Function Designator	Purpose	Limitations on the Parameter (It May Be of Integer or Real Type)	Result
abs (x)	absolute value: $|x|$		
sqr (x)	square: x^2	such that $x^2 \leq maxint$	same type as x
sqrt (x)	square root: $\sqrt{x}$	$x \geq 0$	
exp (x)	exponential: e^x		
ln (x)	natural logarithm: ln x	$x > 0$	real
sin (x)	sine	expressed in radians;	
cos (x)	cosine	1 radian $\simeq 57°$	
arctan (x)	arctangent (principal value)		real—expressed in radians

3. Other than the two functions that test files, discussed later in the text (their parameter, if present, specifies a file).

Note that, as Table 3–2 shows:

(1) In all arithmetic functions, the parameter may be integer or real.
(2) Only for the functions *abs* and *sqr* is the result of the same type as the parameter; the result of all other functions is real.

The Pascal system also provides two *transfer functions,* for transfer from the real into the integer type:

(1) *trunc (x),*
for a real parameter x, the integer result is obtained by truncating (discarding) the fractional part; thus

$$trunc \ (-4.9) \ \text{yields} \ -4$$

(2) *round (x),*
for a real parameter x, the integer result is obtained by rounding off to the closest integer, thus

$$round \ (-4.9) \ \text{yields} \ -5$$

EXAMPLE 3–13
Note the order of evaluation of these expressions.

(1) the real expression

$$3.5 + sqr \ (6.5 - (sqrt \ (1.44) + 3.3))$$

will be evaluated in this order:

$3.5 + sqr \ (6.5 - (1.2 + 3.3))$
$3.5 + sqr \ (6.5 - 4.5)$
$3.5 + sqr \ (2.0)$
$3.5 + 4.0$
7.5

(2) the integer expression

$$14 \ \textbf{mod} \ trunc \ (3.5) + 5 * 15 \ \textbf{div} \ 4$$

may be correctly evaluated in this order:

$14 \ \textbf{mod} \ 3 + 5 * 15 \ \textbf{div} \ 4$
$2 + 5 * 15 \ \textbf{div} \ 4$
$2 + 75 \ \textbf{div} \ 4$
$2 + 18$
20

The following example illustrates the use of functions.

EXAMPLE 3-14

A single-chip microcomputer consists of a square area holding the processor and memory, and the area surrounding them, as shown in Fig. 3–3. This surrounding area contains buffers and bonding pads, and is 20 mils wide (a mil is one thousandth of an inch). Thus, the total area of such a square chip is:

$$\text{chip area} = (\sqrt{\text{processor area} + \text{memory area}} + 40)^2$$

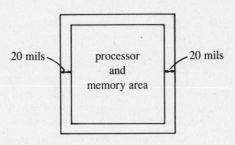

FIGURE 3-3. A microcomputer chip.

This program, prepared for batch execution, computes the chip area:

```
program chipArea (input, output);
        {determine the area of a single-chip computer}
const
   padWidth = 40;
var
   processorArea, memoryArea, chipArea: integer; {specified in mils}
begin
   writeln ('All data in square mils.');
   writeln;
   readln (processorArea, memoryArea);
   writeln ('Processor area :', processorArea,
            '     Memory area: ', memoryArea);
   chipArea := sqr (round ( sqrt (processorArea + memoryArea)) + 40);
   writeln ('Chip area:', chipArea)
end.
```

A typical output:

```
Processor area :        6000     Memory area:        15000
Chip area:       34225
```

H. CONTROLLING THE OUTPUT FORMAT

As discussed earlier, a Pascal processor has a default format for printing or displaying integer and real values. Output with this format is sometimes difficult to read, however; in particular, the exponential output format for real numbers may be unnatural in the context of a specific problem.

The programmer may override the default by providing an explicit output field specification for any value on the output list. The general format of such specification for all data with the exception of real numbers in positional notation is:

value: total width

where the total width is the width of the field in which the value is to be presented (in other words, the number of output columns allotted to it).

For example:

writeln (count: 5);

The total width may, in general, be an integer expression; thus the spacing may depend on the value of program variables. The Pascal processor automatically protects the integrity of numerical output if insufficient total width of the field was provided by expanding it to accommodate the numbers, as described below.

Use consistent formats for the output of numerical data.

1. OUTPUT OF FIXED CHARACTER STRINGS

If the string is shorter than the total width, it will be presented right-justified in the field allotted, with the leading columns left blank. If the string is longer than the field (usually an error), its rightmost characters will be discarded (truncated). For example,

writeln (' ': 10, 'Attention!': 15, ' Provide the value!': 8);

will produce this output line:

	Attention!	Provide
10 spaces	15	8

Note the handy way of specifying spaces.

2. OUTPUT OF INTEGERS

If the total width allotted for an integer is "wider" than the integer, it will be presented right-justified. If, on the other hand, the field is insufficient, it will be expanded to present the integer in the smallest possible space (i.e., without any surrounding blanks). Hence, if no surrounding blanks are desired, this will always do to avoid the leading spaces of the default format:

writeln (count: 1); {count is of integer type}

3. OUTPUT OF REAL NUMBERS

"Formatted" real numbers may be presented either in positional or in exponential notation.

When printing (displaying) a real value, select the precision befitting the problem and the input data.

---

a. Positional Format

This formatted output style is used most frequently because it suppresses the default exponential format output.

The general form is:

value: total width: number of fractional digits

where total width and number of fractional digits are integer expressions (they may be constants, of course).

For example,

writeln (volume: 10: 2);

specifies that the value of the real variable *volume* is to be placed right-justified in a field of total width 10, with 2 digits after the decimal point. This, for example, might be a requested output:

$$\underbrace{\qquad -35.11}_{4}$$

Note that the same result will be achieved by each of these legal output statements:

writeln (−35.11: 10: 2);

or

writeln ((partial − 15.11): 10: 2);

assuming that the current value of the variable *partial* is −20.0.

Extra fractional digits are rounded to the number specified. However, if the total width is insufficient, it will be expanded to show the complete value.

EXAMPLE 3–15

Problem

Convert a temperature reading from the Fahrenheit to the Celsius scale.

Solution

In this program, attention has been paid to the precision of values:

```
program temperature (input, output);
        {convert temperature from Fahrenheit to Celsius scale}

const
    integerDigits = 3;
    precision = 2;
var
    Fahrenheit: real;
    width: integer;

begin
    readln (Fahrenheit);
    width := integerDigits + precision + 1;
    writeln (Fahrenheit: width: precision, ' degrees Fahrenheit equals ',
            5 * (Fahrenheit - 32)/9: width: precision, ' degrees Celsius.')
end.
```

Output:

```
400.00 degrees Fahrenheit equals 204.44 degrees Celsius.
```

b. Exponential Format

The general form is, as for integers,

value: total width

Since in most implementations the exponent is represented with two digits, a minimum of eight columns is required to represent a number in this format, according to this layout:

sd.dEsdd

where s is a sign, and d is a digit. For example:

$-5.3E-02$

Higher precision requires more space. Additional space will be given if needed to show the value.

Many implementations provide a space before every real number in the output, thus requiring more columns as a minimum.

4. PRINTING ON A NEW PAGE

To start a new page the programmer issues this statement:

page

For example:

page;
writeln (income: 8: 2);

The programmer can keep a count of lines printed so far, and "throw a page" when reaching a count that corresponds to a full page on the printer that is being used.

I. TECHNIQUE 2: STYLISTIC GUIDELINES FOR READABLE PROGRAMS AND OUTPUTS

The programmer should follow a consistent pattern of presenting the program and its output in a readable fashion. Following are some of the guidelines which may help in this task.

1. GUIDELINES FOR PROGRAM READABILITY

Program code has to be almost self-documenting. Both a reader of the program and its author should be able to understand its operation and modify it, if so desired, sometime in the future. The following should help.

(a) Use identifiers that describe the meaning of the entities being named in the problem.
(b) Supply all comments needed to understand how the problem is handled by the program. Do not overcomment, however; in particular, do not allow the comments to duplicate or smother the code. Make the comments stand out from the code itself.
(c) Meaningful segments of code may be grouped by surrounding them with blank lines. Blank spaces may be used within the code lines to enhance their readability.
(d) In general, place a single declaration/definition or statement per line.
(e) Indent declarations/definitions and statements from the keywords, such as **begin, var,** etc., by a consistent number of spaces. Indentation by 3 spaces is used by many Pascal programmers.

2. GUIDELINES FOR OUTPUT READABILITY

All programs should produce an output. Usually, interactive programs, which are oriented toward a terminal screen output, are written to produce less output than batch programs which, in general, result in printed output.
It is well to remember that while the program code will be read in most

instances by other programmers, the output is oriented toward the so-called end user, a nonprogrammer. Hence, it needs to be eminently legible. These guidelines may be followed.

(a) Use character strings to explain the meaning of every output value. Use a consistent format for the values themselves.
(b) Design the layout of the output carefully, possibly using the formatting features of Section H.
(c) Echo all the input that does not come from large files. This is particularly important during program testing. Without the input values, the output values are, in general, meaningless.
(d) For printed output, paginate correctly.
(e) Interactive programming should include prompts to the terminal user for input data (best one at a time), and in an established system, immediate rejection of inappropriate input data, with another prompt to the user.

The program and its printed output constitute important components of the overall program documentation.

J. TECHNIQUE 3: PROGRAMMING BY STEPWISE REFINEMENT WITH PSEUDOCODE

For most tasks worth programming, we would find it impossible to code directly from the problem statement, even following the analysis of the problem: the details of coding in the given language, Pascal in our case, would overwhelm our thinking about the problem solution. Program design, therefore, is a distinct step that should follow problem analysis. We need a vehicle to express this problem solution as it gradually emerges; in other words, we need a notation for the algorithm that has to be developed before the program will be coded.

A widely accepted algorithmic notation is *pseudocode,* an outline-like specification of an algorithm that lists needed actions in brief statements in English, imposing strict sequencing on them. As we will see later (in Chapters 5 and 7), this notation incorporates the control structures of programming that provide the logic of the algorithm (and later of the program itself). In other words, these control structures specify the order in which the statements are to be carried out (if it is different from the sequence in which they appear).

Development of a large program is a complex task. Like any complex task, it has to be accomplished gradually, beginning with the most general (abstract) outline of the solution, which is progressively fleshed out with detail.

The design of an algorithm which proceeds from a general to a more detailed description is called *stepwise refinement.* Several stages of refinement for the initial version of the algorithm may be needed: the algorithm is thus designed in a top-down fashion. As we will see in Chapter 8, in the process of stepwise refinement of non-trivial algorithms we will be able to identify program modules: relatively independent components responsible for handling well-defined aspects of the problem. The stepwise refinement process stops when we are able to code directly in Pascal from the most recent version of the algorithm.

Pseudocode obtained during the stepwise refinement process serves as an important part of the program documentation since it explains the program in a hierarchical fashion: its first version excludes almost all detail, while subsequent refinements provide further explanation. Pseudocode may also serve as a source of comments for the program.

Pseudocode used as a vehicle for stepwise refinement thus serves two basic purposes:

- it is a design tool;
- it becomes a component of the documentation for the finished product, thus assisting in program maintenance.

The format of pseudocode is flexible, aiming at the best way to express and communicate the algorithmic solution. The following guidelines will be of assistance:

- the statements ought to be brief imperative calls for action;
- an indentation pattern (to be seen in more detail when the control structures are discussed in Chapters 5 and 7) should be maintained;
- comments may be included;
- the pseudocode of the later refinement steps may become very close to the actual Pascal code in some of its fragments. This occurs, in particular, when the complexity of a specific subtask requires a bottom-up (details first) investigation of it. Thus, some of the variables that will become part of the code may be identified at the time of pseudocoding.

The following example illustrates the use of pseudocode in a rather simple program.

EXAMPLE 3–16

Problem

Develop a change-making program: for a given amount of change (smaller than a dollar), produce this change with the minimum number of coins and specify these coins.

Solution

(1) Pseudocode of the algorithm in initial form:

program *produceChange;*
begin
    read in the amount of change required;
    starting with the largest-denomination coin, determine the
           number of various coins in the change;
    write out the coin counts
end.

(2) Pseudocode of the first refinement:

program *produceChange;*
begin
    read in the amount of change required;
    determine the number of half dollars;
    determine the number of quarters in the remainder;
    determine the number of dimes in the remainder;
    determine the number of nickels in the remainder;
    determine the number of pennies in the remainder;
    write the total number of coins;
    write the number of coins of each denomination
end.

(3) Based on the last refinement, this program is produced:

```
program produceChange (input, output);
        {compute the minimum number of coins needed to produce
         change in an amount smaller than one dollar, and
         specify the coins required}

var
    amountOfChange, remainder,      {original and remaining change}
    halfdollars, quarters, dimes, nickels, pennies: integer; {coin counts}

begin
    readln (amountOfChange);
    halfdollars := amountOfChange div 50;
    remainder := amountOfChange mod 50;
    quarters := remainder div 25;
    remainder := remainder mod 25;
    dimes := remainder div 10;
    remainder := remainder mod 10;
    nickels := remainder div 5;
    pennies := remainder mod 5;
    writeln ('To produce ', amountOfChange:1, ' cents, the minimum number of',
             ' coins is ', halfdollars + quarters + dimes + nickels +
             pennies: 1, ', namely:');
    writeln (halfdollars: 1, ' in half dollars');
    writeln (quarters:1, ' in quarters');
    writeln (dimes: 1, ' in dimes');
    writeln (nickels: 1, ' in nickels');
    writeln (pennies: 1, ' in pennies')
end.
```

This is a typical output:

```
To produce 98 cents, the minimum number of coins is 7, namely:
1 in half dollars
1 in quarters
2 in dimes
0 in nickels
3 in pennies
```

You may note that the initial version of the algorithm in the above example conforms to this pseudocode outline, typical for most programs:

```
begin
    read in data;
    process data;
    output results
end.
```

4

BOOLEAN AND CHARACTER DATA

The Boolean data type serves to define data whose value may be either *true* or *false*. Boolean expressions, which may include relational, Boolean, and arithmetic operations, are most often used to specify program "logic," that is, its alternative execution sequences. During program execution, the value of such expressions included in the control statements (see Chapters 5 and 7) is tested, and the appropriate execution sequence is thus established.

Character (text) data are sometimes manipulated with the use of the *char* data type, whose values are single characters from the character set of the computer.

Boolean and *char* data types, together with the integer type (and user-defined types discussed in Chapter 6) belong to the category of ordinal data types. The values of such data types are strictly ordered, from the smallest to the largest, and thus relational operators and ordinal functions are applicable to them.

A. BOOLEAN DATA AND BOOLEAN EXPRESSIONS

The Boolean data type provides only two possible values for its items: *false* and *true*. Data of this type may be combined in Boolean expressions with relational and Boolean operators to specify the conditions for selecting alternative execution paths in a program.

1. BOOLEAN DATA

The power of digital computers rests to a large extent on the programmer's ability to specify alternative actions. One of these is to be taken by the computer if a certain condition is *true* or *false* at the time it is being tested during program execution.

The means for specifying such conditions are provided through the Boolean[1] data type, along with the operations rendering the value *true* or *false*. In some cases, data items of the type Boolean are also used directly to store and manipulate data which may assume only one of these two values[2] (for example, to process responses to a yes/no quiz) in a fashion similar to, say, integer data.

The two Boolean constants *false* and *true* are predefined in Pascal and other Boolean constants may be defined in terms of these. Boolean variables may be declared in the routine fashion. Assignment of a Boolean value to a Boolean variable may be performed.

EXAMPLE 4–1a

This is a valid program fragment:

> ⋮
>
> **const**
>   *fair* = *true;*
> **var**
>   *assertion: Boolean;*
> **begin**
>   *assertion* := *fair;*
> ⋮

Boolean expressions are discussed in the next section.

To output a Boolean value, we may use the *write* or *writeln* procedures. Depending on the value, the string *true* or *false* (the case of the letters—upper or lower—depends on the implementation) will be presented. To provide the desired leading spaces, total width may be specified (as shown in Chapter 3–H).

EXAMPLE 4–1b

Continuing the program from Example 4–1a, this statement:

writeln (assertion: 10);

will provide this output:

>   true
>   ⎣‾‾‾‾‾⎦
>   6

or

>   TRUE
>   ⎣‾‾‾‾‾⎦
>   6

---

1. The English mathematician George Boole created the algebra of two-valued logic in the mid-19th century.

2. We may say that Boolean data have the cardinality of two, since **cardinality** is the number of distinct values in a given data type.

However, Pascal provides no means for the input of Boolean values. This limitation may be circumvented easily.

Three required (standard) Boolean functions[3] are available: *odd, eoln, eof.* The two last functions are used to control input and are described in Chapter 5–E. The function *odd (x),* whose parameter *x* has to be an integer expression, has the value *true* if *x* is odd, and *false* if *x* is even.

EXAMPLE 4–2

The use of *odd (x)* is illustrated by the following pseudocode fragment:

{classify the integer *x* and count it appropriately}
    if *odd (x)* **then**
        increment the counter of odd numbers
    else
        increment the counter of even numbers

Thus, if *odd (x)* yields false, only the counter of even numbers is incremented.

The values of Boolean expressions (or simply variables) may be compared using the relational operators discussed in the next section. The value *false* is by definition smaller than *true.*

2. BOOLEAN EXPRESSIONS

Boolean expressions, evaluating to a logical value of *false* or *true,* play an extremely important role in programming. Their use allows the programmer "to steer" the program execution sequence depending on the conditions which arise during the processing. Thus, for example, the program may specify: "if the computed *revenue* is greater than *limit,* then execute a sequence of statements computing *tax,* otherwise execute the statements which compute *credit.*" The statements which allow us to express such decisions are presented in Chapter 5; here we will learn to represent the conditions which are to be tested.

A condition whose outcome (i.e., value) may be only *false* or *true* is represented as a Boolean expression.

Boolean expressions may include relational, Boolean, and arithmetic operators. Such an expression may be used in an assignment to a Boolean variable or in an output list (similar to an arithmetic expression). However, the most frequent use of Boolean expressions is to express a condition in a decision or a loop statement, as discussed in Chapter 5.

---

3. Boolean functions are also called *predicates.*

There are six general-purpose relational operators[4] in Pascal, shown in Table 4–1.

TABLE 4–1. Relational Operators of Pascal

Pascal Operator	Meaning	Algebraic Notation
=	is equal to	=
< >	is not equal to	≠
<	is less than	<
< =	is less than or equal to	≤
> =	is greater than or equal to	≥
>	is greater than	>

Two operands joined by a relational operator produce a simple condition, often called a *relation*. Such a relation asserts the truth of a certain equality or inequality, and produces the value of *false* or *true*.

Thus, for example, the Boolean expression

$$twoscore \; < > \; 40$$

will give the value *false* if the current value of *twoscore* (which has to be of integer or real type) is 40, and *true* if it differs from 40.

The operands joined by a relational operator need to be compatible. Compatibility is discussed more fully in Chapter 6–E; suffice it to say now that the operands have to be of the same type, with the exception that one may be an integer and the other real.

A condition may also include arithmetic operators, which take precedence over relational operators. It may also include arithmetic and transfer functions.

EXAMPLE 4–3

(a) The following test on integer variables:

$$sqr \; (b) \; - \; 4 \; * \; a \; * \; c \; = \; 0$$

checks whether

$$b^2 \; - \; 4ac \; equals \; 0.$$

(b) To test whether two real variables, *next* and *current,* have close enough values to be considered equal, we may employ this condition:

$$abs \; (next \; - \; current) \; < = \; 0.00001$$

4. The seventh relational operator, **in,** applies to sets and is discussed in Chapter 16.

(c) If both *tall* and *young* are Boolean variables, the relation

$$tall <> young$$

has the value *true* only if *tall* and *young* have different truth values. This is known as the *exclusive-or* operation.

On the other hand,

$$tall = young$$

has the value *true* only when *tall* and *young* are both either *true* or *false*. This is the *equivalence* operation.

Do not forget that relational operators do apply to Boolean values; but both values compared by them have to be Boolean.

Note that multiple relations are not allowed. For example, the following double relation:

$$50000 \le bracket \le 60000$$

cannot be directly transcribed into Pascal code. To express such a condition, we need Boolean operators.

Thus, when a condition more complex than a single relation is to be expressed, the Boolean operators **or, and, not** are used. The truth table for these operators is shown as Table 4–2. Note that these operators apply only to entities of Boolean value (for example, P and Q may be Boolean variables or relations).

TABLE 4–2. Truth Table for Boolean Operators

Values of Operands		Result of Operation		
P	**Q**	**not P**	**P and Q**	**P or Q**
false	false	true	false	false
false	true	true	false	true
true	false	false	false	true
true	true	false	true	true

It is easy to think of the three Boolean operators as follows:

(1) The unary (acting on a single operand) operator **not** inverts the value of the operand. If the operand's value is *false,* it becomes *true,* and vice versa.
(2) The **or** operator yields the value *true* if either of its two operands has the value *true.*
(3) The more restrictive **and** operator yields the value *true* only if both of its operands have the value *true.*

With the use of these operators, we have no difficulty in representing the double relation above as

(bracket > = 50000) **and** *(bracket < = 60000)*

Note the need for the parentheses: they impose the desired order of evaluation for this condition. They are necessary, since the three sets of operators which may appear in Boolean expressions have the following order of precedence:

(1) highest: **not**
(2)   ***, /, div, mod, and** (so-called multiplying operators)
(3)   **+, −, or** (so-called adding operators)
(4) lowest: =, < >, <, < =, > =, > (relational operators)

Operations of equal precedence are performed from left to right; parentheses (round only!) may be used to change this order of precedence.

Since the relational operators are of the lowest precedence, it is necessary to place relations in parentheses if Boolean operators are present in the expression.
Parenthesize not only when in doubt, but also to make the Boolean expression easier to understand.

EXAMPLE 4–4
It is assumed that all variables have been declared real.

(1) To encode the following:

both *growth* and *rate* are negative while *total* is not positive

the following Boolean expression may be used:

(growth < 0) **and** *(rate < 0)* **and** *(total < = 0)*

Notes:

(a) The parentheses are required, since without them an attempt will be made by the processor to apply **and** as follows:

0 **and** *rate*

Neither 0 nor *rate* is Boolean, of course, and the program will fail.

(b) A frequent error is to write:

growth **and** *rate* < 0   {wrong!}

Again, the error may be avoided by remembering that Boolean operators apply only to Boolean values.

(2) To encode:

> temperature is neither freezing nor boiling

we may use

> (temperature <> freezing) **and** (temperature <> boiling)

(3) To encode:

> the square root of volume is greater than 5.5 or pressure lies between 10.1 and 17.3 exclusively

we may write

> (sqrt (volume) > 5.5) **or** (pressure > 10.1) **and** (pressure < 17.3)

While Boolean values are most often used directly in statements, such as decisions and loops, which control program flow during execution, sometimes they are assigned to Boolean variables.

EXAMPLE 4–5
The assignment of Boolean values is exemplified by this code fragment:

```
var
    zeroTest, check, greater: Boolean;
    size, nominal: integer;
begin
        ⋮
    check := (size >= nominal);
    greater := (2 * size > nominal − 17);
    zeroTest := (nominal = 0);
        ⋮
```

Note that in all cases parentheses are not necessary, but they do clarify the statements.

Observe that it would be enough for a Pascal processor to evaluate the first true operand of an **or** clause (since then the entire expression is then true), or the first false operand of an **and** clause (since then the expression is false). While some implementations indeed cease the evaluation of a Boolean expression in such cases, we need to assume, in general, that every Boolean expression is completely evaluated.

EXAMPLE 4–6

We cannot write this condition:

(*smaller* = 0) **or** (*greater* **div** *smaller* <= 10)

under the assumption that if *smaller* equals 0 the second operand of the **or** clause will not be evaluated. The attempt may be made to divide by 0, and the program will fail.

The following program operates on Boolean variables.

EXAMPLE 4–7

We will obtain the truth tables for the exclusive-or and equivalence operations, discussed in Example 4–3c:

```
program truthTable (input, output);
        {produce the truth tables for the exclusive-or and
         equivalence operations}

var
    P,Q: Boolean;

begin
    writeln ('Values of Operands      Result of Operation');
    writeln;
    writeln ('    P        Q        exclusive-or    equivalence');
    writeln; writeln;
    P := false;
    Q := false;
    writeln (P: 7, Q: 8, P <> Q: 15, P = Q: 15);
    Q := true;
    writeln (P: 7, Q: 8, P <> Q: 15, P = Q: 15);
    P := true;
    Q := false;
    writeln (P: 7, Q: 8, P <> Q: 15, P = Q: 15);
    Q := true;
    writeln (P: 7, Q: 8, P <> Q: 15, P = Q: 15)
end.
```

These are the truth tables obtained:

Values of Operands		Result of Operation	
P	Q	exclusive-or	equivalence
FALSE	FALSE	FALSE	TRUE
FALSE	TRUE	TRUE	FALSE
TRUE	FALSE	TRUE	FALSE
TRUE	TRUE	FALSE	TRUE

B. CHARACTER DATA

Word (text) processing is an important application of computers. As a limited tool for this task, Pascal offers the *char* data type, whose values are single characters. A more general tool is available as variable character strings, discussed in Chapter 14.

1. *CHAR* DATA TYPE AND CHARACTER SETS

To communicate with computers, people use text, which of course consists of individual characters. For example, lines of text may be presented through a terminal keyboard. Similarly, the output is presented as text via printers or screens. Much of data manipulation consists of character processing: consider text editing or mailing list preparation.

To represent text, the *char* (short for "character") data type is provided by Pascal. The value of a data item of *char* type is, however, only a single character drawn from the character set used by the implementation. (To represent longer variable character strings, packed arrays of characters are used in Pascal, as discussed in Chapter 14.)

Characters available for use depend to an extent on the implementation. In computer memories, characters are stored in binary form. Every computer has its **character set** that determines the correspondence between the individual characters and their internal numerical value in binary code. The two most popular codes, ASCII (pronounced "askee") and EBCDIC (pronounced "ebsedik") are shown in Appendix C.

Regardless of the character set, the following characters are included:

- upper-case letters from "A" through "Z";
- often (but not always) lower-case letters from "a" through "z";
- digits from "0" through "9";
- the blank (space);
- special printable characters, such as arithmetic operators, punctuation marks, and special signs (e.g., @, $);
- control (nonprintable) characters, such as backspace, carriage return, etc.

2. CHARACTER CONSTANTS AND VARIABLES

A character constant, that is, a constant of the type *char,* is specified by enclosing the character in apostrophes (single quotes). If an apostrophe itself is the constant, it is written twice. (Do not use the double-quote symbol for this!)

These are examples of character constants:

$$'M', '?', 'd', ' ', '9', ''''$$

A constant definition may be used to provide an identifier for a character constant; for example:

const
    space = ' ';
    hey = '!';

Note that the apostrophes are necessary to distinguish a character constant from an identifier.

Observe also the distinction between the one-character-long character constants and the potentially longer fixed character strings (discussed in Chapter 2–E).

EXAMPLE 4–8

(a) This statement:

    code := *x*;

assigns the value of the constant or variable *x* to the variable *code*. The two variables must be compatible in type. On the other hand,

    code := 'x';

assigns the value "x" to the variable *code* which ought to have been declared to be of type *char*.

(b) If this statement

    digit := '5';

appears in the program, *digit* must have been declared as type *char*; but in this case

    digit := 5;

digit must be declared as integer or real type.

Variables of type *char* may be declared:

var
    letter, digit: char;

An assignment of a *char* value (that is, the value of another *char* variable or *char* constant) to such a variable may be performed, as shown in Example 4–8.

The only operations defined for character-valued data are input, output, and comparisons, all discussed later in this chapter. No arithmetic is, of course, possible.

The manipulation of text with the use of *char*-type data has to occur character by character. Loop control structures (see Chapter 5) are used for this purpose.

3. INPUT AND OUTPUT OF CHARACTER DATA

To read in a character value, we use *read* or *readln* statements (see Chapter 3–E). The data presented by you as input ought to have no enclosing apostrophes!

The important distinction between numerical and character data is that in *char*-type input, blanks are not skipped during input, as they are with numerical data. Thus, care needs to be exercised in the layout of data for input.

EXAMPLE 4–9
If, following this declaration:

var
    firstInitial, middleInitial: char;

these statements are executed:

read (firstInitial);
read (middleInitial);

on this input data:

W C FIELDS

the value of *firstInitial* becomes "W," but the value of *middleInitial* becomes blank (' ')!

For the output of character data *write* and *writeln* are used. By default, one space is allocated to every character (thus, no surrounding blanks are provided). If spacing is desired, the total field width is to be provided; in that case the leading columns will be blank (similar to the output of character strings, described in Chapter 3–H–1).

EXAMPLE 4–10

(a) If *letter* is a *char* variable, the statement

    writeln (letter: 10);

    will provide 9 spaces, followed by the character value of *letter,* and terminates the current line.

(b) This statement

write (' ': n);

where *n* is an integer constant or variable, will write n blanks on the current output line. Such statements may be used to space out the output data.

4. ORDERING OF *CHAR* VALUES

Character values may be compared using the six relational operators described in Section A–2. Different character sets have somewhat different orderings of character representations (called the *collating sequence* of the set).

However, all sets provide correct alphabetical ordering, that is, ensure the following:

'A' < 'B' < . . . < 'Z'
'a' < 'b' < . . . < 'z'

as well as the numerical ordering of digits:

'0' < '1' < . . . < '9'.

But in some Pascal processors the representations of letters are not consecutive. For example, there may be other (non-letter) characters placed in the collating sequence between, say, "M" and "N."

The main distinction between the two most popular character sets (see Appendix C) is that the letters are "smaller" than the digits in EBCDIC, as opposed to ASCII where they are "larger"; in both cases, however, the blank is smaller than both letters and digits.

In programming, avoid if possible program dependence on a specific character set, since such a program may be difficult to transfer to another computer.

C. ORDINAL FUNCTIONS

Integer, Boolean, and *char* data types share a common property: each value of such a type has a single predecessor value and a single successor value (the exceptions are the first value which has no predecessor, and the last one, without a successor). In other words, these values are ordered, and the three data types listed belong to the so-called *ordinal data types* (see the classification of simple data types in Chapter 6).

Aside from the six relational operators which apply to all ordinal data types, four standard ordinal functions are defined.

The first pair of functions allows the programmer to "step through" the set of values of the data type. These are: *succ (x)* which returns the successor of the value of *x;* and *pred (x)* which returns the predecessor of the value of *x.*

In both cases, *x* is an expression of an ordinal type. The following apply:

(1) The value of the function is of the same type as *x.*
(2) It is an error to request the predecessor of the first element of the type or the successor of the last.
(3) The order of values is determined as follows:

- in the case of *char* type, by the collating sequence of the character set;
- in the case of Boolean type, *true* is the successor of *false;*
- in the case of integer i,

succ (i) equals $i + 1$ (e.g., *succ* (21) is 22);
pred (i) equals $i - 1$ (e.g., *pred* (21) is 20);

and thus these functions are rarely used on integer values.

EXAMPLE 4–11

(a) In the ASCII character set (see Appendix C):

succ ('9') is ':';
pred ('A') is '@'.

(b) These are examples of erroneous use of these functions:

pred (false), succ (maxint)   {wrong!}

The two remaining ordinal functions provide a mapping between the values of an ordinal type and the integers. Every value of an ordinal type has its *ordinal number,* which specifies its position in the set of values, ordered starting with the smallest (whose ordinal number is 0).

Thus, for example,

for Boolean values: *false true*
the ordinal numbers are: 0   1

The required function:

ord (x) returns the ordinal number of the value of the expression *x* (where *x* is any expression of ordinal type);

chr (x) the inverse of *ord (x)*, is defined exclusively for type *char*. Its value is the character whose ordinal number is *x*. Thus, *x* has to be an integer expression.

Note that for any value of *letter* (of *char* type):

chr (ord (letter)) equals *letter*.

EXAMPLE 4–12

For the ASCII character set (only!), as shown in Appendix C:

ord ('A') is 65	*chr (65)* is 'A'
ord ('z') is 122	*chr (80)* is 'P'
ord ('9') is 57	*chr (122)* is 'z'
ord (' ') is 32	*chr (50)* is '2'

Note that the following is true for any character *c* in a Pascal character set, for which these functions are defined:

pred (c) = chr (ord (c) − 1)
succ (c) = chr (ord (c) + 1)

According to the Pascal standard,

ord ('A') < ord ('Z')
ord ('0') < ord ('9')

but the relationship between *ord ('A')* and *ord ('0')* depends on the character set.

EXAMPLE 4–13

The following assignment will produce a lower-case letter *lowLetter* from its upper-case equivalent *upLetter,* for any letter of the Latin alphabet, provided that the ASCII code is employed:

lowLetter := chr (ord (upLetter) + 32);   {*ASCII only!*}

In general, for a character code with consecutive representation of upper- and lower-case letters, respectively, we may use this sequence of statements:

difference := ord ('a') − ord ('A');
lowLetter := chr (ord (upLetter) + difference);

5

CONTROL OF PROGRAM
EXECUTION FLOW:
FUNDAMENTAL STRUCTURES

To guide the flow of program execution, structured statements of Pascal are used. Three fundamental constructs of structured programming—sequence, selection, and repetition (loop)—may be implemented, respectively, with the compound, conditional, and repetitive statements of Pascal. The **if** conditional statement and the **while** repetitive statement are discussed in this chapter (supplementary control structures are presented in Chapter 7). The control of data input with loops and *eof* and *eoln* tests is also analyzed here.

A. WHAT ARE CONTROL STRUCTURES?

Unless directed otherwise by appropriate control statements, program execution proceeds from the first statement in its statement part to the last. However, such sequential execution is satisfactory only for the simplest programming situations.

The real power of computers rests on our ability to provide alternative paths for program execution (of which one may be selected during the execution itself, based on the existence of a specified condition), and to provide for reuse of certain program statements in order to achieve the cumulative effect of their actions.

The following basic control structures are sufficient to represent any programming "logic," that is, a desired flow of control from statement to statement:

- sequence, providing for the execution of included statements in the order in which they have been written (this is what happens when other control structures do not give orders to the contrary);
- selection (decision), specifying two alternative paths (statement se-

quences), one of which will be taken during program execution based on the truth or falsity of the condition stated in the decision statement;

- repetition (loop), which specifies that a sequence of statements included in it be executed repeatedly, and provides the condition for ceasing this iteration (repeated execution).

These three are the fundamental control structures of structured programming, a systematic program implementation method based on the use of proper control structures. In terms of the flow of execution control, each of these structures has a single entry point (at the top, where the structure begins), and a single exit point (at the bottom, where the structure ends). Therefore, with the use of these structures programming may proceed in a natural, top-down fashion, as a far superior alternative to undisciplined transfer of control up and down the code. (Such transfers can be made with **goto** statements, discussed in Chapter 7–D, but only in exceptional situations.) The reading of the program is correspondingly simplified. This, in turn, leads to easier modification.

As we said, the above three structures have been proven sufficient for controlling execution flow. Pascal provides a number of structured statements (as opposed to its simple statements, such as assignment) serving to control program execution flow. The essential Pascal statements implementing the fundamental structures are discussed in the present chapter.

In addition, Pascal offers several supplementary structured statements, discussed in Chapter 7. In many situations, the use of these is more expressive of the program logic. The structured statements available in Pascal to control program flow are shown in Fig. 5–1. The structures discussed in the present chapter are outlined; the others, with the exception of **with**,[1] are discussed in Chapter 7.

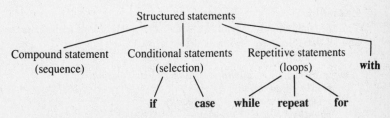

FIGURE 5–1. Structured statements of Pascal.

1. The **with** statement controls record processing and is analyzed in Chapter 15.

As we have discussed in Chapter 3–J, pseudocode is often employed during program design to express the algorithm, possibly in several refinement steps. Control structures will be included in the pseudocode to express the logic of the algorithm. The actual format of these structures is as close to those of Pascal as warranted by the level of abstraction maintained during the given development step. When Pascal code is developed from pseudocode, a control structure different from the one employed in the pseudocode may be chosen to implement the particular logic fragment, for reasons of code readability or efficiency.

B. SEQUENCE

To show that several statements are to be executed sequentially, they are included in a *compound statement* of Pascal and separated from one another by semicolons. Such statements are treated as if they were a single statement, carrying out the actions specified by its components.

The general format of a compound statement is:

begin
    statement; ⎫
    statement; ⎬ optional
    ⋮ ⎭
    statement
end

The statements enclosed in the **begin-end** brackets (which may be simple statements or other structures) are executed top-down, in the order in which they appear.

EXAMPLE 5–1a

This is a compound statement (we assume that g is a defined real constant, and all variables have also been declared real):

```
begin {velocity and quantity of fluid flow are computed}
    readln (head, area);
    velocity := sqrt (2.0 * g * head);
    quantity := area * velocity;
    writeln (head, area, velocity, quantity)
end; {computation of velocity and quantity of fluid flow}
```

Corresponding comments are often used on matching **begin-end** brackets in order to explain a meaningful segment of the program, as shown in Example 5–1a. Particularly in a large program containing many **begin-end** pairs, this enhances readability.

The indentation shown for the compound statement is a matter of style, rather than necessity. We need to remember that Pascal offers free-format program layout, and semicolons (rather than line termination) serve as statement separators.

Indentation of structure components from the structured statement is an important aspect of assuring program readability. A consistent pattern should be followed by the programmer; three spaces are often chosen, and such a pattern is followed here.

EXAMPLE 5–1b

The compound statement of Example 5–1a may also be written as follows:

begin *readln (head, area); velocity := sqrt (2 * g * head);*
        quantity := area * velocity;
        writeln (head, area, velocity, quantity) **end;**

In general, the one-statement-per-line format is more readable.

Observe that no semicolon needs to be placed before the **end** symbol, since semicolons separate individual statements within the construct, and the last statement does not have to be followed by a separator. However, placing a semicolon before **end** would cause no problem. The Pascal processor would assume then that the last statement is followed by the so-called *empty statement,* a valid (if illusory!) Pascal statement having no effect (it is sometimes used to place labels, as discussed in Chapter 7–D).

Some programmers do indeed place a semicolon before **end,** to make it easier to insert another statement there during a possible program modification.

An example of a compound statement is the entire statement part of every program (see Chapter 2–D). The main use of the **begin-end** brackets, however, is to place the statements enclosed by them within a branch of a conditional statement, or as the body of a repetitive statement, as though the enclosed statements were a single one.

Note that, in its general format, a compound statement could enclose a single statement rather than a sequence. Again, some programmers use this form to allow insertion of additional statements during a program modification.

C. SELECTION WITH *IF* STATEMENT

A two-way selection (decision) construct is used to specify two alternative paths in the program execution. During the execution, one of these is selected, based on testing the truth or falsity of the condition specified in the construct. By nesting such constructs, as described below (or by using the **case** selection statement), we can provide for multiple selection.

In other words, with the two-way selection construct, we want to achieve the effect specified by this pseudocode:

if a condition is true **then**
    statement-1 shall be executed
else
    statement-2 shall be executed

This construct is implemented with the Pascal **if** statement (note how close it is to the above pseudocode) of this general format:

if Boolean expression **then**
    statement-1
else   } optional
    statement-2

where either or both statement-1 and statement-2 may be simple (e.g., an assignment or a *read*) or compound (delimited by **begin** and **end**). Observe that there is no semicolon before **else.**

Placing a semicolon before **else** is a frequent error which will lead to program failure.

An **if** statement is executed as follows:

(1) The Boolean expression is evaluated (according to the rules of Chapter 4–A–2).
(2) If the value obtained is *true, only* statement-1 is executed; otherwise (i.e., the value of the Boolean expression is *false*), in the presence of the **else** part, *only* statement-2 is executed. In either case, control passes to the statement following the entire **if** statement.

In many programming situations, the alternative to the action to be taken if the Boolean expression is true is no action. Then the optional **else** part is absent:

if Boolean expression **then**
   statement

Note that since we can invert a Boolean expression, we have no need for a statement with an **else** part only.

Observe the indentation pattern for the construct (we use 3 spaces consistently).

EXAMPLE 5-2
Study the following Pascal code fragments.

(a) To assign the larger of the two integer values, *previous* or *present*, to the integer variable *maximum*, we may employ this **if** statement:

```
if previous > present then
   maximum := previous
else
   maximum := present;
```

Note that, like any other statement, an **if** statement is separated from its successor by a semicolon.

(b) In this case, no **else** part is needed:

```
if received = '.' then
   writeln ('Do you wish to terminate the session?');
```

(c) In the following code segment, both branches of the **if** statement are compound statements:

```
{compute the tax and count the number of payers in each bracket}
if income <= bracketLimit then
   begin {tax for low income}
      tax := income * lowRate/100;
      lowCount := lowCount + 1
   end
else
   begin {tax for high income}
      tax := floor + (income - bracketLimit) * highRate/100;
      highCount := highCount + 1
   end;
```

(d) A frequent error is to use the following sequence of statements instead of the **if-then-else** statement of example (a) above to handle that situation:

```
{this sequence is wrong:}
if previous > present then
    maximum := previous;
maximum := present;
```

In this case, the **if** statement has no effect; the value of *maximum* will always be that of *present* (analyze!).

(e) Often more complex conditions (Boolean expressions) are called for:

```
{the next character of a message is accepted if the transmission has
            not yet ended, provided fewer than 80 characters have
            been received}
if not endTransmission and (messageLength < 80) then
    begin {obtain next character}
        read (character);
        write (character);
        messageLength := messageLength + 1
    end
else {prepare for next transmission}
    messageLength := 0;
```

You may conclude that *endTransmission* is Boolean; such a Boolean variable indicating a certain condition is often called a flag.

(f) This **if** statement should not have been written:

```
if (pressure >= lowLimit) and (pressure <= highLimit) then
    nominal := true
else
    nominal := false;
```

since it may be replaced by this simpler statement:

```
nominal := (pressure >= lowLimit) and
            (pressure <= highLimit);
```

The statement included in either branch of an **if** statement may be (consistent with the general format shown above) itself an **if** statement. Thus, nested **if** statements are formed, allowing us to express more complex decisions.

> Deep nesting is to be avoided, since it leads to errors and difficult to understand programs. A simpler form of expression should always be sought.

For example, here nesting is done on the **if** branch (there is no **else** clause):

if condition-1 **then**
   if condition-2 **then**
      statement-1;

The above statement may be rephrased as follows in most situations:

if condition-1 **and** condition-2 **then**
   statement-1;

The latter is easier to understand and thus preferable. A possible reason to use the former, nested, **if** statement is the desire to bypass the evaluation of condition-2, should condition-1 prove false. This is necessary in the following example.

EXAMPLE 5–3

We have to write (all variables are of integer type):

if *smaller* $< >$ *0* **then**
   if *odd (greater* **div** *smaller)* **then**
      writeln ('It''s odd!');

since **and**-ing the two conditions in a single **if** may cause program failure if the value of *smaller* is 0, as discussed in Example 4–6. In the above nested statement, the second condition is not tested (and thus no division is performed) in this case.

With nested **if** statements, the following situation (called the "dangling **else**") may be considered ambiguous:

   if condition-1 **then if** condition-2 **then** statement-1 **else** statement-2;

(remember that a Pascal processor does not recognize indentation!).

In Pascal, the following rule resolves the apparent ambiguity: an **else** part is always associated with the closest preceding **if** which has no other matching **else**. Thus, using our indentation pattern, the above statement could be written as follows:

```
if condition-1 then
    begin
        if condition-2 then      {this if is associated with . . .}
            statement-1
        else                     {. . . this else}
            statement-2
    end;
```

In this statement, **begin-end** brackets have been placed solely to stress the structure (it is legitimate, since a compound statement may contain a single statement).

In general, a nested **if** statement is usually easier to understand if the nesting is done on the **else**-branch (a rephrasing of the statement into such form can always be done). The general format of such a nested **if** statement is:

```
if condition-1 then
    statement-1
else if condition-2 then
    statement-2
else if condition-3 then
    statement-3
        ⋮
else          ⎫ optional
    statement-n ⎭
```

Note:

(1) Only one of the n alternatives will be selected and executed (assuming that there is the **else** part); this will be the statement (possibly compound) following the first true condition, or following **else.**

(2) Since this is a single structured statement, there are no semicolons other than those found within statements 1–n, should any of these be compound.

(3) Customarily, the above indentation format is used for such a nested **if** statement (again, indentation has no influence on the effect of the statement, but a great one on its readability).

EXAMPLE 5–4
This code fragment illustrates the use of nested **if** statements:

```
writeln ('Do you wish to play again?');
writeln ('Please answer Y for yes, or N for no.');
if (answer = 'y') or (answer = 'Y') then
    writeln ('You are on!')
else if (answer = 'n') or (answer = 'N') then
    begin
        writeln ('Thank you for the game.');
        writeln ('Your best score was ', score)
    end
else
    begin
        writeln ('I do not understand your answer.');
        writeln ('Please answer Y for yes, or N for no.')
    end;
```

In many cases, when multiway selection is desired, the **case** statement (discussed in Chapter 7–A) is preferable to the nested **if,** both for readability and execution efficiency.

The following program illustrates the use of nested **if** statements.

EXAMPLE 5–5

Obtain the roots of a quadratic equation.

Pseudocode of the algorithm

```
program roots;
            {compute roots of ax² + bx + c = 0}
begin
    read a, b, c;
    if (a = 0) and (b = 0) then
        write message on degenerate case
    else if a = 0 then
        compute single root equal to −c/b
    else if c = 0 then
        compute 2 roots, equal to −b/a, 0
    else
        begin
            discriminant := b² − 4ac;
            if discriminant ≥ 0 then
                compute 2 real roots
            else
                compute 2 complex roots
        end
end.
```

```
program roots (input, output);
        {compute roots of quadratic equation
        a * (x * x) + b * x + c = 0 }

const
   precision = 2;
var
   a, b, c, discriminant, bTwoA, rootDiscr: real;

begin
   readln (a, b, c);
   writeln ('Coefficients:  a = ', a: 10: precision,
            ',  b = ', b: 10: precision, ',   c = ', c: 10: precision);

   if (a = 0) and (b = 0) then
      writeln ('Check the coefficients!')

   else if a = 0 then
      writeln ('The single root is: ', -c/b: 10: precision)

   else if c = 0 then
      writeln ('The roots are: ', -b/a: 10: precision, ', ', 0:1)

   else                     {general case}
      begin
         discriminant := sqr (b) - 4 * a * c;
         rootDiscr := sqrt ( abs (discriminant)) / (2 * a);
         bTwoA := -b / (2 * a);
         if discriminant >= 0 then
            writeln ('The roots are:',
                    (bTwoA + rootDiscr): 10: precision, ', ',
                    (bTwoA - rootDiscr): 10: precision)
         else
            writeln ('The complex roots are: (', bTwoA: 10: precision, ',',
                    rootDiscr: 10: precision, 'i), (', bTwoA: 10: precision,
                    ', ', -rootDiscr: 10: precision, 'i)')
      end
end.
```

Two output printouts

(1)

```
Coefficients:  a =       2.00,  b =        5.00,  c =       2.00
The roots are:    -0.50,      -2.00
```

(2)

```
Coefficients:  a =       2.00,  b =        2.00,  c =       2.00
The complex roots are: (     -0.50,      0.87i), (     -0.50,       -0.87i)
```

D. REPETITION WITH *WHILE* STATEMENT

Repetition, also called a **loop,** allows for the repeated execution of a statement (simple or, most often, compound) contained within it. As this contained statement (often called the *loop body*) is executed, certain actions are taken by the computer, and thus multiple execution of this statement has a cumulative effect. This repetitive execution (known as *iteration*) is stopped when the terminating condition specified in the repetitive statement occurs.

There are three kinds of repetitive statements in Pascal (see Section A of this chapter). The **while** statement, perhaps the most generally useful, is discussed in this section.

The general form of the **while** statement is:

while Boolean expression **do**
    statement

where the statement included as the loop body may, of course, be compound (bracketed by **begin-end**).

A **while** statement is executed as follows:

(1) The Boolean expression is evaluated (according to the rules of Chapter 4–A–2).
(2) If the value obtained is *true,* the statement is executed, and control is returned to the **while** and thus to step (1); otherwise, the execution of the **while** statement is completed.

Thus, while the condition presented by the Boolean expression remains *true,* the loop body is repeatedly executed. Observe that the Boolean expression is tested *only before* every iteration; it is *not* constantly tested while the statement is being executed. Thus, once the existence of the condition has been verified, the **while** statement orders that its entire body be executed.

EXAMPLE 5–6

    {write out the even natural numbers up to 100, inclusive}
    even := 2;
    while *even* $< =$ *100* **do**
        begin
            writeln (even);
            even := even + 2
        end;

Note the following:

(1) If the condition for entry into the loop (i.e., the value of the Boolean expression) is false to begin with, the loop body is not executed at all (the **while** statement is skipped, as it were). Thus, the **while** statement "protects" its body; this is one of its advantages.

(2) If the loop is entered, the execution of its body must ultimately reverse the value of the Boolean expression, to make it false. A loop where this does not occur during the execution is a so-called infinite loop, and represents a serious error (program execution will have to be stopped by external—usually system—means). Note that if you place a semicolon after **do:**

while Boolean expression **do;**   {error!}

you have a potential infinite loop consisting of an empty statement!

(3) To use a **while** statement, the programmer does not have to know how many iterations through the loop will have to occur (even in terms of the value of a program variable established before the loop is executed). In fact, if we know this value, the **for** statement (see Chapter 7–C) is often preferred for presenting the loop.

(4) The Boolean expression must be ready for testing before the loop body is executed even once; that is, all entities appearing in it must have been given values. Care needs to be taken to insure this. If it is desired (and safe!) to first execute the body and then check the completion condition, the **repeat** statement may be used (see Chapter 7–B).

---

(5) Avoid "off-by-one" errors: be sure that the first and the last times the loop is entered are the correct ones.

EXAMPLE 5–7

Euclid's algorithm

We need to find the greatest common divisor (GCD) of two positive integers. (The GCD of two integers is the largest integer by which both of them can be divided exactly.)

(1)

This algorithm (known as Euclid's algorithm) may be used:

The larger integer is divided by the smaller one. If the remainder is 0, the smaller integer is the required result; otherwise, the larger integer is discarded and the smaller integer is treated as the larger one and the remainder as the smaller one, whereupon the procedure is repeated from the beginning.

This Pascal program implements Euclid's algorithm:

```
program findGCD (input, output);
        {find greatest common divisor of two positive integers}

var
   m, n, remainder: integer;

begin
   readln (m, n);    {integers whose GCD is sought}
   writeln ('for ', m:1, ' and ', n:1);
   remainder := m mod n;
   while remainder <> 0 do
      begin
         m := n;
         n := remainder;
         remainder := m mod n
      end;
   writeln ('greatest common divisor is ', n:1)
end.
```

A typical output:

```
for 12 and 46
greatest common divisor is 2
```

These traces of the values of variables will help to understand the operation of the **while** statement:

(a) for these data: $m = 8$, $n = 2$, we have:

> *remainder* $= 0$;
> loop is not entered;
> GCD (value of n) is 2.

(b) for these data: $m = 12$, $n = 46$ (note that the second integer is the larger one), we have:

$$remainder = 10;$$

	m	n	*remainder*
after the first execution of the loop:	46	12	10 (the values are exchanged)
after the second execution of the loop:	12	10	2
after the third execution of the loop:	10	2	0

GCD (value of n) is 2

Note that when $m < n$, the first time through the loop serves to exchange the values of the variables.

Perform a similar trace with values of your choice.

(2)

This is an alternative version of Euclid's algorithm, using subtraction instead of division. It is based on the fact that the GCD of two positive integers is always a divisor of their difference. This version also uses the **while** statement (only the statement part of the program is shown):

```
readln (m, n);
writeln ('for ', m: 1, ' and ', n: 1);
while m  < >  n do
   if m  >  n then
       m := m − n
   else
       n := n − m;
writeln ('greatest common divisor is ', n: 1);  {m  =  n here!}
```

Trace the values of the variables and their differences, as in part (1) of this example. Note that more iterations are required here.

The following program further illustrates the use of **while** statements in a typical situation where they are employed: when we do not know the number of iterations.

EXAMPLE 5–8

Count the number of characters in a one-line exclamation; assume that at least the terminating exclamation mark is present.

Pseudocode of the solution

```
program countCharacters;
begin
    read current character;
    increment the count;
    while current character is not the terminator do
        begin
            increment the count;
            read next character
        end;
    write the count
end.
```

```
program countCharacters (input, output);
       {count the number of characters in an exclamation}
const
   terminator = '!';
var
   count: integer;
   current: char;       {the character being counted}
                        {comments here explain the code itself}
begin
   count := 0;               {initialize the counter}
   read (current);           {"prime the pump"}
   write (current);
   count := count + 1;
   while current <> terminator do
      begin
         count := count + 1;
         read (current);
         write (current)
      end;
   writeln;
   writeln ('The above exclamation contains ', count: 1, ' characters.')
end.
```

This is an output:

```
Leaping lizards!
The above exclamation contains 16 characters.
```

Note that, typically for a **while** statement, we have to read once before the statement itself in order to establish values for the Boolean expression. This consequently calls for the shown order of statements within the loop body. We will see in Chapter 7–B that this situation may be handled more naturally with a **repeat** statement.

If desired, before reading the first character we may check whether there are any data to be read in at all, as we shall see in Section E.

Trace carefully the value of all the variables when applied to, say, "Hi!"

EXAMPLE 5–9

This is an example of an erroneous, infinite loop:

> **while** *ready* **do**   *{error!}*
>   *writeln ('Hi, I am ready.');*

Since the value of the flag *ready* is not changed by the loop body, an attempt will be made to write out an infinite number of salutation lines.

More examples of the **while** statement, operating in conjunction with the tests for the end of current input line or end of input data file, are provided in the next section.

Because the body of a loop may itself be a **while** statement, or may include one, **while** statements may, of course, be nested. During execution, an inner loop runs its full course for every iteration of the outer one.

EXAMPLE 5–10

This example illustrates the last point (for such a programming situation, **for** loops are used in practice, as we will see in Example 7–8). Note that this is strictly practice code.

```
{practice nested while statements}
total := 0;
i := 1;
while i <= 5 do
    begin
        j := 1;
        while j <= 3 do
            begin
                total := total + 1;      {the accumulation}
                j := j + 1
            end;
        i = i + 1
    end;
writeln ('the total is ', total: 1);
```

The value of *total* will be 15 (5 iterations of the outer loop, times 3 iterations of the inner one for each of these). Note the need to reinitialize the inner loop. Observe the matching **begin-end** brackets.

The following example uses nested **while** statements.

EXAMPLE 5–11

This code fragment counts the number of sequences (runs) of identical letters placed on a single line and terminated by a period. Thus, for example, for

AZCCCDD.

the count is 4 sequences.

```
{count the runs of letters}
count := 0;
read (next);
while next <> '.' do
    begin
        count := count + 1;
        changed := false;
        previous := next;     {remember the previous letter}
        while not changed do      {scan a run of identical letters}
            begin
                read (next);
                changed := next <> previous {has the run changed?}
            end
    end;
writeln ('We have ', count, ' sequences.');
```

To test this code fragment, trace the values of its variables (as in Example 5–7(1)) for these sequences:

ABC.　　　(3 runs)
AAA.　　　(1 run)
AXAC.　　(4 runs)

E. LOOP-CONTROLLED DATA INPUT

A frequent programming task is that of reading in an input file to process its data. The termination of the reading is to occur when the data have been exhausted. But how do we recognize this condition?

One method is to use a *sentinel (trailer)*, a special value placed immediately after the actual data; another is to precede the actual data by a count of the values (or sets of values) to be read in. The second method is to be avoided, in general, since the data would have to be counted by us, instead of having the computer do the work more reliably.

A more universal technique is the use of the standard function *eof,* which tests for the end of the input file (collection of the input data). This function is frequently used together with another required function of Pascal, *eoln,* which tests for the end of the current input line.

1. SENTINEL AND COUNT TECHNIQUES

A sentinel is a special data item placed in an input file right after the last actual data item. It is not one of the input data items and has to be selected outside of their range of values so as to be recognizable. For example, if we read age data, the sentinel may be any negative value (e.g., -1), etc. But the sentinel must be of the same type as the input data, otherwise the *read/readln* statement reading it will fail.[2]

While reading an input data item, the program checks that it is not the sentinel; when the sentinel is encountered, the input is stopped.

The schematic program fragment is:

```
{read in the data using a sentinel}
read (next);
while next < > sentinel do
   begin
      :      {processing of the input data}
      read (next)
   end;
```

2. When reading Chapter 6, note that the use of sentinels with subrange data types is inconvenient (the subrange needs to be artificially broadened to include the sentinel value).

Note:

(1) Typically, the first *read* needs to be done before the **while** statement, to establish its condition for testing. Within the loop, the *read* statement is, correspondingly, placed last.

(2) The sentinel itself is discarded when read (check that this is so); in particular, if an empty file is read (containing the sentinel only), the loop is not executed at all.

Sentinels are used to advantage when the input file contains several sequentially laid out groups of data; each of them would be delimited by its own sentinel.

If the count of input data items is available, it may be used instead of a sentinel to control the reading of the input file. In this case, the count is placed before the actual values.

The schematic program fragment is:

```
{read in the data using a count}
read (count);
while count > 0 do
    begin
        read (item);
        ⋮      {processing of the input data}
        count := count − 1
    end;
```

This fragment may be conveniently coded with the **for** repetitive statement (see Example 7–6(c)).

2. END-OF-LINE AND END-OF-FILE DETECTION

An input file of Pascal is structured as a sequence of lines containing data (it is a file of text).

Pascal provides two Boolean functions, *eoln* and *eof* (usually pronounced by spelling), to recognize, respectively, end of line and end of file. As Boolean functions, they give the value *false* or *true*.

As is discussed in detail in Chapter 17, *eoln* applies to any textfile and *eof* to any file whatever. When used to test the predefined input file, the file does not need to be specified as a parameter (by default, *eof*, for example, refers to the input file). Thus, the function names stand alone in this case.

Both functions test the file without disturbing it, that is, no reading from a file is necessary to see whether *eof* or *eoln* is *true* or *false*.

a. End-of-Line Test

Every line of the input file is terminated (and stored in memory) with an end-of-line marker. This is a nonprintable control character which corresponds, for example, to a carriage return in an interactive system or a card termination in a batch system. If written out as a *char*-type value, it is presented as a blank space. (An end-of-line marker may be placed into the output file by programming means through executing the *writeln* statement.)

The Boolean function *eoln* (without a parameter, thus applied to the input file) yields *true* if the current position in the input file is that of the end-of-line marker (all data on the line having been already read in); otherwise it is *false*. It is an error to execute *eoln* after end of file has been reached (i.e., when *eof* is true).

EXAMPLE 5-12

This **while** loop serves to read in and echo a line of data:

```
while not eoln do
    begin
        read (character);
        write (character)
    end;
```

Note that if the current line contains no data (this possibility always has to be considered!), no action will be taken.

Remember (or see Chapter 3–E–1) that after *readln* is executed, the reading position is at the beginning of the next line (past the previous end-of-line marker).

b. End-of-File Test

Every file is terminated by a nonprintable end-of-file marker (it cannot be read in at all).

The Boolean function *eof* (without a parameter, thus applied to the input file) yields *true* if the current position in the file is on the end-of-file marker (that is, beyond the last end-of-line marker); otherwise it is *false*. No *read, readln* or *eoln* may be executed on a file for which *eof* is *true*.

Use of the *eof* test is an essential technique for the termination of input in batch programs.

This example illustrates the interaction between the input/output statements and the *eoln* and *eof* tests.

EXAMPLE 5–13

The following program echoes (copies) the input file into the output file:

```
program echo (input, output);
      {a copy of the input is obtained on output}

var
   c: char;

begin
   while not eof do
      begin
         while not eoln do        {copy a line}
            begin
               read (c);
               write (c)          {copy a character}
            end;
         writeln;                 {terminate the current output line}
         readln                   {go to the next input line}
      end
end.
```

> Programs have to work even if their input files are empty!

A special consideration is necessary when *eof* is employed to terminate the input of integer or real data. As we saw in Chapter 3–E–1, numerical data items are separated by blank spaces, so when *read* or *readln* is executed with a numerical-valued entity, a scan takes place for the first non-blank item, which is assumed to be (and better be!) of a type compatible with this entity.

Thus, in a loop with *eof* test, having read the last datum, the program will pass the end-of-line marker (since it is treated as a space!) and attempt to read past the end of file—and fail. To prevent such a failure, integer and real values must be read in line by line. After the last line has been read, end of file may be detected. Depending on the data layout, there are two ways of doing it.

The following simple method is possible if the input data are presented one line at a time (that is, *readln* will read in all the data on a given input line):

```
{a set of complete input lines is processed}
while not eof do
   begin
      readln ( . . . );   {read a line into corresponding entities}
         :} process input data
      writeln ( . . . )   {if wanted, write a line of output}
   end;
```

A more complicated approach has to be used when the input data are freely laid out in the input file (but the last item is not followed by a blank):

```
{general schema for reading in integer or real items}
while not eof do
    begin
        while not eoln do
            begin
                read (item);
                  :} process item
                writeln ( . . . ) {if wanted, write a line of output}
            end;
        readln      {go past the end-of-line marker}
    end;
```

Note that this approach is similar to the one employed for reading characters (in Example 5–13).

EXAMPLE 5–14

Information stored in computer memories or transmitted via communication networks is often protected by cryptographic techniques. The importance of these methods is growing with the proliferation of data managed by computers. Cryptography is the science (or art?) of "secret writing": converting the original message, called plaintext, into a scrambled message by encryption techniques, and recovering the original message by decryption. Two fundamental methods are employed: code, where a whole word (or phrase) is encoded by a group of symbols, and cipher. In a cipher, individual characters of the message are represented by other symbols (substitution cipher), or the characters of the plaintext are transposed to obtain the ciphertext.

Problem

Design a program to produce a Caesar cipher. This substitution cipher is designed for single-case letters: it replaces every letter by the one three positions down in the alphabet (as used by Julius Caesar in his campaign in Gaul). Wraparound is performed on the last three letters; thus, "X" is replaced by "A," "Y" by "B," and "Z" by "C." This shift by 3, called the shift key, which was used in the original cipher, may, of course, be changed.

Algorithm

program *encipherInCaesar;*
begin
    define limits of representable characters;
    while there is more plaintext **do**
        begin
            read next plaintext character;
            if character is outside the limits **then**
                terminate encryption with message
            else
                begin
                    shift character with wraparound;
                    write ciphertext character
                end
        end
end.

Implementation

```
program encipherInCaesar (input, output);
        {encipher alphabetic text in Caesar cipher;
         consecutive alphabet of capital letters without blanks assumed}

const
    shiftKey = 3;
    firstLetter = 'A';
    lastLetter = 'Z';
var
    plainLetter, cipherLetter: char;
    origin, limit,              {ordinal numbers of first and last letter}
    position: integer;          {expected ordinal number of cipher letter
                                 before wraparound}
    valid: Boolean;             {indicates valid character}
```

```
begin
   origin := ord (firstLetter);
   limit := ord (lastLetter);
   writeln (' ': 10, 'plaintext', ' ': 10, 'ciphertext');
   writeln;
               {read in and encipher valid text}
   valid := true;
   while not eof and valid do
      begin
         while not eoln and valid do
            begin
               read (plainLetter);
               if (ord (plainLetter) < origin) or
                  (ord (plainLetter) > limit)   then
                  begin
                     valid := false;
                     writeln ('Encryption terminated due to invalid',
                              ' character ', plainLetter)
                  end
               else                 {encrypt the character}
                  begin
                     position := ord (plainLetter) + shiftKey;
                     if position > limit then      {wrap around}
                        position := position - 26;
                     cipherLetter := chr (position);
                     writeln (' ': 14, plainLetter, ' ': 19, cipherLetter)
                  end
            end;
         readln
      end
end.
```

An Output

plaintext	ciphertext
B	E
A	D
Z	C
O	R
O	R
K	N
A	D
S	V
I	L
N	Q
B	E
O	R
X	A
E	H
S	V

If the reader wants to become familiar at this point with the basic use of procedures, he or she may study the Introduction to Part II and Chapter 8.

6

TYPE DEFINITION. NEW ORDINAL DATA TYPES

Pascal provides the type definition facility with which the programmer may define the types of data desired in the program. New ordinal data types are some that may be so defined. Others will be discussed in Part III. New ordinal data may be:

- enumerated types, specified by listing in order the identifiers of the type values, or
- subrange types, specified as an allowed range of values of another ordinal data type.

Since these programmer-defined types are ordinal, relational operators and ordinal functions (discussed in Chapter 4) apply.

All expressions used in Pascal must include only compatible data entities. Also, assignment-compatibility rules may be enforced by Pascal processors.[1] This, along with the requirement for declaration and definition of the type of all data entities, facilitates error detection.

A. CLASSIFICATION OF SIMPLE DATA TYPES OF PASCAL

Type definition facilities are among the strengths of Pascal. The programmer is able to define a data type which reflects the nature of the real-world objects of concern in the program. Subsequently, variables may be declared as being of this new type. Every program variable must be declared explicitly as being of a certain type. This allows for error checking by the Pascal processor.

1. But in many implementations only some rules are actually enforced.

Pascal provides a rather elaborate spectrum of possible data types. *Simple data types* are those whose instances are single data values. The simple types offered by Pascal may be classified as shown in Fig. 6–1.[2] Aside from the simple types, the language offers structured types, which consist of simple data as components, and pointer types, whose values identify other variables rather than being data values themselves (see Part III for all of these data types).

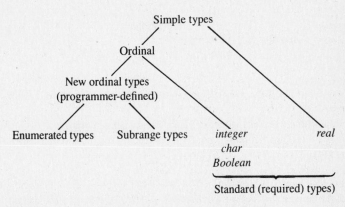

FIGURE 6–1. Classification of simple data types in Pascal.

As can be seen from Fig. 6–1, Pascal provides four required data types, which we have discussed: *integer, char, Boolean,* and *real.* Programmers may also define their own simple data types by enumerating their possible values (as enumerated types), or by defining a range of the values of another type to be the set of possible values of a new (subrange) type. These types may be named using the type definition facility.

Given the opportunity to define their own data types, programmers are able to think in terms of the problem which is being solved by the program, rather than in terms of programming details. Also, by defining problem-oriented types, one precludes the possibility of many erroneous computations, such as, for example, adding the day of the week to the marital status, which could happen if both were treated as integer data.

The *real* data type is an exception: it is not ordinal and thus the four ordinal functions of Chapter 4–C do not apply to it. The real type also may not serve as a host type for the definition of a subrange type.

---

2. In an older classification, all the simple types, with the exception of the subrange types, were called scalar types.

B. HOW TO DEFINE A NEW TYPE

To define a new type, the specification may be included directly in the variable declarations (as shown in the following sections), or the type definition facility may be used.

The general form of the type definition is:

type
    type identifier = type denoter;
            ⋮   } optional
    type identifier = type denoter;

where

    type identifier is the name (identifier) given by the programmer to the new type;
    type denoter may be the name of a previously defined type (thus two names may be used for the same type) or, more frequently, the specification of the new type.

In this chapter, type definitions will include specifications of enumerated and subrange types. As we will see in Part III of the book, type definitions may also be used to define structured and pointer types.

Type definitions have to be placed in the declarative part of the program between the constant definitions and the variable declarations. Thus the template of a program including type definitions is:

program heading;
const definitions;
type definitions;
var declarations;
begin
    ⋮ } statement part
end.

After a type has been defined, variables of this type may be declared.

Note that since the type specification may be provided directly in a variable declaration, it is not necessary to provide type definitions. However, in a manner similar to constant definitions, type definitions serve to document the program by assigning explanatory names to the types. They also introduce consistency and thus should be employed (and are sometimes necessary) if the same type is used for several variables. They also play a role in modular programming, as discussed in Part II.

C. ENUMERATED TYPES

The programmer often wishes to define a data type whose values correspond to the meaning of data to be manipulated by the program. An ordered set of such values may be specified as an *enumerated type*, whose specification lists all the possible values (constant identifiers) of the type in the order desired, enclosed in parentheses.

The general format of an enumerated type specification is:

(identifier, . . . , identifier)
        optional

For example, in a program which computes an insurance payment, we may want to define the *maritalStatus* data type as follows:

type
    maritalStatus = (single, married, separated, divorced, widowed);

Thus, any variable of the type *maritalStatus* may assume only one of the five listed values (e.g., its value may be *single*).

Variables of a type so defined may be declared, for example:

var
    beneficiary, insured: maritalStatus;

Alternatively, a type specification may be used directly in variable declarations; thus the two declarative statements above would be replaced by a single one:

var
    beneficiary, insured: (single, married, separated, divorced, widowed);

As argued in the preceding section, it is preferable to define a type in any case when it is shared by several variables.

The following are further examples of enumerated type definitions:

type
    workingDay = (Monday, Tuesday, Wednesday, Thursday, Friday);
    weekend = (Saturday, Sunday);
    coin = (penny, nickel, dime, quarter, halfdollar, dollar);
    sport = (swimming, bridge, running, chess);
    weekday = workingDay; {provides another name for the type}

Note that this type declaration is illegal:

type
    vowel = ('A', 'E', 'I', 'O', 'U');   {invalid!}

since *char* constants are not identifiers!

A variable of an enumerated type may assume only the values listed in its specification. It is extremely important to realize that the enumerated identifiers are the values of the type (similar to *true* being a value of the required type *Boolean*) and not variable names. For example, a variable of the type *weekend* may assume only the value *Saturday* or *Sunday*.

An identifier listed in a type specification is thereby declared, and each such value may then be listed only in a single type specification in the given set of definitions (in other words, no value may belong to more than one enumerated type). Therefore, the type definitions below are incorrect

type   *{invalid definition!}*
    hairColor = (black, blond, brown);
    eyeColor = (blue, brown, green);

since they overlap in the value *brown.*

A variable of an enumerated type may be assigned exclusively one of the values of its type.

EXAMPLE 6–1
In a program with these definitions and declarations:

  type
     spectrum = (red, orange, yellow, green, blue, indigo, violet);
     contrast = (black, white);
  var
     flag, coatOfArms: spectrum;

we may use these assignments:

    flag := blue;
    coatOfArms := flag;

since *blue* is one of the values enumerated for the type *spectrum,* declared for *flag,* and *flag* and *coatOfArms* are of the same type. We could not assign *white* to *flag.*

To go systematically through the values of an enumerated type, the **for** statement may be employed (see Chapter 7–C), as in Example 7–6b. The **case** statement (see Chapter 7–A) is useful in some situations as well.

The meaningful relationship between the values of an enumerated type is their ordering. Thus, as in the case of any other ordinal type, relational operators and the three ordinal functions (see Chapter 4–C) may be applied. In the type specification, values of the type are listed in the desired increasing order.

EXAMPLE 6–2
The ordinal numbers (see Chapter 4–C) of identifiers of the type defined in Example 6–1 are:

$$spectrum \;=\; (red, \; orange, \; yellow, \; green, \; blue, \; indigo, \; violet);$$
$$ 0 \qquad 1 \qquad 2 \qquad 3 \qquad 4 \qquad 5 \qquad 6$$

Let us consider the values of variables whose type is *spectrum:*

(a) The relation

$$violet \; > \; blue$$

yields the value *true,* but

$$indigo \; <= \; orange$$

yields the value *false.*

(b) Ordinal functions yield, for example, these values:

succ (yellow) is *green;*
pred (blue) is *green;*
ord (indigo) is 5.

Of course, only values of the same type may be compared. Thus, this comparison, if made on the data of Example 6–1, would be illegal:

$$flag \; <> \; black \qquad \{Wrong!\}$$

since the entities are of different types.

Arithmetic or Boolean operators are not applicable to data of an enumerated type (what sense could adding *Tuesday* to *Friday* or **and**-ing *penny* and *quarter* possibly have?).

In Standard Pascal, the values of an enumerated type cannot be presented on input or output (in order to write out such a value, we may use the equivalent character string). Many implementations allow this, however.

Since constant definitions precede type definitions in a Pascal program, enumerated-type values may not be used to define constants.

D. SUBRANGE TYPES

In many programming situations, the values of data are limited to a certain subrange of values of an ordinal type. Thus, for example, an integer variable *age* may assume only positive values up to a certain limit, or the *char* variable *digit* may range only from "0" to "9."

Such a meaningful range of values may be specified for variables of a subrange type. The specification of a subrange type identifies the smallest and the largest of the values included in the subrange, with all the values in between implicitly belonging to it. These two values have to be constants of the same ordinal type, which becomes the *host type* of the subrange type.

Any standard simple type, with the exception of *real*, may serve as host; also, any new (programmer-defined) type whose definition precedes the given one may be used as the host. The general format of a subrange type specification is:

$$\text{constant-1} \ . \ . \ \text{constant-2}$$

where

$$\text{constant-1} <= \text{constant-2}$$

in the system- or programmer-supplied definition of the host type. Either of the constants may be defined with a **const** definition. Note that the value limits for the subrange type are fixed as constants at the time the program is written.

The following are examples of type definitions which include subrange specifications; note how the type identifiers explain their meaning:

```
type
    twentiethCentury = 1901 . . 2000;
    pennies = 0 . . 99;
    letter = 'A' . . 'Z';        {in ASCII, no other characters are interspersed}
    natural = 1 . . maxint;
    weekday = (Mon, Tue, Wed, Thu, Fri, Sat, Sun);     {enumerated type}
    workday = Mon . . Fri;       {subrange type using weekday as host}
```

Subsequently, variables of a defined subrange type may be declared in the program:

```
var
    change: pennies;
    initial, code: letter;
    today: workday;
```

Alternatively, the type specification may be used directly in variable declarations.

The limits of a subrange type defined on a standard host type may be, as we said, defined constants, for example:

```
const
    employmentAge = 16;
    retirementAge = 70;
type
    workingAge = employmentAge . . retirementAge;
```

Subrange types may legitimately overlap (as opposed to enumerated types). For example, these definitions are syntactically correct:

```
type
    youngAge = 16 . . 49;
    middleAge = 40 . . 69;
```

A subrange type retains all the properties of its host type (including input and output), but the range of its correct values is limited as prescribed by its specification. For example, arithmetic may be performed on the variables of the type *youngAge,* so long as the values of expressions remain within the 16 to 49 limit. Since subrange types are ordinal, relational operators and appropriate ordinal functions, of course, apply.

EXAMPLE 6–3
Assuming the above declarations of variables *change* and *today,* we have:

(a) *ord (change)* equals *change;*
Remember that the ordinal number of a nonnegative integer is the integer itself.
(b) If the value of *today* is *Friday,* then

> *pred (today)* is *Thursday,*
> *succ (today)* is *Saturday.*

The essential merit of subrange types is in presenting the allowable limits for data values. During program execution, the processor is able to check whether values assigned to variables of subrange types are within the declared limits.[3] An attempt to assign a value falling outside the limits is an error and usually causes program failure, just as an attempt to assign a Boolean value to an integer variable would.

Whenever the range of values of a variable is limited and known at the time the program is being written, it is desirable to define a subrange type for this variable. The advantages are:

- improved error detection, with the processor's support;
- increased program readability;
- possibly, protection against program misuse, for example with these statements:

type
    pay = *10000 . . 100000;*
var
    paycheck: pay;

- possible saving of memory space, since the cardinality of a subrange type is smaller than that of its host, which may lead to smaller space needs for a datum of the given subrange type.

---

3. This happens in most systems only when the so-called debug mode of processing is specified.

Note the use of subranges in the following example.

EXAMPLE 6–4
We need to display and total the number of slams (i.e., contracts to take 12 or 13 tricks out of a possible 13) won by us over years of playing bridge. The number of days on which slams were won is also displayed.

As data, we submit the results for individual years.

```pascal
program countSlams (input, output);
        {count the number of slams and the days of their occurrence}
const
   startYear = 1965;
   endYear = 1985;
type
   natural = 1 .. maxint;
   daysInYear = 0 .. 366;
var
   slams, totalSlams : natural;
   year : startYear .. endYear;
   slamDays : daysInYear;

begin
   writeln ('Year      Number of slams      Slam Days');
   writeln;
   totalSlams := 0;
   while not eof do
      begin
         readln (year, slams, slamDays);
         writeln (year: 1, slams: 14, slamDays: 17);
         totalSlams := totalSlams + slams
      end;
   writeln;
   writeln ('Total slams won in ', startYear: 1, ' to ',
            endYear: 1, ': ', totalSlams: 1)
end.
```

An Output

Year	Number of slams	Slam Days
1973	2	1
1975	25	12
1980	40	15
1983	11	5

Total slams won in 1965 to 1985: 78

E. COMPATIBILITY AND
ASSIGNMENT-COMPATIBILITY FOR
SIMPLE DATA TYPES

The strong typing[4] of Pascal (see Chapter 3–A), with its requirement that the types of all data be declared, makes it possible for the processor to enforce type consistency rules in expressions and assignment statements, thus preventing many programming errors.

In expressions, the operands need to be *compatible.* That is, the type of the values joined by a binary operator needs to be the same (only integer and real data may be mixed), and compatible with the operator. A subrange type retains the characteristics of its host type (other than the value limits); the data of both of these types may be used together in expressions.

In an assignment statement (see Chapter 3–F), the expression must be *assignment-compatible* with the variable on the left-hand side of the assignment operator. This means that one of these conditions has to be fulfilled:

- both are of the same type;
- an integer value is being asigned to a real variable;
- they are subranges of the same host type, or one is a subrange of another, and the value of the expression is within the limits specified for the variable to which the assignment is being made.

Compatibility and assignment-compatibility rules for data types other than simple ones are further elaborated in the appropriate chapters.

4. Almost, since there are certain deviations from this principle in the more advanced facilities of the language.

7

SUPPLEMENTARY CONTROL STATEMENTS

The three structures presented in Chapter 5: the sequence, **if** statement, and the **while** loop, are sufficient to represent any programming logic. However, in many circumstances, other selection and repetitive statements are more expressive of the problem handled by the program and better support the programmer's thinking, leading to more understandable programs. The following Pascal statements are provided:

- multiple selection—the **case** conditional statement—is a better alternative than nested **if** statements in some situations;
- **repeat** and **for** repetitive statements are two alternatives to **while** repetition.

Together with the three fundamental control structures, these support structured programming.

In exceptional circumstances only, the **goto** statement can be used to transfer control to another point in the program, the point bearing a specified label.

A. MULTIPLE SELECTION WITH *CASE* STATEMENT

The **if** conditional statement (see Chapter 5–C) offers a selection of one of two alternative execution sequences, based on the truth value of a Boolean expression. Often, a programmer may want to provide more than two possible execution paths. This may be expressively accomplished with a **case** statement of the following general form:

```
        case index
         ‿
case expression of
    case constant list: statement;⎤
                               ⎬ optional
                 ⋮             ⎦
    case constant list: statement
    end
```

where the case index[1] expression has to be of the same ordinal type (see Chapter 6) as all the listed case constants (thus, no real values!); the statements may be simple or compound, of course. For example:

```
{tests with scores from 0 to 100 are graded}
case testScore div 10 of
    0,1,2,3,4:  begin
                    grade :=  'F';
                    writeln (' Test failed completely.')
                end;
    5,6:        grade = 'D';
    7:          begin
                    grade := 'C';
                    writeln (' Unexceptional performance.')
                end;
    8,9:        grade := 'B';
    10:         begin
                    grade := 'A';
                    writeln (' Your score was ', testScore)
                end
    end;
    writeln (' Your grade is ', grade);
```

The **case** statement is executed as follows:

(1) The case index expression is evaluated (it acts as the selector for the **case** statement);
(2) The constant value obtained "selects" for execution the statement preceded by this constant in its case constant list. This statement is executed, after which control passes to the statement following the **end** closing the **case** statement.

Thus, only one of the statements (it may be compound) included in the **case-end** brackets is executed.

---

1. The case index is sometimes called *selector*.

It is an error if there is no case constant equal to the value of the case index! You may test the case index before the **case** statement, to see that it is within the desired range.

Note the following:

(1) All case constants must be distinct;
(2) Several constants appearing on one list indicate that the same action is to be taken in several cases;
(3) The case constants are not constrained to appear in any particular order.

As a matter of style, the **case** statement should be presented to best reflect the logic of the problem being handled.

Since the program will fail if there is no statement specified for a possible value of the case index, the values for which no action is to be taken must be followed by an empty statement (introduced in Chapter 5–B).

EXAMPLE 7–1

We have these definitions and declarations:

```
type
    dayOfWeek = (Monday, Tuesday, Wednesday, Thursday, Friday,
            Saturday, Sunday);
var
    day: dayOfWeek;
```

(a) We may specify:

```
{weekly activities}
case day of
    Monday, Tuesday, Thursday: writeln ('Project X');
    Wednesday, Sunday:          ;      {an empty statement!}
    Friday, Saturday:      begin
                                writeln ('Project X to be completed.');
                                writeln ('Project Y')
                           end
end;
```

(b) We may use the **case** statement to output the value of a variable of an enumerated type (which, as we know, cannot be written out directly):

```
case day of
    Monday:     writeln ('Monday');
    Tuesday:    writeln ('Tuesday');
    Wednesday:  writeln ('Wednesday');
    Thursday:   writeln ('Thursday');
    Friday:     writeln ('Friday');
    Saturday:   writeln ('Saturday');
    Sunday:     writeln ('Sunday')
end;
```

Case statements are a superior replacement for nested **if** statements whenever several parallel logic paths are required. They are, in particular, a complement for enumerated data types, as illustrated by the above example.

EXAMPLE 7–2

Problem

Write a program to imitate the operation of a pocket calculator.

Analysis

Pocket calculators perform arithmetic in the order the operators are entered. Our program will thus accept as input an expression (with no embedded blanks) consisting of real operands and the four arithmetic operators, terminated by the equals sign.

This is an example of such an evaluation:

$$\underbrace{\underbrace{\underbrace{10.5 + 2.3}}_{\textstyle 12.8/3.2}}_{\textstyle 4.0*6.6} = 26.4$$

terminator

Program

```
program pocketCalculator (input, output);
        {operators are applied to operands in the sequence
         they are entered; the expression contains no blanks and
         is terminated by '='}

const
    terminator = '=';
var
    value, answer: real;        {operand}
    operator : char;
```

```
begin
   if eof then
      writeln ('No expression entered.')
   else
      begin
         writeln ('This is pocket-calculator arithmetic:');
         writeln;
         read (answer);
         write (answer: 7: 3);
         read (operator);
         write (operator);
         while operator <> terminator do
            begin
               read (value);
               write (value: 7: 3);
               case operator of
                  '+': answer := answer + value;
                  '-': answer := answer - value;
                  '*': answer := answer * value;
                  '/': answer := answer / value
               end;
               read (operator);
               write (operator)
            end;
         writeln (answer: 7: 3)
      end;
end.
```

An Output

```
This is pocket-calculator arithmetic:

10.500-  4.500/  2.000*  2.500=  7.500
```

B. REPETITION WITH *REPEAT* STATEMENT

In certain cases where a repetitive execution of a sequence of statements is desired, these statements are always to be executed at least once, and, moreover, it appears natural to express the condition for ceasing the repetition as follows: "Keep doing the work until such-and-such condition arises." In such cases, the **repeat** statement (loop) is usually preferred to **while** repetition (discussed in Chapter 5–D).

The general form of the **repeat** statement is:

repeat
    statement;
      ⋮ } optional
    statement
until Boolean expression

A **repeat** statement is executed as follows:

(1) The sequence of statements enclosed between **repeat** and **until** is executed.
(2) The Boolean expression is evaluated (according to the rules of Chapter 4–A–2).
(3) If the value obtained is *false*, control is returned to **repeat** and thus to step 1; otherwise the execution of the **repeat** statement is completed.

EXAMPLE 7–3
In order to appreciate the difference between the **repeat** and **while** loops, compare this code fragment with Example 5–6:

```
{write out positive even numbers up to 100, inclusive}
even := 2;
repeat
    writeln (even);
    even := even + 2
until even > 100;
```

Note the following:

(1) A **repeat** loop is always executed at least once; this should be correct under the circumstances of the program.
(2) The Boolean expression must become *true* after a finite number of iterations—otherwise we have an "infinite" loop.
(3) As in the case of the **while** loop, the number of iterations does not have to be known before the loop is entered.
(4) Since **repeat** and **until** symbols delimit the body of the loop, there is no need to present it as a compound statement with additional **begin** and **end** brackets.

The **repeat** statement is especially useful when the completion condition for the iteration is not established before the loop is entered. If we wanted to use the **while** statement instead, we would need either to "force through" the condition by providing its variables with artificial values, or write out a part of its body before the loop (and consequently modify the loop itself).

EXAMPLE 7–4
As a superior alternative to Example 5–8, this fragment may be employed to count characters in a single-line exclamation:

```
count := 0;
repeat
    read (current);
    count := count + 1
until current = '!';
```

Note that the Boolean expression is inverted in such a transformation from **while** to **repeat.** The resulting fragment is terser and easier to understand.

Trace the values of the variables, using "Hi!" as input, and compare with the trace obtained for Example 5–8.

C. VARIABLE-CONTROLLED REPETITION WITH *FOR* STATEMENT

Situations when the number of iterations to be performed by a repetitive statement is known before the statement is to be executed are quite common. The **for** statement is a very convenient implementation of such a loop. This statement uses a *control variable,* whose initial and final values for the loop execution are specified, to count out the iterations. The values of this variable proceed **to** a higher value, or (in other loops) **downto** a lower value.

The general form of the **for** statement is:

$$\text{expression} \qquad \text{expression}$$

for control variable := $\overbrace{\text{initial value}}$ **to/downto** $\overbrace{\text{final value}}$ **do**
    statement

where:

- the control variable is of an ordinal type (not real!) compatible (see Chapter 6–E) with both the expression for its initial value and the expression for its final value;
- the statement included may be, of course, simple or compound.

EXAMPLE 7–5
Here are two **for** loops:

(a) **for** character := 'A' **to** 'Z' **do**

    write (character);

(b) **for** count := n **downto** n − 10 **do**

    total := total + count;

The **for** statement is executed as follows:

(1) The values of the initial-value and final-value expressions are obtained and stored; they will not change throughout the entire iteration (even if the variables included in them will).

(2) The control variable is assigned the initial value.

(3) This condition is evaluated:

in a **to** loop: control variable > final value,
in a **downto** loop: control variable < final value.

If the value obtained is *true,* the execution of the loop ceases and control passes to the next program statement.

(4) If the value is *false,* the body of the loop is executed, and the control variable is incremented or decremented as follows:

in a **to** loop: control variable := *succ* (control variable),
in a **downto** loop: control variable := *pred* (control variable).

In order to test whether the loop is to be entered again, step 3 is carried out again and so forth.

Observe carefully that when the control variable equals the final value, the loop *is* entered!

EXAMPLE 7-6

(a) This loop (where *counter* is an integer variable):

for *counter* := −*10* **to** *10* **do**
    writeln (counter);

will present the integers −10, −9, . . . , 0, . . . , 10, one per line. Note that the last value presented is the final value.

(b) In a program with the definition and declaration of Example 7–1, we may have this loop:

totalGolf := 0;
for *day* := *Sunday* **downto** *Wednesday* **do**
    begin
        readln (golfHours);
        totalGolf := *totalGolf* + *golfHours*
    end;

(c) To encode the schematic code fragment of Chapter 5–E–1 for reading in data using its count, we may employ this fragment:

```
read (count);
for i := 1 to count do
    begin
        read (item);
        :        {processing of the input data}
    end;
```

Note that in this case we could equally well use this loop:

```
for i := count downto 1 do
    :
```

Note this:

(1) Like the **while** statement, the **for** statement is "protective": the included statement will not be executed at all unless the entry condition is initially fulfilled;

(2) The stepping up or down (**to/downto**) through the progression of values of the control variable is always to its immediate successor or predecessor value, respectively. Thus, for an integer control variable we have only increments (or decrements) of 1. If other increment/decrement values are desired, **while** or **repeat** loops may be used. Alternatively, certain values of the control variable may be "ignored" or other values may be derived from the progression of the control variable values, as in the following examples:

EXAMPLE 7–7

(a) *{sum of positive odd integers no greater than n is obtained}*
```
total := 0;
read (n);
for item := 1 to n do
    if odd (item) then
        total := total + item;
```

(b) *{square roots of the sequence: 0.5, 1.5, 2.5, ..., n + 0.5 are presented}*
```
read (n);
for index := 0 to n do
    begin
        rootee := index + 0.5;
        writeln ('Square root of ', rootee: 10: 2, ' is ',
                    sqrt (rootee): 10: 2)
    end;
```

The following should be understood about the (ordinal) control variable itself:

(1) It must be a so-called entire variable (see the Introduction to Part III) declared via a **var** declaration, and never a component of a data structure.

(2) The declaration of the control variable has to be located in the same block (see Part II) that contains the **for** statement itself.[2]

(3) The value of the control variable may be, and very often is, used (referenced) during the iteration (see the above examples), but statements included in the loop must be unable to cause a change in the value of the control variable (for example, through an assignment to it). Changes in the value of the control variable must be caused solely by its progression from the initial to the final value, caused by the looping mechanism itself.

(4) After the loop has been completed, the value of the control variable is undefined; thus, it cannot be used after the normal exit from the loop. (It is, however, available if the loop was left, exceptionally, via a **goto** statement—see the next section.)

(5) The initial and final values of the **for** statement must be assignment-compatible (see Chapter 6–E) with the control variable if the loop is entered at all. Thus, for example, if these values are outside the subrange defined for a subrange-type control variable, the **for** statement is in error.

In conclusion, the most important features to remember: the initial and final values never change during the execution of the **for** loop, and the control variable's value may be changed (implicitly) only through the looping mechanism.

The crucial point in writing **for** loops is to ensure that the initial and final values are precisely the values desired. Often hand-checking helps to avoid "off-by-one" errors.

The **for** loops may, of course, be nested, often in conjunction with other repetitive or conditional statements.

---

2. In particular, the control variable cannot be a formal parameter.

EXAMPLE 7-8

(a) The code fragment presented in Example 5-10 may, with a great increase in readability, be recoded so:

```
total := 0;
for i := 1 to 5 do
    for j := 1 to 3 do
        total := total + 1;
writeln ('the total is ', total: 1);
```

(b) This code fragment:

```
readln (n);
for i := 1 to n do
    begin
        for j := n downto i do
            write ('*');
        writeln
    end;
```

will print this figure for *n* equal to 5:

```
*****
****
***
**
*
```

The **for** statement is particularly well suited for processing arrays (see Chapter 13).

Nested loops are employed in the following program:

EXAMPLE 7-9

Problem

Display a diamond outlined by capital letters as illustrated by this example:

```
        A
      B–B
     C——C
    D———D
     E——E
      F–F
        G
```

The letter in the middle row may be selected from the meaningful range A to M.

Algorithm

(a) Initial version

program *displayDiamond;*
begin
    write the upper part of the diamond, including the middle row;
    write the lower part of the diamond
end.

(b) First refinement

program *displayDiamond;*
begin
    read the *letter selected* to appear in the middle row;
    for *letter* **from** 'A' **to** *selected* **do**   {upper part}
        begin {write out the row bounded by this letter}
            write leading blanks as appropriate for the row;
            write the letter;
            write *filler* characters;
            write the letter
        end;
    determine the *lastLetter* to appear at the bottom of the diamond;
    for *letter* **from** successor of *selected* **to** *lastLetter* **do**   {lower
                                          part}
            {write out the row bounded by this letter}
            . . . as in the upper part . . .
end.

Implementation

```
program displayDiamond (input, output);
        {alphabetic diamond is displayed, with selected letter
         A to M in the middle row}

const
    filler = '-';   {character filling the diamond}
var
    selected,          {letter in the middle row}
    letter,            {letter in the row being displayed}
    lastLetter: char;  {letter in the last row}
    blankSpan,         {leading blanks in the row}
    fillerCount,       {number of fillers in the row}
    i: integer;
```

```
begin
    readln (selected);
    if (selected < 'A') or (selected > 'M') then
        writeln ('Wrong character selected: ', selected)
    else
        begin
            {write the upper part of the diamond, including middle row}
            for letter := 'A' to selected do
                begin
                    blankSpan := ord (selected) - ord (letter);
                    if blankSpan > 0 then
                        write (' ': blankSpan);
                    write (letter);
                    fillerCount := (ord (letter) - ord ('A')) * 2 - 1;
                    for i := 1 to fillerCount do
                        write (filler);
                    if (fillerCount > 0) then
                        writeln (letter)
                    else
                        writeln
                end;
            {write the lower part of the diamond}
            lastLetter := chr (ord (selected) + (ord (selected) - ord ('A')));
            for letter := succ (selected) to lastLetter do
                begin
                    blankSpan := ord (letter) - ord (selected);
                    write (' ': blankSpan, letter);
                    fillerCount := (ord (lastLetter) - ord (letter)) * 2 - 1;
                    for i := 1 to fillerCount do
                        write (filler);
                    if fillerCount > 0 then
                        writeln (letter)
                    else
                        writeln
                end
        end
end.
```

An Output

```
                        A
                       B-B
                      C---C
                     D-----D
                    E-------E
                   F---------F
                  G-----------G
                 H-------------H
                I---------------I
               J-----------------J
              K-------------------K
             L---------------------L
              M-------------------M
               N-----------------N
                O---------------O
                 P-------------P
                  Q-----------Q
                   R---------R
                    S-------S
                     T-----T
                      U---U
                       V-V
                        W
```

If desired, the reader may learn about one-dimensional arrays at this point by studying Chapter 13, sections A through D.

D. EXCEPTIONAL TRANSFER OF CONTROL WITH *GOTO* STATEMENT

Any programming situation can be handled with the structured statements of Pascal that were presented in Chapter 5 and the preceding sections of this chapter. The use of these single-entry, single-exit statements in a disciplined fashion, called structured programming, enhances the readability of a program, making it easier to understand and modify.

In exceptional circumstances (which arise very rarely in uncomplicated programs), the program may be simplified if an unconditional transfer of control to another place in the program is specified with a **goto** statement. Typical situations are:

(1) A loop, possibly nested with other constructs, needs to be left before completion of the current execution of its body. This may happen in a search program when the item is found, or in any program processing an input data file when an exceptional data item is encountered.
(2) An exceptional condition is discovered during execution of one of the procedures or functions of a program (see Part II), and an immediate exit to the main program is wanted.

Thus a **goto** plays the role of an exit statement from the current execution environment to the point specified by that statement.

The general form of the **goto** statement (it is a simple statement) is:

goto label

where the label is the marker of the place to which control will be transferred as the sole effect of the execution of the **goto** statement. Subsequently, program execution will continue from the "labeled" point. For example,

goto *1000;*

A label is employed in a Pascal program only so it can become the target of a **goto** statement. The label must be declared, like other entities created by the programmer.

(1) A label is an unsigned integer (but its numeric value is of no significance, since it is simply a marker, within the range from 0 to 9999. Implementations frequently further restrict the magnitude of labels.

(2) A label must be declared before all other declarations and definitions, using a **label** declaration of the following general form:

label
    label, . . . , label;
         optional

For example,

label
    1000, 1010;

(3) Each label can be used only once in the block for which it is declared; the scope rules (see Part II) for labels are the same as for identifiers.

A label is used by prefixing it, followed by a colon, to a statement, possibly empty, which is to become the target of a **goto**. Empty statements are used to transfer control to the end of a compound statement, as shown in the following example.

EXAMPLE 7–10

(a) In a program with this declaration:

label
    99, 101;

we may have these statements:

      ⋮
    goto *101;*   *{immediate shutdown}*
      ⋮
    goto *99;*   *{main switch failed}*
      ⋮
   99: writeln ('Failure of the main switch!');
   101:   *{shutdown}*
   end.

Note that since the label 101 is attached to an empty statement (here, **goto** 101 causes program termination), it has to be preceded by a semicolon.

(b) Study this code fragment:

```
    ⋮
while not eof do
    begin
        read (character);
        if character = '$' then
            goto 100;      {input file in error, stop processing}
        ⋮ }process data
    end;
    ⋮
100: writeln ('Incorrect input file') {error termination}
end.
```

But remember that a labeled statement will be executed regardless of whether or not it has been reached through a **goto**! Also note that the use of a **goto** may be avoided by reading this fragment with an **if-then-else** statement.

Unconstrained use of **goto**'s leads to unreliable and unmaintainable programs. These statements may be used, if at all, only occasionally, when the alternative constructs have been considered and rejected as inferior. These additional restrictions apply:

(1) No **goto** may be used whose target would be a statement included in a repetitive or conditional statement.

(2) No **goto** may lead into a procedure or function (see Part II), but a **goto** may lead out of it into the main program.

---

(3) "Backward" **goto**'s (that is, ones leading to a statement above them) are to be entirely avoided (use a loop instead).

(4) Comments should be provided both with the **goto** and its target to explain the purpose of the statement.

Our final template for a program without procedures and functions (to be discussed in Part II) is thus:

```
program heading;
label declarations;
const definitions;
type definitions;
var declarations;
begin ⎤
    ⋮ ⎬ statement part
end. ⎦
```

Note that each of the word symbols **label, const, type, var** may appear only once.

Part Two

MODULAR
PROGRAMMING

INTRODUCTION. GOALS OF MODULAR PROGRAMMING

Writing a meaningful program is often a large task, in many cases resulting in thousands of lines of code. The complexity of such a task is manageable only if the program itself, and hence also the process of designing and writing it, can be broken down into components which handle certain aspects of the problem. Smaller programs also profit in clarity of design by being structured of functional components rather than written as a sequence of statements.

Designing a program of such larger components, which will subsequently be coded, the developer is able to manage the profuse detail involved in programming. Such detail is brought in gradually, as program development progresses.

These self-contained program components, which perform well-defined tasks in the handling of the problem and may be activated by name, are called *modules*. A purposeful program design of such units is called *modular programming*. This process of design proceeds in a hierarchical (top-down) fashion, from the briefest and most abstract description of the solution algorithm to the handling of all of the detail. Thus, modular programming complements the process of stepwise refinement: as our view of the program algorithm is being refined, modules that will handle increasingly detailed tasks are identified. The modules communicate by exchanging data (via parameters) or accessing certain data entities commonly available to them (called nonlocal entities).

Modules may be written relatively independently by different programmers, and the complete program tested incrementally, by adding finished and individually tested modules to the ones completed so far.

Modular programming has significant advantages over straight-line coding without modularization (larger programs are always written in a modular fashion):

- A modular program is easier to design and implement (code and test); for large programs, the straight-line approach is virtually impossible.
- A modular program, if well documented, is far easier to understand. In particular, meaningful module and parameter names explain the major components of the program.
- A modular program is easier to modify, since during a modification of a well-designed program the changes will be limited to the modules affected, with the rest remaining intact.
- Overall programming effort lends itself to a better organization when more than one programmer is involved, which is the practice with larger programs. Members of a programming team work on separate modules.
- Multiple use of tested modules (as an alternative to repetition of the code) in a program, when possible, results in increased program readability, as well as in savings of programming effort and memory space. Certain modules that perform frequently needed tasks in a given environment may be placed in module libraries, to be available for use in different programs.

While hard-and-fast rules cannot be offered since the complexity and goals of modules differ, a module should be no longer than approximately a page of code, that is, about 50–100 lines. For large programs, a two-page maximum length may be recommended, about 150–200 lines.

Pascal program modules include the main program (always present, of course) and two types of *subprograms:* procedures and functions (see Fig. II–1). Subprograms are declared in the program and activated by the main program, other subprograms, or even themselves (via recursive calls), when needed.

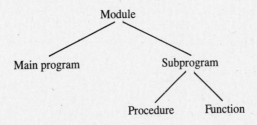

FIGURE II–1. Classification of program modules.

When activated, a procedure or a function may be communicated the data values it needs for its computational task. A subprogram may also communicate any number of values computed by it back to the activating module. Good programming practice, however, demands the use of procedures as a more general vehicle for module implementation when several values are to be returned, and the use of a function when a single result is sought. A function is invoked directly in the expression where its result is needed.

Communication with subprograms is established either through parameters listed in subprogram headings, or through nonlocal variables accessible to subprograms under the scope (accessibility) rules of the language. In the case of a function, its single result is always returned, to be substituted for the function designator which activated it.

Aside from programmer-declared procedures and functions, Pascal offers a complement of standard procedures and functions that may be used (activated) without declaring them. These are discussed throughout the book in the chapters describing their domain of application.

8

PROCEDURES

The procedure is the more general of the two types of subprograms offered by Pascal. A procedure is declared, that is, named and specified, with the use of a procedure declaration. It may be subsequently activated through the execution of a procedure statement stating the name of the procedure and specifying its parameters if it has any.

The generality of a procedure (as compared to a function) consists in the fact that it may be properly employed to compute any number of values for the activating program.

In its computation, a procedure declared in the main program has access to all the variables declared in the main program (i.e., global variables), unless the same identifier has been used in the procedure itself. Some procedures are declared within other subprograms, thus having access to the nonlocal variables declared in these (unless these variables are redeclared in the procedure). The rules of scope of identifiers are discussed in greater detail in Chapter 9.

A. WHY DO WE NEED PROCEDURES?

Let us consider a solution to the following simple problem: find the largest of three positive integers and highlight the answer by framing it.

We are looking to the following output, for example:

```
******
* 57 *
******
```

This is the highest-level pseudocode of the solution:

```
program presentMaximum;
{present the largest of three integers in a frame}
begin
    find the maximum of three integers;
    format the output in a frame
end.
```

Thus, our problem is reduced to solving two simpler problems, each with its own solution algorithm. The general programming facility for handling a subtask of the program is a procedure. Through the use of procedures, larger programming problems can be solved by being subdivided into subproblems, each corresponding to a complete aspect of the entire solution. These subproblems may, in their own turn, be decomposed, with a hierarchy of procedures as the result. Such a "divide and conquer" strategy is the essence of problem solving in most situations.

Thus, in our case we can allot the work to two procedures as shown by this pseudocode:

```
program presentMaximum;
begin
    findMaximum;
    formatFrame
end.
```

The program will then include two procedures we have called *findMaximum* and *formatFrame;* the task of the main program in this case will be simply to activate these procedures in the proper sequence.

As we will see in Section C of this chapter, where this program will be coded, lower-level procedures may be employed to further subdivide the task.

A *procedure* is a named, self-contained sequence of declarations and definitions, and statements, which may communicate with other parts of the program via specific data entities. It may be activated (called) when needed during program execution by a statement that states the identifier of the procedure and, if the given procedure requires it, presents necessary data.

As we will see in Chapter 11, another kind of subtask may be conveniently allotted to a similar facility, called a *function*. When activated, a function returns a value which replaces the function activation. We may think of a function as replacing an expression (even though a function declaration itself may contain any statements) whose value is returned as a substitute for the activation, while procedures stand in place of a series of statements assigning values to a number of variables.

Procedures and functions, often called collectively subprograms, obey in most respects the same rules of communication with the remainder of the program through nonlocal data (see Chapter 9) and parameters (see Chapter 10). Execution always begins with the main program, the subprograms being activated as specified by appropriate statements during the course of the execution. A subprogram is not executed unless it has been activated.

Our search for a solution to the above problem has illustrated the usefulness of pseudocode in the modular programming process. As stepwise refinement progresses, procedures and functions which will handle specific aspects of the problem are identified. Further, these procedures and functions may themselves be pseudocoded independently.

B. DECLARATION AND ACTIVATION OF PROCEDURES

To be used, a procedure must be:

(1) declared, that is, coded and included as a procedure declaration; this makes the procedure ready for use (but, like any declaration, it does not cause the execution of the procedure);
(2) activated (called), that is, brought into action in the place within the program where the procedure's task is to be accomplished.

The placement of procedure declarations is determined by the Pascal language itself; the activations, on the other hand, are placed as needed to accomplish the task of the program.

Several standard procedures are provided in the Pascal system (for example, *read* and *write*); these procedures are used without declaration.

A *procedure declaration* consists of the procedure heading, which names the procedure, and the procedure block. For procedures that use them, the heading also identifies their parameters, that is, data to be communicated to and/or by them (this is discussed in Chapter 10). Since a procedure, like the entire program, is an implementation of a self-contained algorithm, a procedure block has the same structure as the entire program block. It follows that a procedure may declare its own entities for internal use, among them also other procedures. The relative jurisdiction of these declarations is discussed in Chapter 9.

A *procedure heading*, which opens the declaration of every procedure, has the following general form:

procedure identifier (formal parameter list);
                         _____
                                optional

where the list of formal parameters (further discussed in Chapter 10) names the data whose values will be "imported" into the procedure from the point of its activation and/or "exported" by the procedure into that point. Formal parameters are the procedure's own (dummy) names for these entities.

Thus, the general template of procedure declarations is:

procedure identifier (formal parameter list);

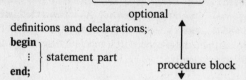

definitions and declarations;
begin
   ⋮   } statement part
end;

procedure block

Note that this template is the same as the general program template of Fig. 2–1, with the exception of the heading and the semicolon after **end** (as in other declarations).

> Definitions, declarations, and the statement part of a procedure are conveniently indented from the heading in order to distinguish them from the environment in which the procedure is embedded.

Procedure declarations are placed at the end of the definition and declaration sequence of a given block. These declarations may be placed in any order in the proper block, with an important constraint: the declaration of a procedure has to precede its use.

The entities declared in the main program block are accessible to the procedure unless other entities with the same name are declared in the procedure itself. The entities declared in the main program are *global* entities. On the other hand, the entities declared in the procedure are *local* to it; they are not accessible to the main program. Thus, the procedure may keep secrets from the main program (but not vice versa). This is desirable because the procedure may fully "hide" certain details of its operation from other modules, leading to an overall simplicity of program design. The general rules of existence and accessibility of entities, known as scope rules, are discussed in Chapter 9.

EXAMPLE 8–1
The following procedure swaps the values of two integer variables, *this* and *that*:

```
procedure swap;
{swap the values of two integer variables}
   var
       temporary: integer;
   begin
       temporary := this;
       this := that;
       that := temporary
   end;
```

Note a most important point: the variables *this* and *that* are not declared in the procedure. This is entirely proper, since they are assumed to have been declared in the main program block where the procedure itself is declared. They are global variables and constitute the means of communication between the main program and the procedure *swap*.

Had these variables been declared in the procedure itself, then as local variables they would have been invisible to the remainder of the program, and the procedure would have no effect.

The variable *temporary* is declared locally, on the other hand, since it is used by the procedure for internal purposes.

To activate (call) a procedure, a *procedure statement* is employed. It simply names the procedure to be executed and, if needed by the procedure, provides the list of actual parameters, corresponding to the formal parameter list of the procedure heading (this correspondence is discussed in detail in Chapter 10).

A procedure statement has the following general form:

identifier (actual parameter list);
 of the   optional
procedure

For example, to activate the procedure *swap* of Example 8–1, it suffices to state:

swap;

The procedure statement is a simple statement of Pascal and may be used as such in the statement part of the main program or a subprogram.

The execution of every program always begins with its own statement part. When a procedure statement is encountered in the course of the execution, the statements of the named procedure are executed. In other words, the execution of a procedure statement results in the execution control being diverted to the statement part of the procedure. After its execution has been completed, control returns to the statement following the procedure statement.

Let us investigate in detail the very simple communication of values between a main program and the procedure *swap*, which is called by the program in two places.

EXAMPLE 8–2
This is the outline of a program utilizing the procedure *swap* of Example 8–1:

```
    program sort (input, output);
      ⋮
    var
        this, that: integer;
      ⋮
    procedure swap;
        var
            temporary: integer;
        begin {swap}
          ⋮
        end; {swap}
    begin {sort}
      ⋮
        if this < that then
            swap;
        that := that + 1;
      ⋮
        swap;
      ⋮
    end. {sort}
```

The following junctions in the program execution are of interest:

1. The execution begins with **begin** {sort} and continues until the **if** statement.
2. If the test succeeds, swap is activated. The current values of variables this and that are exchanged by the procedure as if they were its own variables. In doing so, the procedure uses its local variable temporary, whose existence is "unknown" to the main program, since it is not declared there.
3. Control returns from swap to the assignment statement in the main program.
4. The procedure is called again, this time unconditionally, to exchange the now current values of this and that. (Note that due to the intervening processing these values may be different from the values left in these variables following the first activation of swap.) Subsequently, a return to the next statement in the main program occurs.

C. TECHNIQUE 4: DESIGN OF A MODULAR PROGRAM

Let us complete the design of the program began in Section A. This is a refinement of its pseudocode:

```
program presentMaximum;
{present the largest of three integers in a frame}
begin
    findMaximum; {find the maximum of three integers}
    formatFrame {format the output in a frame}
end.
procedure formatFrame;
    begin
        drawSurface; {draw the top of the frame}
        place the maximum value in a box;
        drawSurface {draw the bottom of the frame}
    end;
```

During the stepwise refinement of the algorithm, we have thus identified the need for three procedures, one of which was worth pseudocoding independently. The modular structure of the program is best seen in its structure chart. A *structure chart* shows program modules as boxes, with the main program on top and activations as lines joining the boxes. The structure chart of our program is shown in Fig. 8–1.[1]

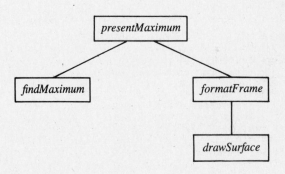

FIGURE 8–1. Structure chart.

From the structure chart, we observe that the procedure *drawSurface* is activated exclusively by the procedure *formatFrame;* it may thus be declared locally within *formatFrame.*

The following example presents the code of the program. Read the code

1. As we will see in Example 17–6, a structure chart may also show parameters, as in Fig. 17–6.

carefully, paying special attention to the communication via accessible variables. Note that the reading of modular programs starts with the statement
part of the main program, and thus close to the bottom!

EXAMPLE 8–3
This is the implementation of our program:

```
program presentMaximum (input, output);
        {present in a frame the largest of three integers}

var
    maximum: integer;

procedure findMaximum;
        {find the maximum of three integers}
    var
        first, second, third: integer;
    begin {findMaximum}
        readln (first, second, third);
        if first > second then
            maximum := first
        else
            maximum := second;
        if third > maximum then
            maximum := third
    end; {findMaximum}

procedure formatFrame;
        {format the output in a frame}
    const
        frameWidth = 8;

    procedure drawSurface;
            {draw top or bottom of the frame}
        var
            index: integer;
        begin {drawSurface}
            for index := 1 to frameWidth do
                write ('*');
            writeln
        end; {drawSurface}

    begin {formatFrame}
        drawSurface;
        write ('*');
        write (maximum: frameWidth - 3);
        write (' *'); writeln;
        drawSurface
    end; {formatFrame}

begin {presentMaximum}
    findMaximum;
    formatFrame
end. {presentMaximum}
```

An output:

```
********
*  555 *
********
```

Note these matters of style in modular programs:

(1) A consistent indentation pattern has to be maintained for readability.
(2) The **begin** and **end** symbols enclosing every statement part are best commented with the name of the module whose statement part this is. Such a practice helps significantly in reading longer programs.

BLOCK STRUCTURE AND SCOPE OF IDENTIFIERS

A Pascal program has a structure of nested blocks. The blocks of the subprograms (procedures and functions) are nested within the main program or within other subprograms. The outermost is the program block, within which global identifiers are defined or declared. Each block may in turn contain definitions (declarations) of identifiers local to it, whose corresponding entities may be used only within the block (which includes other blocks nested within it).

The scope rules of Pascal determine the part of the program where an identifier may be used to refer to a specific entity.

In order to develop reliable, understandable, and modifiable programs, it is necessary to apportion certain aspects of the program's task entirely to various modules. The localization of entities within these modules is the essential technique in such structured design of modular programs.

A. BLOCKS AND LOCAL IDENTIFIERS

With the inclusion of procedure and function declarations (the latter will be discussed in Chapter 11), we now have a complete template for a Pascal program or subprogram, shown in Fig. 9–1.

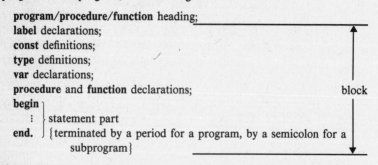

FIGURE 9–1. Complete template of a Pascal program or subprogram.

Thus, programs as well as subprograms consist of the appropriate heading and of the block, where the entities needed in the block are declared or defined, and then manipulated by the statement part. (As a matter of style, the declarations, definitions, and the statement part of a subprogram may be indented from its heading.)

As we remember, some entities are global, that is, defined or declared directly in the main program block; others are local to the subprograms in whose blocks they are defined or declared.

Pascal is a member of the family of so-called *block-structured* languages. In such a language, program entities (e.g., variables or types) may be declared (or defined) within individual blocks, and thus be inaccessible outside of them. Blocks may be nested; for example, procedure A may contain a declaration of another procedure B which is thus available for the exclusive use of A, as it is not known outside of A.

Due to the possibility of block nesting, we speak of *nonlocal* identifiers being known in the procedure. These are the entities defined (declared) in the blocks enclosing the given procedure; of these, the identifiers defined (declared) in the main program are known to us already as global. The main program and the subprograms communicate via nonlocal identifiers; it is through them and through parameters, discussed in Chapter 10, that all the program modules accomplish the work as a whole.

Local identifiers, on the other hand, serve exclusively the subprogram where they are defined (or declared), and any subprograms nested within it. They are known only during execution of that subprogram.

A variable local to a procedure or a function is created, that is, memory space is allocated for it and an identifier associated with that space, when the given subprogram is activated. The local variable ceases to exist with the return from the subprogram to the point of activation. This has the following consequences:

(1) When a subprogram is activated, the value of its local variables is undefined.

(2) Subprograms have no memory between activations: you cannot store a value in a variable during one activation of a procedure and expect to find it there during the next activation. (If you want this effect, the value must be communicated to an activating module.)

(3) Since local variables of a subprogram do not exist between the activations of that subprogram, it clearly follows that they cannot be accessed by the main program or a subprogram not declared inside the given one.

(4) The memory locations which were allotted to local variables during the activation of a procedure may be reused by the Pascal processor following the return from the procedure.

The use of local identifiers—variables in particular—has many advantages, discussed in detail in Section C. The crucial points to be stressed here are:

(1) The use of local identifiers simplifies both the programming process and the understanding of the program, since

   (a) it is not necessary to consider the influence of other parts of the program on the local entities which are isolated by the block structure;
   (b) the identifiers for local entities may be chosen freely, unless they would coincide with nonlocal identifiers needed in the subprogram.

(2) The insulation of local variables makes any reference to them outside the subprogram in which they are declared detectable as an error during program compilation.

(3) Since local variables cease to exist after execution of the subprogram where they are declared, their space may be reused for other variables during program execution.

B. SCOPE RULES

The *scope* of an identifier is the part of the program where a particular identifier may be used to refer to a given entity such as a variable or constant. The scope of identifiers in Pascal programs is determined (as in other block-structured languages) by the *scope rules*, which are of extreme importance.

These are the scope rules of Pascal:

• the main rule:

   the scope of each identifier (or label) is the entire block in which its definition (or declaration) occurs, including all the blocks nested within it, with the exception stated by

• the exclusion rule:

   if an identifier (or a label) declared/defined in block A is redeclared/redefined (that is, the identifier is used again in another set of declarations/definitions) in another block B nested within A, then block B is excluded from the scope of that identifier. (An entirely different entity bearing the same name exists in block B.)

Note that the main rule is also the rule for existence of local variables. The exclusion rule tells us that a subprogram which could have access to a variable but uses its name for a different purpose does not actually have this access.

All the standard identifiers (such as *maxint* or *read,* for example) are assumed to have been defined in an imaginary block enclosing every Pascal program. Hence, they may be redeclared/redefined; this, however, should be avoided to prevent confusion.

Thus the scope rules determine the part of the program where an identifier may be used to denote the same entity.

The following apply:

(1) Throughout the program, every entity must be declared (defined) before it may be used.[1]
(2) However, every declaration (definition) is made for the entire block, regardless of its position in the block.
(3) According to the above scope rules, a subprogram (procedure or function) may be used only within the block where its declaration appears. This means that it may be used in all the blocks nested within that block as well. However, due to the above "declaration before use" rule, a subprogram may activate only itself (such recursive calls are discussed in Chapter 12–A) or other subprograms whose declarations precede its own (this limitation may be circumvented by using the **forward** directive discussed in Chapter 12–B).

EXAMPLE 9–1

In Fig. 9–2 a program and its procedure declarations are shown as boxes:

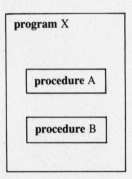

FIGURE 9–2.   A box diagram.

Procedure B may activate procedure A, but not vice versa.

The box diagram employed in Example 9–1 may be used as a mental aid in determining the scope of identifiers by remembering that you may look

1. With the exception of the pointer facility, discussed in Chapter 18.

out of a box (and access the identifiers in enclosing boxes, unless redefined/
redeclared in the box), but you may not look in.

The following important example illustrates scope rules.

EXAMPLE 9–2

The diagram of Fig. 9–3 shows the scope of variables declared in the main
program and in the procedures as cross-hatched areas. You may draw the
equivalent box diagram.

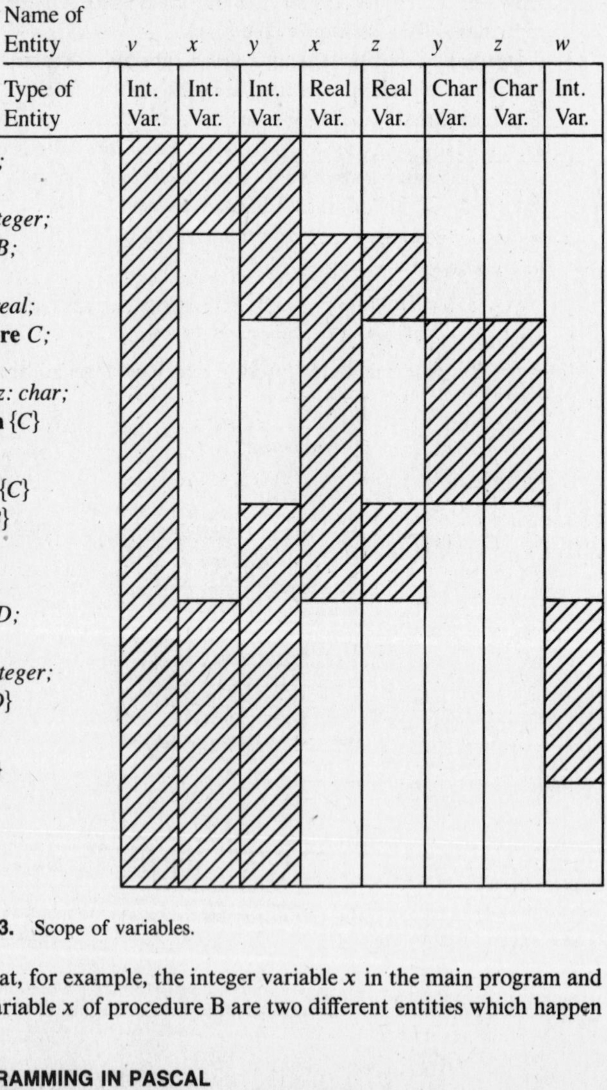

Name of Entity	v	x	y	x	z	y	z	w
Type of Entity	Int. Var.	Int. Var.	Int. Var.	Real Var.	Real Var.	Char Var.	Char Var.	Int. Var.

```
program A;
var
  v,x,y: integer;
procedure B;
  var
    x,z: real;
  procedure C;
    var
      y,z: char;
    begin {C}
      .
      .
    end; {C}
  begin {B}
    .
    .
  end; {B}
procedure D;
  var
    w: integer;
  begin {D}
    .
    .
  end; {D}
begin {A}
  .
  .
end. {A}
```

FIGURE 9–3. Scope of variables.

Note that, for example, the integer variable x in the main program and
the real variable x of procedure B are two different entities which happen

to have the same name. Both exist when procedure B is executed, but B cannot access the integer variable *x*.

The procedures are accessible as follows:

procedure B may be activated by:
    the program A;
    procedure B, that is, itself—such recursive activation is discussed in
            Chapter 12–A;
    procedures C and D;
procedure C may be activated by procedure B and itself;
procedure D may be activated by program A and itself
    (procedure B cannot activate it since it is "unknown" when the
           declaration of B is encountered during program transla-
           tion).

These guidelines apply:

(1) The scope rules are designed to prevent conflict in identifier names among independently written subprograms rather than to economize on the number of identifiers. Having the same identifier stand for several different entities in a program makes it more difficult to understand. If the principle of assigning meaningful identifiers is followed, such coincidences are rather rare.

(2) Be careful to declare/define all local entities. Otherwise, an inadvertent coincidence with a nonlocal identifier may occur and the error will get past the translator resulting in a rather tricky execution error.

(3) Never use nonlocal identifiers to store temporary results during a subprogram execution. Such false economy considerations will surely lead to errors. Do not hesitate to declare local variables as needed.

This is an example of a modular program designed for interactive use.

EXAMPLE 9–3

Problem

Write a program to reconcile the balance in your checking account with the bank statement.

Analysis

The program has to be interactive: it will prompt the user for all the transaction amounts, as well as for both balances, that is, the checkbook balance and the bank statement balance. The actual balance of a proven account will also be shown.

Design

This is the pseudocode of the program, identifying all its procedures and specifying the main ones.

```
program reconcileCheckbook;
begin
    enterChecks;
    enterDeposits;
    proveBalance
end.
procedure enterChecks;
    begin
        for all checks not listed in the bank statement do
            begin
                enter check amount;
                add check amount to check total
            end
    end;
procedure enterDeposits;
    begin
        for all deposits not listed in the bank statement do
            begin
                enter deposit amount;
                add deposit amount to deposit total
            end
    end;
procedure proveBalance;
    begin
        enterBalances; {enter checkbook balance and statement balance}
        otherTransactions; {enter credits and charges}
        actual balance := checkbook balance + credits − charges;
        if statement balance + deposit total − check total ≠
                actual balance then
            indicate the account out of balance
        else
            begin
                indicate the account OK;
                show actual balance
            end
    end;
```

The modular structure of the program is shown by the structure chart of Fig. 9–4.

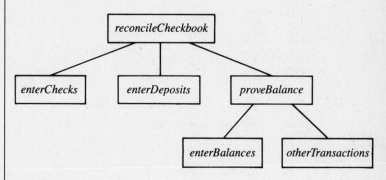

FIGURE 9–4.

Implementation

```
program reconcileCheckbook (input, output);
        {reconcile bank statement balance with checkbook balance}

var
    checkTotal,            {sum of checks not listed in bank statement}
    depositTotal: real; {sum of deposits not listed in bank statement}

procedure enterChecks;
        {check amounts not listed in bank statement are
         entered and totaled}
    var
        thisCheck: real;  {check amount being entered}
    begin {enterChecks}
        writeln ('Please enter check amounts not shown in ');
        writeln ('the bank statement, for example: 22.25');
        writeln ('When done, enter 0.');
        writeln;
        checkTotal := 0;
        repeat
            write ('Check amount: $');
            readln (thisCheck);
            checkTotal := checkTotal + thisCheck
        until thisCheck = 0;
        writeln ('Total amount of checks not considered in the ');
        writeln ('statement is $', checkTotal: 3: 2);
        writeln
    end; {enterChecks}
```

```pascal
procedure enterDeposits;
        {deposit amounts not listed in bank statement
         are entered and totaled}
   var
      thisDeposit: real;
   begin {enterDeposits}
      writeln ('Please enter deposit amounts not listed in ');
      writeln ('the bank statement, for example: 15.45');
      writeln ('When done, enter 0.');
      writeln;
      depositTotal := 0;
      repeat
         write ('Deposit amount: $');
         readln (thisDeposit);
         depositTotal := depositTotal + thisDeposit
      until thisDeposit = 0;
      writeln ('Total amount of deposits not considered in the ');
      writeln ('statement is $', depositTotal: 3: 2);
      writeln
   end; {enterDeposits}

procedure proveBalance;
        {prove statement balance against checkbook balance}
   var
      statementBalance, checkbookBalance, charges, credits,
      actualBalance: real;

 .procedure enterBalances;
           {enter checkbook and statement balances}
      begin {enterBalances}
         write ('Enter the closing balance in your checkbook: $');
         readln (checkbookBalance);
         writeln;
         write ('Enter the closing balance in your statement: $');
         readln (statementBalance);
         writeln; writeln
      end; {enterBalances}

   procedure otherTransactions;
           {enter total amounts of other transactions}
      begin {otherTransactions}
         writeln ('If there are service charges against the account, ');
         write ('enter total of these, otherwise enter 0 : $');
         readln (charges);
         writeln ('If interest or other credits were directed to the ');
         write ('account, enter total of these, otherwise enter 0: $');
         readln (credits);
         writeln; writeln
      end; {otherTransactions}

   begin {proveBalance}
      enterBalances;
      otherTransactions;
      actualBalance := checkbookBalance + credits - charges;
      if statementBalance + depositTotal - checkTotal <>
            actualBalance then
         begin
            writeln ('The account is not reconciled. ');
            writeln ('Please check all transactions.')
         end
      else
         begin
            writeln ('The account is OK.');
            writeln ('The actual balance of your account is $',
                    actualBalance: 3: 2)
         end
   end; {proveBalance}
```

```
begin {reconcileCheckbook}
    writeln ('Reconciliation of Checkbook with Bank Statement');
    writeln;
    enterChecks;
    enterDeposits;
    proveBalance
end. {reconcileCheckbook}
```

This is a session protocol (user entries are underlined in the text):

```
Reconciliation of Checkbook with Bank Statement

Please enter check amounts not shown in
the bank statement, for example: 22.25
When done, enter 0.

Check amount: $100.50
Check amount: $50.25
Check amount: $0
Total amount of checks not considered in the
statement is $150.75

Please enter deposit amounts not listed in
the bank statement, for example: 15.45
When done, enter 0.

Deposit amount: $100
Deposit amount: $0
Total amount of deposits not considered in the
statement is $100.00

Enter the closing balance in your checkbook: $944.25
Enter the closing balance in your statement: $1000

If there are service charges against the account,
enter total of these, otherwise enter 0 : $5
If interest or other credits were directed to the
account, enter total of these, otherwise enter 0: $10

The account is OK.
The actual balance of your account is $949.25
```

In Example 9–3 we have consciously "localized" the accessibility of entities (constants, variables, and procedures), that is, restricted access to them to the lowest possible level on the need-to-know principle. This important consideration of program design is further discussed in the next section.

C. LOCALIZATION OF ENTITIES AND GOOD PROGRAM DESIGN

Properly designed programs limit the existence of entities such as, for example, variables or types to the subprograms where they are needed. In other words, the declarations and definitions of entities are placed as low in the hierarchy of program modules (expressed, for example, by a structure chart such as that of Fig. 8–1) as is compatible with the program's task. The ability to modularize the existence of entities in such a fashion is one of the main advantages of block-structured languages. This is a major tool in controlling the logical complexity of larger programming projects.

Localization of program entities, that is, limiting their existence to the program modules where they are needed, has these important advantages:

(1) During top-down design of the program, entities are introduced as they are required. Thus, the complexity and detail are kept to a minimum at all times. In other words, a level of abstraction compatible with the progress of program development is maintained.

(2) A subprogram with local entities is able to "hide" certain information from other modules, thus becoming the manager of that information. As a result, other modules in the program are not burdened with the details of how this information is managed, which in turn leads to simplification of the overall program.

   If various aspects of the problem are completely apportioned to certain modules, these modules will be the only ones affected by a program modification, should the need arise for a different handling of these aspects. The encapsulation of entities within modules helps to isolate them from the other parts of the program.

(3) The programmer developing a subprogram is free to name and manipulate a local entity as he or she sees fit, independently of other program modules.

(4) The reader of a module does not need to consult other parts of the program in order to understand the meaning of local entities.

(5) Since a local entity cannot be misused outside of its scope, the possibility of programming errors is diminished.

(6) Due to the limited lifetime of local variables, memory space is economized by its dynamic allocation (i.e., allocation during program execution, as the need arises) to the currently existing variables.

Thus, localization strives to keep the entities confined to specific modules. Of course, if all variables were local, no interaction between the modules would be possible (other than via parameters) and in most situations a meaningful modular program could not be constructed. Nonlocal entities (and parameters, as discussed in Chapter 10) provide for necessary passing of information between program components.

These localization guidelines should be followed:

(1) If an entity is not used outside a given program block, declare/define its identifier in that block.

(2) If an entity is needed in more than one block, its identifier should be declared/defined in the block immediately enclosing the blocks using that entity.

(3) If it is desired that a variable used by a procedure not lose its value from one procedure activation to another, the variable must be declared in the block immediately enclosing all activations of the procedure.

However, for the sake of reliable programming and program clarity, explicit communication through parameters is often preferable to using nonlocal variables. This is discussed in the next chapter.

VALUE AND VARIABLE PARAMETERS

Parameters serve to pass to a subprogram such information as:

- values of variables;
- identifiers of designated nonlocal variables which are to be accessible to the subprogram; values of such parameters may then be passed back to the activating module;
- identifiers of procedures and functions to be activated by the subprogram.

The subprogram's parameters are listed in the formal parameter list in its heading; these formal parameters are then used as the identifiers of the corresponding entities in the block of the subprogram.

During activation of the subprogram, the formal parameters are replaced by the corresponding actual parameters, listed in the activating statement: positional correspondence between the actual and formal parameters applies.

Since any actual parameter of the appropriate kind and type may be substituted for a formal parameter, the subprogram may be used in many contexts. Also, the subprogram may be written independently, in terms of its own formal parameters.

We may then have:

- value parameters, which serve to pass a value to the subprogram (but not back from it); or
- variable parameters, through which a value may be passed to the subprogram on its activation and back to the activating module on return.

The testing of modular programs is also discussed in this chapter.

A. WHAT ARE PARAMETERS?

It is desirable to write subprograms (procedures and functions) in a fashion which makes them as independent of the context where they will be used as possible. In other words, it is good if a subprogram uses entities whose names (identifiers) are its own. Such a subprogram can be written as an independent programming task; it may also be activated in several places in the given program, or placed in different programs altogether. The use of parameters provides this independence to subprograms.

Parameters specify the information passed to the subprogram and, in some cases, the values passed back by it on return (other than the nonlocal information available to it under the scope rules).

Parameters are listed in the parameter lists of the procedure heading (see Chapter 8–B) or function heading (see Chapter 11–B). Through them, ready values or identifiers of entities (that is, of variables, procedures, or functions) to be used by a subprogram may be communicated to it by the activating block. The subprogram may, in turn, return the value(s) computed by it.

There are four kinds of parameters in Pascal:

- *value parameters* communicate a value to a subprogram but cannot be used to pass a value back to the calling program;
- *variable parameters,* which by communicating a variable identifier to a subprogram establish a two-way, in-out communication;
- *procedural* and *functional parameters* (two kinds that are used rather rarely and discussed in Chapter 12–C), which communicate to a subprogram the name of a procedure or a function, respectively, to be activated by the subprogram.

A subprogram may employ any combination of these parameters; it is undesirable, however, as argued in Chapter 11, to provide a function with variable parameters.

Parameter communication is established between a subprogram and the point of its activation via the corresponding formal and actual parameter lists, as discussed in the next section.

B. FORMAL AND ACTUAL PARAMETER LISTS

Let us consider the corresponding procedure heading and procedure statement (call), discussed in Chapter 8–B:

heading: **procedure** identifier (formal parameter list);
call: identifier (actual parameter list);
                       of the procedure

The formal parameters specify the information expected by the procedure (the same considerations hold for a function). The actual parameters constitute the information supplied by the activating module. When the procedure is called the actual parameters are substituted for (or the values of the value parameters are assigned to) the corresponding formal parameters. Thus, every formal parameter is a stand-in for the corresponding actual parameter. The positional correspondence of actual and formal parameters determines the substitution[1]: the first actual parameter is substituted for the first formal parameter, the second for the second, et cetera. Subprograms can thus be written in terms of formal parameters (sometimes called dummy parameters, since they are replaced by actual parameters or acquire their initial value from them).

EXAMPLE 10–1

Though the details will be discussed in the next section, this is an example of a matching procedure heading and activation:

> **procedure** *work (days, hours: integer);*
> *work (duration, 5);*

When the procedure call occurs (i.e., the procedure statement is executed), the value of the variable *duration* is assigned to the variable *days*, and the value 5 is assigned to the variable *hours*. The procedure *work* is written in terms of the two variables *days* and *hours* (and any other variables local to it or accessible to it under the scope rules).

In another part of the program, the same procedure might be called as follows:

> *work (17, length);*

A formal parameter list consists of a number of *sections*, separated by semicolons. Each section describes one of these:

- one or more value parameters of the same type;
- one or more variable parameters of the same type;
- a procedural parameter;
- a functional parameter.

Within a section, parameters are separated by commas.
An actual parameter list contains the actual parameters, appropriate for

---

1. Thus note that the association is *not* by name!

their corresponding formal parameters (as discussed below), separated by commas.

The nature of the corresponding formal and actual parameters is described later in this chapter for value and variable parameters, and in Chapter 12–C for procedural and functional parameters. Parameters may be of standard as well as programmer-defined (for example, enumerated) types.

The following must hold for the formal and actual parameter lists of every subprogram:

(1) the number of parameters in both lists must be the same;
(2) the actual and formal parameters in the same position in the respective lists must match as to kind and type (where appropriate); this match is further discussed for parameters of all four kinds;
(3) the order of evaluation of actual parameters (where they are subject to evaluation) depends on the implementation.

In conclusion, actual-formal parameter communication enables us to write the subprogram itself in terms of its formal parameters, and activate it with the actual parameters as required in the given context.

C. VALUE PARAMETERS

When a value has to be passed *to* a subprogram and no communication back to the point of activation is required, a value parameter is used. (Such a parameter is sometimes referred to as an in-parameter.)

In the case of a value parameter, the actual parameter is an expression (which may, in some cases, be a constant value or a variable), and the formal parameter is a variable identifier. The value of the actual parameter must be assignment-compatible (see Chapter 6–E) with the formal parameter (that is, for example, an integer value may be assigned to a real formal parameter).

The corresponding formal parameter is always a variable. The type of the formal parameter (or the sequence of parameters) is specified right in the formal parameter list. Thus, the general form of a section of this list for value parameters of the same type is:

formal parameter(s): type;

For example, here is a procedure with three sections:

procedure *computePercent (total, median: real;*
residual: integer; {percentage for the future}
view: real);

Note:

(1) It is convenient to list one section per line for readability.
(2) The order of parameters in the list depends on the programmer and is usually dictated by readability considerations; thus, there may be more than one section with the same type.
(3) Comments, placed as above, are recommended to explain the role of the parameters, unless the parameter identifier is self-explanatory.

It is an error to declare a formal parameter in the subprogram block; its listing with the type in the formal parameter list serves in place of such a declaration.

The procedure statement calling *computePercent* may be:

computePercent (base + margin, 15.51, 10, estimate);

under the assumption that all the identifiers used as actual parameters are assignment-compatible with the corresponding formal parameters.

When the procedure statement is executed, actual parameters that are not ready values are evaluated at the point of call (as we said, the order of this evaluation depends on the implementation). The value of every actual parameter is assigned to the corresponding formal parameter. In effect, every formal parameter is initialized to the value of the corresponding actual parameter.

If the type of corresponding actual and formal parameters is programmer-defined (which is the case with all structured types, discussed in Part III), it must be defined in the block enclosing the activation as well as the subprogram. Only then can the type identifier be specified in the procedure heading as required.

EXAMPLE 10–2

We would like to modify the procedure *drawSurface* used in the program of Example 8–3 so that it can draw a line of any length, using any character to draw with.

```
procedure drawAnySurface (length: integer;
                          mark: char); {character to draw with}
{draw a surface of desired length}
    var
        index: integer;
    begin {drawAnySurface}
        for index := 1 to length do
            write (mark);
        writeln
    end; {drawAnySurface}
```

The procedure statement needed to activate this procedure in the program of Example 8–3 would become:

drawAnySurface (frameWidth, '');*

The activating statement could also be, for example:

drawAnySurface (frameWidth − 2, chr (43));

Correspondingly, *frameWidth* would be declared as a variable in *formatFrame* and its value would be read in.

Compare carefully the passing of values via parameters with the communication via nonlocal variables in the procedures of Example 8–3.

Value parameters are passed through the so-called call-by-value mechanism: a copy of the actual parameter value (evaluated, if needed) is given to the subprogram. Consequently, the following holds for value parameters:

(1) Formal value parameters are treated as if they were local variables of the subprogram.
(2) It is permissible to make assignments to a formal value parameter within the subprogram. However, like any assignments to a local variable, such assignments will have no effect on any values outside the subprogram. When execution control returns from the subprogram, the formal value parameters cease to exist and their values are not passed back (this is call by value).

This example illustrates the use of programmer-defined parameter types.

EXAMPLE 10–3

With these global definitions:

type
    hue = (brown, blue, red, mauve, taupe);
    count = 1 . . 10;

we may have this call:

displayBoxes (3, blue);

to the following procedure:

```
procedure displayBoxes (number: count;
                              color: hue);
{display the color and number of boxes}
   begin {displayBoxes}
      write (number: 2);
      case color of
         brown: write (' brown');
         blue: write (' blue');
         red: write (' red');
         mauve: write (' mauve');
         taupe: write (' taupe')
      end;
      if number = 1 then
         writeln (' box')
      else
         writeln (' boxes')
   end; {displayBoxes}
```

D. VARIABLE PARAMETERS

In some cases, a parameter has to serve to communicate a result from the subprogram to the activating module or for two-way communication: to pass a value to the subprogram on its activation and another value back to the activating module on return. Variable parameters are used as such out- or in-out parameters.

In the case of a variable parameter, both the actual[2] and formal parameters are variables of the same type.

A variable parameter is identified as such in the formal parameter list by prefixing its section with the word symbol **var**. Thus, the general form of a formal parameter list section for variable parameters of the same type is:

var formal parameter(s): type;

For example:

procedure *assignClass* (**var** *code, class: char;*
                              var *index: integer);*

Note that the symbol **var** has to precede each variable parameter section.

As in the case of value parameters, variable parameters must not be declared in the subprogram.

---

2. The actual parameter may be, more generally, a so-called variable-access, discussed in the Introduction to Part III, and thus either an entire variable or a single component of a structured variable.

Omission of the **var** symbol from a variable parameter section is a frequent error. It leads to the parameter(s) being treated as value parameter(s); the value of such a parameter cannot be passed back to the activating unit on return from the subprogram.

The following happens for every variable parameter when the subprogram is activated: the location of the actual parameter is, as it were, renamed for the duration of the subprogram execution with the formal parameter identifier (this is so-called "call by reference"). Thus, all the references and assignments to the formal parameter by the subprogram statements are equivalent to references and assignments to the variable which is the actual parameter. No copy of the actual parameter is made.

EXAMPLE 10–4

The procedure *swap,* introduced in Example 8–1, swapped the values of two nonlocal variables named *this* and *that.* In many cases, for example in a sorting program, we might want to activate *swap* several times, each time swapping the values of a different pair of variables. To accomplish this, the procedure may be parametrized:

```
procedure swapAny (var first, second; integer);
{swap the values of any two integer variables}
    var
        temporary: integer;
    begin
        temporary := first;
        first := second;
        second := temporary
    end;
```

This procedure may be activated, for example, by this procedure statement:

```
swapAny (flip, flop);
```

In the above example, both parameters are of in-out nature: they transmit a value to the procedure and out of it. In certain cases, a variable parameter serves only as an out-parameter, as do all the parameters in this example:

EXAMPLE 10–5

```
procedure readValid (var a, b, c: real;
                      var valid: Boolean);
  {read and validate a triple of real values}
    begin
        read (a, b, c);
        if a > (b + c) then
            valid := true
        else
            begin
                writeln ('This triple: ', a, b, c, ' is invalid.');
                valid := false
            end
    end; {readValid}
```

This procedure may be activated as follows:

readValid (projection, pastYear, yearBefore);

A variable parameter is a local identifier which refers to a nonlocal variable (the actual parameter). The use of a local name for it permits independent programming of the subprogram.

The corresponding formal and actual variable parameters must be declared with the same type identifier or two equivalent type identifiers (and not be merely assignment compatible). This is illustrated by the following example.

EXAMPLE 10–6

Let us assume these definitions and declarations in a certain block:

```
type
    natural = 1 .. maxint;
    limited = 10 .. 100;
var
    some: limited;
    more: natural;
    all: integer;
procedure compute (var pass: natural);
    ⋮
```

Only the variable *more* among the three variables declared can be passed as the actual parameter to the procedure *compute*.

The requirement for exact identity of the types of corresponding parameters again points up the desirability of **type** definitions, discussed in Chapter 6, since during a program modification it may be desired to pass a variable to a subprogram as an actual parameter.

Naturally, value and variable parameters often coexist in parameter lists. Care must be exercised to provide a separate section for:

- value parameters of a given type,
- variable parameters of a given type.

For example, in this heading:

procedure *getRandom (seed: integer;*
                var *random: integer);*

two sections are needed, even though both parameters are of the same type.

EXAMPLE 10–7

These are correctly matching parameter lists (*x, y, length* are integer variables):

{procedure heading with a formal parameter list}
procedure *graph (scale: integer;* **var** *height: integer; symbol: char);*
values may be
passed as shown:
        graph ((x — y) **div** *2,*   *length,*   *'*');*
{procedure statement with an actual parameter list}

The order of parameters in parameter lists is chosen by the programmer to point up the meaning of the program.

The following simple program highlights the distinction between value and variable parameters. A more elaborate modular program, employing both procedures and functions, is presented in the next chapter.

EXAMPLE 10–8

Problem

Total the scores of each of the two teams, Lions and Tigers, and announce the result.

Program

The input to this batch program is presented with one score per line. The scores of each of the two teams are delimited by a sentinel value −1.

```
program compareScores (input, output);
        {compare the scores attained by two teams, Lions and Tigers}

const
    sentinel = -1;  {separates the two sets of scores
                     and terminates the second set}
var
    LionsScores, TigersScores: integer;
```

```
procedure totalScores (var sum: integer);
        {obtain total score for the team}
    var
        score: integer;
    begin {totalScores}
        sum := 0;
        readln (score);
        while score <> sentinel do
            begin
                write (score: 1, ' ');
                sum := sum + score;
                readln (score)
            end
    end; {totalScores}

procedure report (Lions, Tigers: integer);
        {report the outcome}
    begin {report}
        writeln ('Lions scored ', Lions: 1, ', Tigers scored ', Tigers: 1);
        if Lions = Tigers then
            writeln ('A draw is announced.')
        else if Lions > Tigers then
            writeln ('Congratulations, Lions!')
        else
            writeln ('Congratulations, Tigers!')
    end; {report}

begin {compareScores}
    write ('Lions'' scores: ');
    totalScores (LionsScores);
    writeln;
    write ('Tigers'' scores: ');
    totalScores (TigersScores);
    writeln; writeln;
    report (LionsScores, TigersScores)
end. {compareScores}
```

An Output

```
Lions' scores: 13 5 4 1
Tigers' scores: 2 7 11 4

Lions scored 23, Tigers scored 24
Congratulations, Tigers!
```

E. TECHNIQUE 5: TESTING OF MODULAR PROGRAMS

To locate errors in a program, testing and debugging accompany coding during program implementation, as discussed in Chapter 2–I. Modular programming significantly simplifies this process for larger programs.

Following the coding of an individual module, we can test it in isolation and then add the already tested module to the structure developed so far (consisting of previously coded and tested modules). Such *incremental testing* produces programs built of reliable components, whose interfaces are tested when the modules are being incorporated in the overall structure one-by-one.

In order to test a module in isolation, we have to design a *driver* for it: a short program that will activate the module with the necessary parameters (planned as test cases). The driver should include all the needed definitions and declarations. It will supply the in-parameter values to the module and accept the out-parameter values from it, writing out all the values for testing purposes.

If a module being tested activates another subprogram, we need to substitute for the latter a so-called *stub:* a specially written module replacing the actual one.

In most cases, stubs contain simply *write* or *writeln* statements indicating the activation, and possibly displaying parameter values. Sophisticated stubs may be designed, though, to simulate the action of the real module. When that module is included in the program, the stub will be discarded.

When individually coded and tested modules are being incrementally incorporated into the overall program, particular attention needs to be devoted to their interfaces with other modules: nonlocal variables as well as parameters. Unmatched interfaces are a frequent error in modular programs.

In many structured development projects, coded and tested modules are integrated into the program (as developed so far) in a top-down fashion: the main program is developed first, then the next level of modules, and so on. Top-down implementation provides an early skeleton of the final program and imparts a measure of confidence in the soundness of the design. This method relies on stubs of modules which have not been implemented yet.

In certain cases, bottom-up implementation is preferred, so that the lowest-level modules, which usually access the data files, are developed first. Drivers are necessary in this case.

When it is desired to deliver one or more preliminary versions of a program, realizing only a part of its functionality, a modified top-down implementation technique may be used: we identify and develop completely certain subsets of modules which provide the needed functions.

11
FUNCTIONS

Functions are preferable to procedures in certain programming situations, when a single result is to be computed by a subprogram and used directly in an expression.

A function is activated by its designator, which becomes an operand in an expression in the activating block, or which entirely replaces such an expression. This designator is replaced by the single value, the result of the function. As a consequence, the type of the result has to be specified in the function heading, and the result itself assigned to the function identifier within its block.

The use of functions to compute several values and pass them back via variable parameters should be avoided. Even more dangerous are side effects of functions: changing the value of nonlocal variables as a result of function execution. If such effects are desired, procedures ought to be employed.

A. WHAT IS THE PURPOSE OF FUNCTIONS?

Procedures, discussed in Chapter 8, are employed to compute any number of values. The essential use of a function, on the other hand, is to determine a single value (the result of the function) for direct use in an expression in the activating module. This value replaces the activation of the function. Such usage is in some cases more natural than the use of a procedure.

For example, assuming that we can declare a function *validData*, which will return the value *true* if the data are valid and *false* otherwise, we may easily convert to Pascal code the following pseudocode fragment:

```
if validData then
    process data
else
    write error message;
```

As another example, we may conveniently declare and use as follows: a function *minimum,* which determines the smaller of two numbers:

smallerPlusOne := minimum (x, y) + 1;

Thus, declaration and activation of functions assists the process of programming. A function, like a procedure, is a module, rendering the advantages of modular programming. Its ability to return a single result as the substitute for the activation makes it a convenient tool in certain situations.

A number of standard functions are provided by the language; these may be used without a declaration (for example, the arithmetic and transfer functions discussed in Chapter 3–G). Others are declared by the programmer and activated where needed.

Functions obey the same scope rules and parameter-list correspondence principles as procedures.

B. DECLARATION AND ACTIVATION OF FUNCTIONS

To be used, a function must be:

(1) declared with a function declaration, to be made ready for use;
(2) activated (designated) where its task is to be accomplished.

A function declaration is placed together with other function and/or procedure declarations immediately before the statement part of the block where the declaration is needed (see the template of Fig. 9–1). The relative order of these declarations is chosen by the programmer based on Pascal's "declaration before use" rule and on considerations of program readability.

A function declaration consists of the function heading and the function block.

A function heading has the following general form:

function identifier (formal parameter list): result type;

       of the   optional
       function

For example:

function *mark (first, second, third: real): char;*

The function block has the same properties as the program or procedure block (see Chapter 9–A), and is terminated by a semicolon. Scope rules (see Chapter 9–B) apply. As a matter of style, we indent the function block from its heading.

The essential characteristics of functions which distinguish them from procedures follow from the fact that every function returns (computes) a single result that is substituted for its activation. As a consequence, the following apply:

(1) Every function has the type of its result stated in its heading. This may be any simple type (including enumerated and subrange types defined by the programmer—see Fig. 6–1) or a pointer type (see Chapter 18). If a programmer-defined type is employed as the result, only the type identifier may appear in the function heading. Hence, the type definition (see Chapter 6–B) must be provided in a block enclosing the function declaration and activation(s).

(2) A value assignment-compatible with the result type *must* be assigned to the function identifier by an assignment statement in the function block. Such an assignment statement has to be executed in every path through the function logic.

EXAMPLE 11–1

This function returns as a result the value of the smaller of any two real numbers:

```
function minimum (a, b: real): real;
    begin
        if a < b then
            minimum := a
        else
            minimum := b
    end;
```

Note that, as necessary, an assignment to the function identifier is provided in both logic paths of the above example. In such an assignment, the function identifier stands alone (without parameters), as a variable identifier would. No assignment can be made to a function identifier anywhere in the program outside the function block.

In order to activate a function, its designator (i.e., the function identifier with actual parameters, if any) is included in an expression (or, possibly, stands alone in place of an expression).

The general form of a *function designator* is:

identifier (actual parameter list)

 of the   optional
function

The function designator yields the result of the function.

EXAMPLE 11–2

These are all designators of the function *minimum* of Example 11–1, included in expressions, where needed:

(a) *smaller := minimum (first, last) / 2.5 + floor;*
(b) *writeln ('minimum value: ', minimum (this, that));*
(c) *tiny := minimum (minimum (first, 10.5), third);*

Note that in Example 11–2c above, the minimum of three values is found by using the result of the function as one of the actual parameters. Thus, a function designator may act as an actual value parameter presented to a subprogram. (This is clear, since such a designator may be included in or stand in place of an expression.)

> Do not confuse the function designator with the function identifier! The designator, with its list of actual parameters, serves to activate the function; the function identifier serves as the target of an assignment statement within the function block.

It is very important to realize that even though a value is assigned within the function block to the function identifier, this value *cannot* subsequently be accessed even within that block by referencing the function identifier. In this respect, the function identifier is different from a local variable (remember, this is the value of the function result, not of its identifier!). An auxiliary variable is needed for such a purpose, as illustrated by the following example:

EXAMPLE 11–3

Write and test a function raising a real value to an integer power.

```
program testRaise (input, output);
        {drive the function raise}

var
    a: real;
    n: integer;

function raise (a: real;
                n: integer): real;
        {n-th power of a is computed}
    var
        power: real;
        i: integer;
    begin
        power := 1;
        for i := 1 to n do
            power := a * power;
        raise := power
    end;
```

```
        begin {testRaise}
            readln (a, n);
            writeln (a, n, raise (a, n))
        end. {testRaise}
```

Note that we need the local variable *power* to store the intermediate values. It would not have been legitimate to write the loop body as:

*raise := a * raise;*

since the function identifier *raise* cannot appear on the right-hand side of an assignment.

   This function may be activated as follows, for example:

*capital := raise (rate, years) * capital;*

   The actual parameters of a function designator are associated with the formal parameters of the function's heading according to the rules of positional correspondence (see Chapter 10–B).

   A function may have any number of value parameters; it may also have procedural or functional parameters, discussed in Chapter 12–C.

   Variable parameters may be included in the parameter list of a function as well. However, they serve to return values to the activating module. We are stylistically committed to using a function solely to compute its single result which replaces the function designator. Other use of functions is error-prone. If several values are to be computed by a subprogram, a procedure should be used.

   As pointed out earlier in this chapter, functions aid in the clear expression of conditions. This is an example of a Boolean function for such a purpose:

EXAMPLE 11–4

```
program . . .
    ⋮
function valid (datum: integer): Boolean;
    const
        lowerBracket = 100;
        middleBracket1 = 150;
        middleBracket2 = 175;
        upperBracket = 200;
    begin {valid}
        valid := ((datum > lowerBracket) and
                    (datum < middleBracket1))
                or ((datum > middleBracket2) and
                    (datum < upperBracket))
    end; {valid}
```

```
begin {main program}
    read (weight);
    if valid (weight) then
        ⋮
end. {main program}
```

Note how the use of Boolean functions simplifies the phrasing of conditions.

It would also be a simple matter to change the validation criteria if a program modification required it.

The following two related examples illustrate the use of functions.

EXAMPLE 11–5

Random Number Generation

A frequently used function is a *random number generator:* when activated, it returns (generates) a value seemingly unrelated to the one generated previously. The consecutive activations of the function thus produce a sequence of random numbers.

Random numbers are required in many computer applications, such as:

- simulation: the modeling of the behavior of a physical system by a computer program in order to investigate the properties of the system; for example, the time of arrival of cars at a service station is random with a certain distribution (pattern) of arrivals;
- random sampling from a certain collection;
- certain sorting algorithms, etc.

Random numbers produced with the use of such a generator are reproducible: started in the same way, the same sequence will be obtained (the sequence will also repeat itself after a long—for a good generator—series of activations). Therefore, we are actually producing pseudo-random numbers. This has advantages, for example, in comparative simulation: we may vary the number of pumps in the simulated service station and observe its performance (e.g., mean waiting time) under the same workload.

There are many techniques for random number generation. Most often the numbers are generated in the interval:

$$0 \leq \text{random} < 1$$

This is a frequently used generator function[1]:

```
function random (var seed: integer): real;
    {generate random number: 0 <= random < 1}
    begin
        random := seed / 65536;
        seed := (25173 * seed + 13849) mod 65536
    end;
```

For the first activation of the function, *seed* is assigned a value:

$$0 \leq seed < 65536$$

When *random* is being generated by subsequent activations of the function, the new value of *seed,* randomly distributed in the above interval, is also produced.

The random number generated may be scaled according to program needs. For example, this function (activating, in its turn, the function *random*) produces a random integer in the specified interval:

```
function randomInteger (low, high: integer): integer;
    {generate random integer: low <= randomInteger <= high}
    begin
        randomInteger := low + trunc ((high - low + 1) * random)
    end;
```

The following example illustrates the use of a random number generator (note that the function *random* has been coded as parameterless).

EXAMPLE 11-6

Problem

Simulate the tossing of a coin with a specified bias (or lack of it), i.e., probability of heads as opposed to tails. We need to determine the number of heads tossed.

---

1. Due to the ways they are used, random number generators are usually implemented as functions with **var** parameter or with assignment of value to a nonlocal variable. They are an exception in this regard.

Solution

```
program tossCoins (input, output);
        {simulate tosses of a coin with specified bias}

var
    tosses,                {total number of tosses}
    heads,                 {number of heads tossed}
    seed,                  {for the random number generator}
    i:   integer;
    headProbability,       {specified probability of heads (since
                             coin may be biased)}
    headProportion: real; {proportion of heads tossed}

function random: real;
        {random number generator}

    begin {random}
        random := seed / 65536;
        seed := (25173 * seed + 13849) mod 65536
    end; {random}

begin {tossCoins}
    readln (tosses, headProbability);
    writeln (tosses: 1, ' coin tosses will be performed,');
    writeln ('with probability of heads of ', headProbability: 5: 3);
    writeln;
    seed := 33;      {initialize random number generator}
    heads := 0;
    for i := 1 to tosses do
        if random < headProbability then
            heads := heads + 1;
    headProportion := heads / tosses;
    writeln ('The number of heads was ', heads: 1, ';');
    write ('this constitutes ', headProportion: 5: 3);
    writeln (' of the total number of coin tosses.')
end. {tossCoins}
```

These are the outcomes of three runs, with an increasing number of tosses:

(1)

```
50 coin tosses will be performed,
with probability of heads of 0.600

The number of heads was 31;
this constitutes 0.620 of the total number of coin tosses.
```

(2)

```
150 coin tosses will be performed,
with probability of heads of 0.600

The number of heads was 92;
this constitutes 0.613 of the total number of coin tosses.
```

```
300 coin tosses will be performed,
with probability of heads of 0.600

The number of heads was 182;
this constitutes 0.607 of the total number of coin tosses.
```

C. AVOIDING SIDE EFFECTS

As stressed already, it is best if a function execution is limited to returning a single result. To that end, we avoid using variable parameters with a function, at the same time avoiding side effects.

A *side effect* of a function[2] is a change in the value of a nonlocal variable due to the execution of the function. Side effects are treacherous since they may lead to consequences unanticipated by the programmer and difficult for the reader of the program to fathom.

> **EXAMPLE 11–7**
> Consider this function with a side effect:
>
> > **function** *compute (a, b: real): real;*
> > **begin**
> > $x := x + a;$
> >   *compute := a * b + sqr (a) * sqr (b)*
> > **end;**
>
> The function changes the value of the nonlocal variable x. Let us then consider separately the following two independent assignments in the module which activates *compute* and where x is declared:
>
> $y := x + compute (m, n);$
>
> and
>
> $y := compute (m, n) + x;$
>
> These two statements will (probably unexpectedly) render different results, since it would appear that in the second case the value of x will have been changed by the execution of *compute*. Even this is, in general, uncertain, since in Pascal the order of evaluation of the two operands joined by an arithmetic operator depends on the implementation (see Chapter 3–F–2)!

---

2. One may similarly talk about side effects of procedures; these, however, do not have such undesirable consequences, and are practically unavoidable in many cases.

Hence, to avoid hard-to-locate errors, functions must not change the values of nonlocal variables or call procedures which do so. Of course, functions may *access* the values of nonlocal variables in accordance with the scope rules.

In order to prevent the possibility of assigning a value to a nonlocal variable during function execution, some programmers declare locally within the function all its variables, and communicate values to the function via parameters.

The following example of a modular program presents the use of procedures and functions employing both value and variable parameters.

EXAMPLE 11-8

Problem

Determine the day of the week on which any date in the 20th or 21st century falls. (Calendar programs are frequently used in data processing.)

Analysis

The specified time span extends from January 1, 1901 (a Tuesday) to December 31, 2100 (note this!).

Following an ordinary year, the day of the week on which January 1 of the next year falls advances by one, since 365 days of such a year divided by the number of days in a week—7—will produce a remainder of 1 (365 **mod** 7 is 1). Thus, January 1, 1902, fell on a Wednesday.

In a leap year of 366 days, an additional day of the week will elapse after February 29th. Because of this, in the following year, New Year's Day will advance by two relative to January 1st of leap year.

A year is a leap year if:

- the year number divides evenly by 4, except for the case of the last year of a century (i.e., the year numbers divisible by 100), since
- the last year of a century is *not* a leap year unless it divides evenly by 400; thus, 2000 will be a leap year, but 2100 will not.

An interactive program, prompting for the date and validating the date entered, is desired.

Design

The following is the pseudocode of modules requiring such specification:

```
program determineDay;
    begin
        enterDate; {prompt for a valid date desired}
        nameTheDay; {determine the day of the week on which the date
                    falls}
        displayDay {display the day of the week}
    end.
procedure enterDate;
    begin
        repeat
            prompt for the date
        until validDate {function validDate needed}
    end;
procedure nameTheDay;
    begin
        compute daysPassedInYear; {function, counting the number of
                    days to date in the year, needed}
        compute number of leap years since 1901;
        compute number of day shifts since January 1, 1901;
        determine week day corresponding to this value: number of day
                    shift mod 7
    end;
function validDate;
    begin
        if the day is within the limit for the month,
            with leapYear and          {function leapYear needed}
            February 29th being compatible then
            validDate is true
        else
            begin
                validDate is false;
                display error message
            end
    end;
function daysPassedInYear;
    begin
        daysPassedInYear := days passed till month begins + days of the
                    current month;
        if leapYear and month past February then {function leapYear}
            add 1 to daysPassedInYear
    end;
```

We have thus identified the need for six procedures and functions, whose relationship is represented by the structure chart of Fig. 11–1.

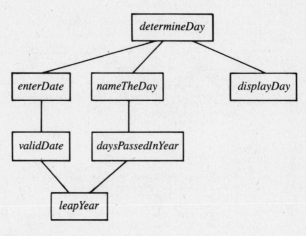

FIGURE 11–1

Note that since the function *leapYear* is activated by two other modules, it has to be declared at the highest level common to both of these, that is, in the main program itself.

The function *validDate*, presented in the program below, may be expressed more succinctly with the use of sets, discussed in Chapter 16.

Implementation

```
program determineDay (input, output);
      {determine the day of the week
        on which any date in the 20th or 21st century falls}

const
   centuryLimit = 2100;
type
   yearType = 1901 .. centuryLimit;
   monthType = 1 .. 12;
   dayType = 1 .. 31;
   daysOfWeek = (Monday, Tuesday, Wednesday, Thursday, Friday,
                 Saturday, Sunday);
```

```
var
    year: yearType;
    month: monthType;
    day: dayType;
    dayName: daysOfWeek;

function leapYear (year: yearType): Boolean;
        {returns true if this is a leap year}
    begin {leapYear}
        leapYear := (year mod 4 = 0) and (not (year mod 100 = 0) or
                    (year mod 400 = 0))
    end; {leapYear}

procedure enterDate (var yearWanted: yearType;
                     var monthWanted: monthType;
                     var dayWanted: dayType);
        {obtain the valid date desired}

    function validDate (year: yearType;
                        month: monthType;
                        day: dayType): Boolean;
            {validate date; returns true if the date is valid}
        var
            OKdate: Boolean;
        begin {validDate}
            OKDate := (day <= 31) and ((month = 1) or (month = 3) or
                        (month = 5) or (month = 7) or (month = 8) or
                        (month = 10) or (month = 12)) or
                      (day <= 30) and ((month = 4) or (month = 6) or
                        (month = 9) or (month = 11)) or
                      (day <= 29) and (month = 2) and leapYear (year) or
                      (day <= 28) and (month = 2);
            if not OKDate then
                begin
                    validDate := false;
                    writeln ('The date entered is invalid. Please repeat.')
                end
            else
                validDate := true
        end; {validDate}

    begin {enterDate}
        repeat
            writeln ('Enter the month, 1 to 12: ');
            readln (monthWanted);
            writeln ('Enter the day, 1 to 31, as appropriate for the month: ');
            readln (dayWanted);
            writeln ('Enter the year, 1901 to 2100: ');
            readln (yearWanted);
            while (yearWanted < 1901) or (yearWanted > 2100) do
                begin
                    writeln ('This program is designed for years 1901 to 2100.');
                    writeln ('Please select the year again:');
                    readln (yearWanted)
                end
        until validDate (yearWanted, monthWanted, dayWanted);
        write ('The day of the week on which ', monthWanted: 1,
               '/', dayWanted: 1, '/', yearWanted: 1, ' falls is ')
    end; {enterDate}
```

```
procedure nameTheDay (thisYear: yearType;
                      thisMonth: monthType;
                      thisDay: dayType;
                      var dayName: daysOfWeek);
          {determine the name of the day specified}
    const
       week = 7;
    type
       daysInYear = 0 ..365;
    var
       originDay: daysOfWeek; {the day of the week on which
                               the first date permitted by the program falls}
       leapsPassed,      {number of leap years from the first date}
       i: integer;
       dayShifts: 0 .. 6;      {shifts in days of the week}

    function daysPassedInYear (thisYear: yearType;
                               thisMonth: monthType;
                               thisDay: dayType): daysInYear;
              {count the number of days to date in specified year}
       var
          toDate: daysInYear;    {days to date in the year}
       begin {daysPassedInYear}
          case thisMonth of
            1: toDate := 0;
            2: toDate := 31;
            3: toDate := 59;
            4: toDate := 90;
            5: toDate := 120;
            6: toDate := 151;
            7: toDate := 181;
            8: toDate := 212;
            9: toDate := 243;
           10: toDate := 273;
           11: toDate := 304;
           12: toDate := 334
          end;
          toDate := toDate + thisDay - 1;
          if leapYear (thisYear) and (month > 2) then
             toDate := toDate + 1;
          daysPassedInYear := toDate
       end; {daysPassedInYear}

    begin {nameTheDay}
       originDay := Tuesday;  {the day of January 1, 1901}
              {count the day-of-week shifts since January 1, 1901}
       leapsPassed := (thisYear - 1901) div 4;
       dayShifts := (thisYear - 1901 + leapsPassed +
                    daysPassedInYear (thisYear, thisMonth, thisDay))
                    mod week;
       dayName := originDay;
       for i := 1 to dayShifts do
          if dayName = Sunday then
             dayName := Monday
          else
             dayName := succ (dayName)
    end; {nameTheDay}

procedure displayDay (theDay: daysOfWeek);
          {display the day of the week}
    begin {displayDay}
       case theDay of
          Monday    : writeln ('Monday.');
          Tuesday   : writeln ('Tuesday.');
          Wednesday : writeln ('Wednesday.');
          Thursday  : writeln ('Thursday.');
          Friday    : writeln ('Friday.');
          Saturday  : writeln ('Saturday.');
          Sunday    : writeln ('Sunday.')
       end
    end; {displayDay}
```

```
begin {determineDay}
   enterDate (year, month, day);
   nameTheDay (year, month, day, dayName);
   displayDay (dayName)
end. {determineDay}
```

A session protocol (user entries underlined):

```
Enter the month, 1 to 12:
2
Enter the day, 1 to 31, as appropriate for the month:
3
Enter the year, 1901 to 2100:
1984
The day of the week on which 2/3/1984 falls is Friday.
```

A session protocol exercising the validation features:

```
Enter the month, 1 to 12:
2
Enter the day, 1 to 31, as appropriate for the month:
29
Enter the year, 1901 to 2100:
1985
The date entered is invalid. Please repeat.
Enter the month, 1 to 12:
3
Enter the day, 1 to 31, as appropriate for the month:
4
Enter the year, 1901 to 2100:
1888
This program is designed for years 1901 to 2100.
Please select the year again:
1990
The day of the week on which 3/4/1990 falls is Sunday.
```

12

ADVANCED USE OF SUBPROGRAMS

A Pascal procedure or function may be designed to activate itself repeatedly (but with different parameters) in order to arrive at the results. Such recursive subprograms are in certain situations superior to their iterative (loop-oriented) equivalents in terms of succinctness and readability.

Indirect recursion, involving two or more subprograms mutually activating one another, is also possible with the use of the **forward** directive.

Along with value and variable parameters, Pascal subprograms may be written with procedural or functional parameters: such a parameter determines a procedure or a function, respectively, which will be activated by the subprogram.

A. RECURSION

Solutions to certain problems are conveniently and naturally represented partially in terms of themselves. Such solution algorithms are called recursive and use recursive definitions. A recursive definition is a computational routine that consists of:

(1) a general rule for obtaining the result(s) for most of the parameter values; this rule is defined in terms of itself, but with different parameters;

(2) explicit (nonrecursive) results for some values of the parameters. Without such ready results, a recursive definition would be circular.

In a correct recursive definition, the progression of parameter values required by the general rule (1) leads to the explicit results of (2).

EXAMPLE 12-1
To compute the factorial n! of a positive integer n, we may use this recursive definition of the factorial:

$$\text{factorial } (n) = n * \text{factorial } (n - 1), n > 0 \qquad (1)$$
$$\text{factorial } (0) = 1 \qquad (2)$$

Thus, as we proceed to evaluate the factorial of a number n, the factorial of its predecessor n − 1 is called for, then the factorial of n − 2, and so on. That is, the factorial is defined in terms of itself, but with decreasing parameter values. When the parameter reaches the value 0, the explicit result is available.

The progression of the evaluation of a factorial value may then be seen as follows:

$$\text{factorial } (3) = 3 * \text{factorial } (2) = 3 * 2 * \text{factorial } (1)$$
$$= 3 * 2 * 1 * \text{factorial } (0) = 3 * 2 * 1 * 1 = 6$$

A recursive solution is to be considered when a problem or its underlying data structure (data structures will be discussed in Part III) is conveniently defined in terms of itself but with the parameters consistently approaching the directly available result(s). This solution technique leads in such cases to succinct programs. In general, however, an iterative equivalent (using loops rather than recursive calls) of such a solution also exists.

In order to enable the programmer to employ recursive algorithms, Pascal makes it possible for a procedure or a function to activate (call) itself. Procedures and functions whose blocks include their own activations are called *recursive*.

We will carefully analyze the mechanism of such recursive activations, since this is necessary to understand recursion.

EXAMPLE 12–2
Let us devise a procedure which reads a sequence of characters of any length, terminated by an asterisk "*", and echoes it out in reverse order.
Here is the procedure with its driver:

```
program testReverse (input, output);
        {test procedure reverseString}

procedure reverseString;
         {reverse a string terminated by an asterisk}
    const
       terminator = '*';
    var
       character: char;
    begin
       read (character);
       if character <> terminator then
          reverseString;                    {recursive call}
       write (character)                {return from recursive calls}
    end;
```

```
begin {testReverse}
    reverseString
end. {testReverse}
```

> (a) When presented with this input:
>
> > This string will be reversed.*
>
> the procedure produced this output:
>
> > *.desrever eb lliw gnirts sihT
>
> (b) The mechanism of a call with the following input:
>
> > The*
>
> is further discussed and illustrated in Fig. 12–1.

> Note that in this case the procedure has no parameter; the recursion will be completed when the end of the string is reached. As the procedure is repeatedly executed through recursive calls, the reading of the string character by character progresses toward this end.

Let us consider what happens when a procedure (or a function) activates itself. To begin with, when such a procedure is first called by another module, space is allocated for the local variables of the procedure (as discussed in Chapter 9–A). However, a recursive procedure does not terminate before the next call to it occurs: it calls itself before returning to the external point of its activation. When such a recursive call occurs, a new set of local variables has to be created for the procedure. This set cannot replace the previous one, since that will be needed to complete the previous activation of the procedure. And so on. Hence multiple collections of local variables must be kept.

In the case of the procedure *reverseString* of Example 12–2, such a series of recursive calls will be issued until the terminator "*" is encountered.

After all the recursive calls have been issued, each one of them has to be completed. The first call that needs to be completed is the one that occurred last, then the previous call can be completed, and so on.

To mark the as-yet-uncompleted calls to the procedure, activation records are used by the language implementation system. An *activation record* contains the values[1] of the local variables and a marker of the point to which execution control is to return from this call (the *return address*). If a recursive subprogram has parameters, the values of its formal parameters (which are, in general, treated as local variables) are also stored in its activation record.

When the "unwinding" of the recursive calls begins, the activation records must be used, as we said, in a last-in-first-out (LIFO) fashion. Therefore,

---

1. Or pointers (see Chapter 18) to larger data structures.

during the recursive calls themselves the activation records are placed in memory in LIFO fashion, thus constituting a so-called *stack* (an often-used data structure).

The run-time stack of activation records created by the Pascal processor for the procedure *reverseString* of Example 12–2 is shown in Fig. 12–1. When a call occurs, a new activation record is placed on top of the stack. After the termination condition for recursion is encountered, recursive descent begins. The activation record on top of the stack is used as the source of local variable values, and the return from the last call is to the return address held in the top activation record. When a return is made from that call, the top activation record is removed from the stack.

Subsequently other activation records are removed from the stack as returns from the corresponding calls occur until the return to the block which activated the procedure is accomplished and the stack is emptied. Note that before recursive descent begins, the activation stack for *reverseString* contains in this case the entire output, which has been automatically placed there by the recursion mechanism.

Recursive functions may be employed in a similar fashion. This is an example.

EXAMPLE 12–3

Let us express the Euclidean algorithm for computing the greatest common divisor (GCD) of two positive integers, presented in Example 5–7, in a recursive form.

Here is the function, together with a driver program.

```
program testGCD (input, output);
        {test function gcd}

var
   m, n: integer;

function gcd (m, n: integer): integer;
        {find recursively greatest common divisor
         of two integers: m and n}
   var
      remainder: integer;
   begin
      remainder := m mod n;
      if remainder = 0 then
         gcd := n
      else
         gcd := gcd (n, remainder)    {recursive activation}
   end;

begin {testGCD}
   readln (m, n);
   writeln (m: 1, ' ', n: 1, ' ', gcd (m, n): 1)
end. {testGCD}
```

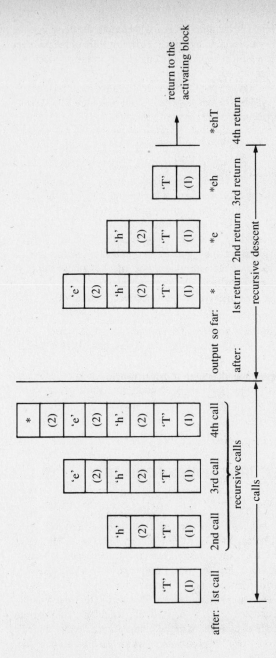

output so far:

after: 1st return 2nd return 3rd return

recursive descent

(1) return point in the activating block (the statement following the procedure statement);

(2) return point from the recursive calls (in the *reverseString* procedure itself)

Composition of an activation record for *reverseString*:

character
return address

FIGURE 12–1. Stack of activation records.

The activation record of the function *gcd* will contain the current value of the local variable *remainder* as well as the current values of the parameters *m* and *n* (and the return address, of course). Trace these values in a manner similar to Fig. 12–1.

Note the difference between the function identifier *gcd* and the function designator, as displayed by the last statement of the function. The variable *remainder* was introduced for the sake of readability.

Comparing the recursive form of the GCD algorithm with its iterative counterpart of Example 5–7, we may agree that as soon as the concept of recursion is understood, the recursive form of expression appears in this case, as in other similar cases, clearer and more natural.

Recursive algorithms have their iterative equivalents, which use loops and often also explicitly managed stacks of data. Only algorithms which gain from the recursive form of expression in conciseness and understandability should be so expressed, since recursive algorithms are, as a rule, less efficient in their use of computer resources than their iterative equivalents.

A programmer using a recursive algorithm needs to ascertain that:

(1) a nonrecursive result is provided for at least one special case;
(2) during the recursive calls, execution converges toward that special case;
(3) the values of the parameters of the procedure or function called recursively are limited; for larger values, the run-time stack of activation records may run out of available memory space.

B. INDIRECT RECURSION AND *FORWARD* DIRECTIVE

Aside from recursion involving a single procedure or function activating itself (sometimes called direct recursion), a program may include two subprograms activating one another. This is known as *indirect* (or mutual) *recursion*. Thus, for example, a subprogram X may activate a subprogram Y which (possibly through a chain of further activations) activates X itself.

The following problem arises. It is a general Pascal rule that every entity has to be declared/defined before it may be used; in particular, a subprogram declaration has to precede all activations of the subprogram. Clearly, this rule cannot be satisfied for any two subprograms of which each calls the other.

To resolve this contradiction, Pascal offers the directive[2] **forward** to provide a preliminary declaration of a subprogram prior to the actual declaration.

Such a preliminary declaration has this general form:

procedure heading; **forward;**

or

function heading; **forward;**

This so-called *forward reference* may be placed anywhere in a sequence of procedure and function declarations in order to make the procedure or function identifier as well as its formal parameters (if any) known to the compiler. The full declaration will follow in the same block, with other subprogram declarations intervening as necessary. After such a preliminary declaration has been made, other subprograms may specify activations of the subprogram so declared.

The procedure or function heading used in an actual (full) declaration that has been preceded by a forward declaration must contain only the identifier of the subprogram; it must not repeat the formal parameter list. In the case of functions, the result type also has to be omitted.

EXAMPLE 12–4

Study this sequence of declarations:

```
program illustrate (input, output);
    ⋮
procedure do (first: integer;
                var second: real); forward;
function make (mark: char): Boolean;
    ⋮
    begin {make}
        ⋮
        do (count, weight);
        ⋮
    end; {make}
procedure do; {note the absence of the formal parameter list}
    ⋮
    begin {do}
        ⋮
        present := make ('*');
        ⋮
    end; {do}
⋮
```

2. Pascal *directives*, of which **forward** is the only standard one, may be, in general, added to a procedure or a function heading, following a semicolon. Such a heading may stand alone, with the proper subprogram declaration coming from another source. This is discussed further in the present section.

> As a matter of consistent style, the formal parameter list may be included in the heading of the full subprogram declaration as a comment. Thus, the program reader will not be misled into thinking that the subprogram is parameterless, and will see all the formal parameter identifiers next to the subprogram block.

Mutual recursion is not the only reason programmers use preliminary declarations. They are also used sometimes to place the full procedure and function declarations in an order that will enhance readability rather than in the order required by the declaration-before-activation rule.

While **forward** is the only standard directive of Pascal, other, implementation-dependent, directives are possible. If defined by the implementation, such a directive may be used, for example, to specify the inclusion of a subprogram from a source external to the program. Thus, often a library of tested subprograms is maintained, and its members may be included in the program with the directive *extern* appended to the heading, which replaces the entire subprogram block (it will come from the external library). For example,

procedure *moveTo (x, y: integer); extern;*

However, subprogram (module) libraries are not a part of standard Pascal.

C. PROCEDURAL AND FUNCTIONAL PARAMETERS

Along with value and variable parameters, under certain circumstances the programmer may wish to pass to a subprogram the identifier of a procedure or a function to be activated by it. Such procedural and functional parameters make it possible to vary the computations performed by the subprogram so parametrized.

For example, we may have a procedure *graph* which produces a graph of a mathematical function. By writing the procedure with the function as its (functional) parameter, we obtain a general graph-making procedure.

A procedural parameter is passed as follows:

(1) the formal parameter is a procedure heading, for example,

    procedure *take* (**procedure** *any (a, b: integer)*);

    where the procedure *any* is the procedural parameter (which itself has two integer value parameters);

(2) the corresponding actual parameter is a procedure identifier.

The procedures denoted by the actual and formal parameters must have congruous (matching) formal parameter lists, as precisely defined below. For example, the procedure statement activating the procedure *take* may be:

take (compute);

under the assumption that the heading of the procedure *compute* is, for example:

procedure *compute (this, that: integer);*

A functional parameter is passed as follows:

(1) the formal parameter is a function heading, for example,

   procedure *give* (**function** *determine (a: integer): real);*

(2) the corresponding actual parameter is a function identifier.

The functions denoted by the formal and actual parameters must have congruous formal parameter lists and the same result type. For example, the procedure statement activating the procedure *give* may be:

give (calculate);

under the assumption that the heading of the function *calculate* is, for example:

function *calculate (i: integer): real;*

As we said, procedures (or functions) used as corresponding actual and formal parameters must have congruous formal parameter lists. This means that:

(1) both must have the same number of parameters;
(2) both lists must have the same number of sections and corresponding sections must be of the same size;
(3) parameters in the same position must match, that is:

  • both are value parameters of the same type, or
  • both are variable parameters of the same type, or
  • both are, in turn, procedural parameters with congruous parameter lists, or
  • both are, in turn, functional parameters with congruous parameter lists and the same result type.

▷ Some implementations allow exclusively value parameters in the formal parameter lists of procedural and functional parameters. ◁

Standard procedures and functions cannot be passed as actual parameters.

In a subprogram whose heading contains a procedural or functional parameter, this formal parameter is used exactly as any procedure or function identifier would be.

EXAMPLE 12–5

The procedure *compare*, included in the following program *driver*, compares the values of two arbitrary functions of a single integer parameter over a range of their parameter values. We use it here to compare the values of the functions *sum* and *raise*; the identifiers of these functions are therefore passed to *compare* as functional parameters.

```
program driver (input, output);
      {test the procedure for comparison of function values}

var
   origin,    {initial parameter value of functions being compared}
   limit,     {final parameter value of functions being compared}
   increment: integer;   {increment of the parameter}

function sum (bound: integer): integer;
      {obtain the sum of integers from 1 to bound}
   var
      index, temp: integer;
   begin {sum}
      temp := 0;
      for index := 1 to bound do
         temp := temp + index;
      sum := temp
   end; {sum}

function raise (power: integer): integer;
      {raise 2 to the integer power}
   const
      base = 2;
   var
      index, temp: integer;
   begin {raise}
      temp := 1;
      for index := 1 to power do
         temp := temp * base;
      raise := temp;
   end; {raise}

procedure compare (function first (i: integer): integer;
                   function second (i: integer): integer;
                   from, upto, step: integer);
      {compare the values of two functions over a range
       of their parameters}
   var
      index, {current value of the parameter of the two functions}
      i: integer;
   begin {compare}
      writeln ( ' Parameter   First Function   Second Function');
      writeln (' ': 18, 'Value', ' ':'12, 'Value');
      index := from;
      for i := 0 to (upto - from) div step do
         begin
            writeln (index: 6, first (index): 15, second (index): 17);
            index := index + step
         end
   end; {compare}
```

```
begin {driver}
    readln (origin, limit, increment);
    writeln ('origin: ', origin: 1, '    limit: ', limit: 1,
        '    increment: ', increment: 1);
    writeln;
    compare (sum, raise, origin, limit, increment)
end. {driver}
```

Here is the output:

```
    origin: 5    limit: 15    increment: 2

    Parameter    First Function    Second Function
                     Value             Value
        5             15                32
        7             28               128
        9             45               512
       11             66              2048
       13             91              8192
       15            120             32768
```

Study carefully the correspondence of parameter lists in all the headings and activations.

It should be noted that the use of procedural and functional parameters hampers program readability and is to be considered only in rather exceptional circumstances.

Part Three

DATA STRUCTURES IN PROGRAMMING

INTRODUCTION. WHAT ARE DATA STRUCTURES?

The simple data types—discussed in Part I of the book—allow us to declare variables which assume a single value of a given type. In programming, however, we often need variables with a number of values, organized as required by the problem. The *structured types* of Pascal are templates which allow us to create corresponding *data structures:* organized collections of data objects together with operations applicable to them.

From the programmer's point of view, there are three aspects to a data structure: the relationship among its components (i.e., the structuring), the values of the components, and the operations applicable to the given structure.

Like structured statements, which group actions and organize them into a program according to an algorithm, data structures group data into larger entities that are meaningful in the program. The use of data structures, as opposed to unrelated equivalent data items:

- simplifies the manipulation of data and thus the algorithm which complements the data structure by performing the manipulation;
- supports modular programming by enabling us to create modules which completely manage a given structure, "hiding" the details of its organization from other modules to make these simpler and more independent;
- explains the nature of data items included in the structure, and the relationships among them, leading to clearer programs.

Pascal provides structured types corresponding to four essential data structures: array, record, set, and file (see Fig. III–1). The components of arrays, records, and files may in turn be some of the other data structures. Such recursive definition of types leads to great programming power in data structuring. The type definition facility of Pascal is a fundamental strength of the language.

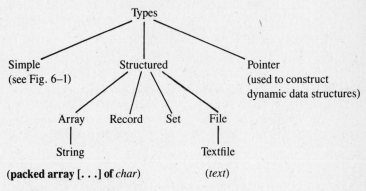

FIGURE III–1. Pascal types.

The data structure selected to organize a collection of data items ought to reflect the real-world relationships among the entities represented by these items. As shown in Fig. III–1, the following data structures are supported by structured types of Pascal.

1. ARRAYS

In this structure, consisting of a fixed[1] number of components of the same type, all the components have a single collective identifier. An individual component is identified by its coordinates within the array; these are called indices of the array. The number of indices (this number is also called the dimensionality of the array) corresponds to the number of characteristics used to classify the components of the array.

For example, we may have an array of Boolean values, describing the availability of tickets in a theater. Every seat is identified by its row letter and seat number, and thus we need a two-dimensional array of components whose value is *true* (available) or *false* (not). Note that if we had orchestra, mezzanine, and balcony sections in our theater, we would need a third dimension in our array, to indicate the placement of the seat.

1. There are no dynamic arrays in Pascal.

2. RECORDS

A record stores all the data relevant to a problem about a certain object or event. It consists of fields; every field describes a certain attribute of the record's object.

As in the real world, records are usually organized, in turn, into larger collections, such as an array or a file of records.

For example, we may have a record representing a theater performance, with such fields as the date, the name of the play, names of its author, director, and leading actors, the number of tickets sold.

3. SETS

Like its counterpart in mathematics, a Pascal set may contain a varying number of distinct values of a certain (ordinal) type.

Your hobbies may be represented as a set of components of an enumerated type. Together with your friends' hobbies, they may be stored in an array of sets.

Sets also offer a convenient way to test certain conditions in programming. For example, to test whether a given day of the week is a performance day, we need a single condition testing the presence of a given value (e.g., Monday) in the performance days set, whose value is the days of the week when the play is performed.

4. FILES

A large collection of components of the same type may be stored as a file. As such, it may be kept in the secondary memory of our system for a long time, independently of the program which created it or of other programs which may use or maintain it. The files of Standard Pascal have an important limitation: they are sequential. Once such a file has been created, its components may be accessed only in the order in which they were written, without any updates.

Note that, as opposed to the Pascal file, arrays are a random-access structure: we may access any component by specifying its indices.

A file of records on the season's daily performances would help a repertory theater to analyze its activity. A more mundane example would be an invoice file of an accounts-receivable system, with records describing individual invoices.

There are two aspects to employing a variable of a structured type. It has to be declared, possibly by using the identifier of a type defined previously. Then, during processing, its components are accessed and manipulated, or the entire structure may be manipulated by such operations as assignment or passing it as a parameter.

In addition to simple and structured types, Pascal offers a pointer facility. Using this data type, we are able to create variables according to a pattern (defined as a type, often a record type), organize them into a desired data structure, and modify this structure (change the relationship between its components)—all during program execution. Such structures, which may be modified as the program is running, are called dynamic.

Any structured type may be specified as **packed,** to save memory (at a certain cost in processing time). This is particularly practicable in the case of arrays.

In addition to its fundamental data types, Pascal recognizes a one-dimensional packed array of characters as a string type and a file of characters as a textfile (of predefined type *text*), both to support text processing.

The discussion of structured types broadens the notion of a Pascal variable. Thus, we can pass as an actual parameter to a procedure or a function a so-called *variable-access*, which may be any of the entities shown in Fig. III–2 (note that a set variable has no components, even though it may have several values).

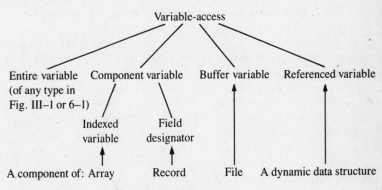

FIGURE III–2. Variable in Pascal (variable-access).

13

ARRAYS

Arrays are ordered collections of data items of the same type bearing the same name. Individual components of an array are identified by their indices. Indices of the array provide the values which classify its components among the others; every component has a unique combination of index values.

The number of indices corresponds to the number of dimensions in the given array; one- and two-dimensional arrays are used most often, but in certain cases arrays using more dimensions are employed.

An array type is specified in a **type** definition or directly in the declaration of the variable(s) of this type. Arrays are, in general, manipulated through their individual components, called indexed variables, but assignment and passing of an entire array as a parameter are possible.

To save memory space, an array may be specified as **packed;** using standard transfer procedures it is further possible to *unpack* such an array for local processing, and then *pack* it back.

Certain implementations offer the conformant array parameter facility (included in ISO Standard Pascal at Level 1) that permits us to write procedures or functions for generalized array processing, irrespective of the index bounds of the actual parameter.

A. WHAT AN ARRAY IS

Frequently, a collection of data items of the same kind, and thus the same type, must be stored and manipulated in a uniform fashion. Such items may be conveniently assembled into a single structured (composite) data entity, called an array. An *array* consists of a collection of data items of the same type, grouped under a single name; its individual components are identified by their *index* (or indices). An index is a value that classifies and identifies a given component of the collection.

The following example illustrates the important programming convenience offered by the use of arrays.

EXAMPLE 13–1a

We have a list of temperature measurements taken in a room every hour from midnight until the next midnight. These measurements are shown in Fig. 13–1.

Hour (military time)	Temperature (stored in memory locations)	Location names: treated as variables	Location names: treated as an array
0	67.11	temp0	temp[0]
1	66.71	temp1	temp[1]
2	66.40	temp2	temp[2]
⋮	⋮	⋮	⋮
23	68.18	temp23	temp[23]

FIGURE 13–1. A collection of variables vs. a one-dimensional array.

Let us take a typical problem: we need to count the number of measurements falling within a certain bracket, for example, from 67 to 67.5, inclusively.

If every one of the measurements has been declared as an individual real variable named, say, *temp0, temp1, . . . , temp23*, then we need the following sequence of statements to accomplish the above task:

```
count := 0;
if (temp0 >= 67) and (temp0 <= 67.5) then
    count := count + 1;
if (temp1 >= 67) and (temp1 <= 67.5) then
    count := count + 1;
    ⋮
if (temp23 >= 67) and (temp23 <= 67.5) then
    count := count + 1;
```
(24)

This is clearly cumbersome (and what if we had 1000 measurements?). The array facility offers a solution to this class of problems.

By using the array facility, we are able to give a collective name to data items that are grouped to reflect their similar nature, and we can identify the individual components by their index within this collection.

In our example, we would declare (as discussed in detail below)

var
    temp: **array** [*0 . . 23*] **of** *real;*

Thus, we have declared the array named *temp* of real-valued components (temperatures in our case). To identify an individual component, an index (in our case the hour when the measurement was taken) will be used. This index type is appropriately declared as an integer subrange, with values from 0 to 23.

Note carefully (see Fig. 13–1) the dependence between the value of the index and the value of the array component. Thus, for example, the value of the component *temp*[*1*] is 66.71.

Our array has a single index, reflecting the fact that its components have a single identifying (and declared) characteristic. Thus, the array has a single *dimension* or, in other words, it is a one-dimensional array. We will see in Section E that multidimensional arrays are also employed. Following mathematical usage, array components are sometimes called elements, and indices are called subscripts.

After an array has been declared, its components may be accessed by specifying the appropriate index value. The power of the index specification rests on the fact that it may be provided as a variable or, in general, an expression of the appropriate type.

EXAMPLE 13–1b

Assuming that the array *temp* has been declared as discussed above, these statements solve the problem posited in Example 13–1a:

```
count := 0;
for i := 0 to 23 do
    if (temp[i] >= 67) and (temp[i] <= 67.5) then
        count := count + 1;
```

Note how the varying index *i* allows us to traverse the entire array. The **for** loop is an especially good tool for uniform processing of all or selected array components.

The components of an array may be of a simple type (for example, integers), or of a structured type (for example, records, discussed in Chapter 15).

B. DECLARATION OF ARRAYS

Like any structured type, an array type has to be defined. In a fashion similar to the definition of new ordinal types (see Chapter 6), the **type** definition may be used for this purpose, or the type specification may be provided directly in an array variable declaration.

An array type specification has the following general form[1]:

array [index type, . . . , index type] **of** component type

optional
(for multidimensional
arrays only)

For example, this declares a one-dimensional array whose index is of a subrange type:

array [*1 . . 100*] **of** *Boolean;*

Thus, an array type is defined as consisting of components of the given component type, with the individual components to be identified by values of the index (or indices, in the case of multidimensional arrays) of the specified index type (or types).

A component type may be any type denoter.[2] This means that:

- We may have an array of any simple-type values, such as an array of integers, *char,* Boolean or real values, or an array of values of an enumerated or subrange type.
- We may also have an array of pointers (discussed in Chapter 18).
- We may have an array of structures. This may be an array of arrays—a multidimensional array, as discussed in Section E—or, to give another important example, an array of records, discussed in Chapter 15.

An index type may be any ordinal type,[3] with the integer type, however, limited in practice to integer subranges. To elaborate:

- the real type may not serve as an index type;
- an index type specifies a limited *range* or enumeration of values which may be assumed by the given array index.

1. In some standard implementations, (. and .) are used instead of [and].
2. As discussed in Chapter 6–B, this is the identifier of a previously defined type or a full type specification.
3. Again, either the identifier of a previously defined ordinal type or a full specification may be given.

The crucial point is that the index type is defined with a constant number of values. Thus, the size of the array is fixed at the time the program is being written; in other words, no dynamic (execution-time) memory allocation for arrays is possible in Pascal. For a one-dimensional array we have:

array size = *ord* (upper limit of index) − *ord* (lower limit of index) + 1

If the actual number of components will vary during program execution, the programmer needs to provide an array size sufficient for the maximum number and keep track of the actual number.

> Care should be exercised in specifying the index type to avoid allocating unneeded memory locations for arrays. Particularly with multidimensional arrays, it is easy to specify large integer subranges as index values without actually using these locations, thus wasting memory space.

We will concentrate, until Section E, on one-dimensional arrays.

In the example above, we have specified an array of 100 components, identified by their index, ranging from 1 to 100. Each of the components is Boolean, that is, the values stored in the array are only *true* or *false*.

Given the above general form of array specification, an array variable may be declared in two ways:

(a) by presenting the type specification directly in the variable declaration, for example:

    var
        temp: **array** [0 . ..23] **of** *real;*

(b) by defining an array type and then using the type identifier to declare variables of this type; such a declaration might be used to ensure that two or more arrays are of identical type, for example:

    type
        measurement = **array** [0 . . 23] **of** *real;*
    var
        temp, pressure, humidity: measurement;

> The use of type definitions is a good programming practice. If a type definition is used to declare an array, do not confuse the type identifier with a variable identifier naming a specific array of this type. Remember that type identifiers may be used only in order to declare variables of that type. Type identifiers may **not** appear in the statement part of a program or subprogram.

Of course, the index and component types may themselves be defined before use, as illustrated by the following example:

EXAMPLE 13–2

Study these definitions and declarations which declare several one-dimensional array variables:

```
const
    lower = 1;
    upper = 10;
type
    percentage = 5 .. 15;
    daysInMonth = 0 .. 31;
    summer = (June, July, August);
    letter = array ['A' .. 'Z'] of integer;
var
    score: array [1 .. 100] of real;
    interest: array [lower .. upper] of percentage;
    daysWorked: array [summer] of daysInMonth;
    charCount: array [char] of 0 .. maxint;
    initialCount, letterCount: letter;
```

Thus, for example, the array *daysWorked* consists of 3 components, whose integer value ranges from 0 to 31, and whose index value is, respectively, *June, July,* and *August.* A sample array is stored in memory as shown in Fig. 13–2.

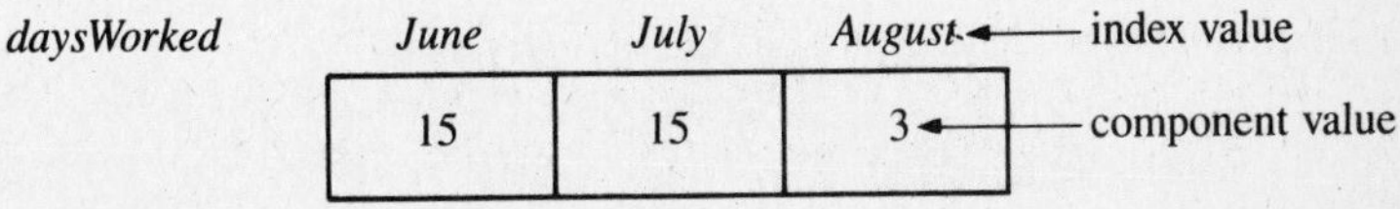

FIGURE 13–2.

Note how the index type is chosen to reflect the nature of the classification of array components.

One-dimensional arrays, with their single index, are a convenient representation of lists of simple data items of the same type. Such an array is the equivalent of a vector used in mathematics, where the index is written as a subscript, e.g., $temp_i$.

C. INDEX VALUES AND SELECTION OF ARRAY COMPONENTS (INDEXED VARIABLES)

Arrays are, in general, manipulated through their individual components (the only whole-array operations—discussed in Section F—are assignment and the passing of an array as a parameter). A component of an array is specified by providing the value of the array index (or indices, in the case of multidimensional arrays). Such a component can be manipulated in the same fashion as a simple variable of the same type; indeed, it is called an *indexed variable.* An indexed variable may appear anywhere in the program a plain variable can, except as the control variable in a **for** statement.

To specify the index value of an indexed variable, an expression, assignment-compatible (see Chapter 6–E) with the index, must be provided. In other words, the expression has to yield one of the values specified for the array index in the array declaration. Thus, an indexed variable has this general form:

array variable[index expression, . . . , index expression]

$$\underbrace{\qquad\qquad\qquad\qquad\qquad\qquad}$$

optional
(for multidimensional
arrays only)

For example,

$$temp[2 * i - 5]$$

assuming that i currently has the value 4, specifies the component of the array *temp* with index 3.

EXAMPLE 13–3

Let us assume these definitions and declarations:

    type
        vowel = (a, e, i, o, u, y);
    var
        vowelCount: array [vowel] of integer;
        initial: vowel;

The array *vowelCount* is shown in Fig. 13–3.

vowelCount

	a	e	i	o	u	y
	8	9	5	10	2	0

vowelCount [u]

FIGURE 13–3.

Assuming that the current value of the variable *initial* is *e*,

the value of *vowelCount*[*initial*] is 9;
the value of *vowelCount*[*succ (initial)*] is 5;
the value of *vowelCount*[*y*] is 0.

The following are typical mistakes of array indexing:

(1) The index value falls beyond the range declared for the array ("index out of range"); this happens particularly frequently when "looping" through the array and overstepping its boundary by going to the nonexistent "next component";
(2) The index specified for the indexed variable differs in type from the declaration ("incorrect type").

D. MANIPULATION OF ARRAY COMPONENTS: ONE-DIMENSIONAL ARRAYS

In order to read, access, update, or write out the values of array components, their indices must be specified as discussed in Section C. Typically, part or all of the array components are processed in the same fashion with the use of a loop. The following pseudocode construct is thus implemented:

while there are more components subject to processing **do**
    begin
        get the next array component;
        manipulate it
    end

In most cases, a **for** loop (see Chapter 7–C) is used instead of a **while** loop, since its control variable may be used as the index (or part of the index expression) to access the desired array components.

An indexed variable may be read in, manipulated, passed as an actual parameter, or written out in the same fashion a plain variable of the same type as the component type would be. If an array component is passed as an actual parameter to a subprogram, the indexing is completed (that is, the component is selected) before the subprogram block is activated.

EXAMPLE 13–4
These code fragments handle typical tasks of array processing.

(1)

We have these declarations:

```
type
    weekday = (Monday, Tuesday, Wednesday, Thursday, Friday);
var
    commuteTime: array [weekday] of real; {minutes with fractions}
    day, longestDay: weekday;
    totalTime, longestTime: real;
```

The following tasks may be accomplished:

(a) To read in the values of the array components, we use:

```
for day := Monday to Friday do
    read (commuteTime[day]);
```

(b) To find the total time spent commuting during the week and identify the day the longest time was spent, we use:

```
totalTime := 0;
longestTime := 0;
for day := Monday to Friday do
    begin
        totalTime := totalTime + commuteTime[day];
        if commuteTime[day] > longestTime then
            begin
                longestTime := commuteTime[day];
                longestDay := day
            end
    end;
writeln ('Total time spent commuting was ', totalTime: 6: 1,
    ' minutes.');
write ('The longest commute was on ');
case longestDay of
    Monday:    write ('Monday');
    Tuesday:   write ('Tuesday');
    Wednesday: write ('Wednesday');
    Thursday:  write ('Thursday');
    Friday:    write ('Friday')
end;
writeln (': ', longestTime: 5: 1, ' minutes.');
```

(2)

We have these declarations:

```
var
    scores: array [1 . . 25] of integer;
    i: integer;
```

To perform a sequential (that is, component by component) search for an array component with a certain value, this code may be employed:

```
{write out the index of the first array component whose value is 0}
i := 1;
while (scores[i] <> 0) and (i < 25) do
    i := i + 1;
if scores[i] = 0 then
    writeln ('The score with index ', i: 2, ' is 0.')
else
    writeln ('There are no 0 scores.');
```

Note:

(a) we need the second relation in the **while** statement to prevent an attempt to search beyond the declared index range, thus causing an execution error;

(b) consequently, when the **while** loop has been terminated we have to establish which of the two relations became *false*.

While using a loop to traverse an array, it is good to hand-check the termination condition of the loop to ensure that the index does not go out of its range.

We may observe that array components may be accessed in a sequential (or selectively sequential—for example, every third component) fashion, as well as randomly. *Random access* means that the component desired can be selected "at random," without any need to access any other components, and it takes approximately the same time to access any of the array components. In this, Pascal arrays are superior to Pascal files (discussed in Chapter 17) which afford only sequential access to their components (however, files may contain far more components).

Efficient search for a needed component requires that the items be ordered or, in other words, sorted.

EXAMPLE 13-5

Bubble Sort

Sorting and searching of data are the most common computer applications. We search a collection of data in order to access a specific component. Since an unordered collection can only be searched in a very inefficient sequential fashion, we usually maintain the items in sorted order. Sorted data may be accessed far more efficiently (a binary search algorithm for accessing such data is shown in Example 15–12).

There exist numerous sorting algorithms. Due to its simplicity, the bubble sort presented here is a good technique for sorting small arrays (up to about a dozen components).

Problem

A set of integers is to be sorted. Ascending order is desired: the larger the number, the higher it should stand in the final list. (In an application, these integers may be the values of the so-called keys, identifying other data.)

Solution via Bubble Sort

(1) Verbal Description of the Algorithm

A bubble sort consists of a pairwise comparison of adjacent numbers starting at one end of an array of numbers. The pair is exchanged if the numbers are in the opposite order to the desired one. One pass through all the numbers does not, in general, suffice. Passes are repeated until, on the last pass, no exchanges are necessary. This confirms that the numbers are in order.

Application of this algorithm to a sample array of numbers is shown below.

The consecutive passes are:

	unsorted array	after pass 1	after pass 2	after pass 3	after pass 4	
i=N →	13	17	17	17	17	
	10	13	13	13	13	
	-10	10	10	10	10	
	17	-10	2	2	2	signifies
	-15	2	-10	-3	-3	"bubbling"
	2	-15	-3	-10	-10	
i=1 →	-3	-3	-15	-15	-15	

(no exchanges)

The details of pass 1 follow:

initial order	following 1st comparison	2nd	3rd	4th	5th	6th	
13	13	13	13	13	13	17	
10	10	10	10	10	17	13	
-10	-10	-10	-10	17	10	10	no exchange
17	17	17	17	-10	-10	-10	
-15	-15	2	2	2	2	2	
2	2	-15	-15	-15	-15	-15	
-3	-3	-3	-3	-3	-3	-3	exchange

Since numbers "bubble up" to take their final place in the array, the algorithm is so named.

It may be observed that the last number moved up during any pass arrives at its final position. An enhanced bubble sort contains a timesaving provision based on this observation: we do not move beyond the number that was moved last at the previous pass. Moreover, if the last number was moved into the position second from "the bottom," the sort has been completed and there is no necessity to make any additional pass without any exchanges.

(2) Pseudocode of the Algorithm[4]

(a) Initial version

```
program bubbleSort;
    begin
        read theArray;
        while exchanges are expected do
            perform next pass over theArray;
        write theArray (now sorted)
    end.
```

(b) Refinement

```
program bubbleSort;
    begin
        read theArray;
        mark scanLimit; {index of the last item to be compared}
                {perform consecutive passes}
        while exchanges are expected do
            begin
                start at the bottom of theArray;
                    {perform a single pass}
                while below scanLimit and scanLimit > 1 do
                    begin
                        compare pairwise and exchange if out of
                                    order;
                        move to next pair
                    end;
                mark new scanLimit
            end;
        write theArray (now sorted)
    end.
```

4. The sorting routine is presented as a program to enable the reader to study it before reading Part II of the book. It may be easily converted to a procedure.

Implementation

```
program bubbleSort (input, output);
        {sort an array into ascending order using bubble sort algorithm}

const
   maxArrayLength = 20;    {limit on the array length}
type
   numericArray = array [1 .. maxArrayLength] of integer;
var
   theArray: numericArray;    {array to be sorted}
   arrayLength,               {actual length of array to be sorted}
   scanLimit, {position of last component to be considered during the pass}
   lastSwap,  {position of last component moved down during the pass}
   temp, i: integer;

begin
              {read in and echo the array}
   writeln ('The array to be sorted:');
   arrayLength := 0;
   while not eof do
      begin
         arrayLength := arrayLength + 1;
         readln (theArray[arrayLength]);
         writeln (theArray[arrayLength])
      end;
   writeln;

              {sort the array}
   scanLimit := arrayLength;
                 {perform consecutive passes}
   while scanLimit > 0 do
      begin
                        {perform next pass}
         lastSwap := 0;
         for i := 1 to scanLimit - 1 do
                        {exchange the pair if necessary}
            if theArray[i] > theArray[i + 1] then
               begin
                  temp := theArray[i];
                  theArray[i] := theArray[i + 1];
                  theArray[i + 1] := temp;
                  lastSwap := i    {last component moved down}
               end;
         scanLimit := lastSwap     {for the next pass}
      end;

                 {present the sorted array}
   writeln ('The sorted array:');
   for i := 1 to arrayLength do
      writeln (theArray[i])
end.
```

Sample Output

```
            The array to be sorted:
                  12345
                    321
                    -10
                     20
                     -1
                      0
                  25000
                  -1111
                    351
                 -40000
```

```
The sorted array:
    -40000
     -1111
       -10
        -1
         0
        20
       321
       351
     12345
     25000
```

E. MULTIDIMENSIONAL ARRAYS

When array components must be classified according to more than one characteristic, multidimensional arrays are employed.

In a one-dimensional array, as discussed above, the value of the single index (subscript) identifies the needed array component. The number of indices in a multidimensional array equals the number of dimensions needed to identify its components.

The concept of a two-dimensional array is illustrated with the following example.

EXAMPLE 13–6

The experiment described in Example 13–1 is modified so that the temperature measurement taken every hour will be triplicated (three copies, replicas, of every measurement are obtained). For further processing, it is desirable to identify every measurement by its two characteristics: the hour when it was taken, and its position within the triple readings taken at this particular hour. The array resulting from such an identification is shown in Fig. 13–4.

Hour (military time)	Number of replica		
	1	2	3
0	67.18	67.01	67.32
1	66.13	65.98	67.12
2	66.01	66.93	66.50
⋮	⋮	⋮	⋮
23	68.80	68.01	68.25

temp[0,3]

FIGURE 13–4. A two-dimensional array.

Having represented our data in such a fashion, we may process them to answer, for example, these questions:

- What is the average temperature taken every hour?
- Is it true that the average of the first replica throughout the day is higher than the average of the second?
- What is the mean daily temperature in the room?

Using the general form of array specification of Section B, the array shown in Example 13–6 may be declared as follows:

var
    temp: **array** [*0 . . 23, 1 . . 3*] **of** *real;*

As seen in Fig. 13–4, a two-dimensional array may be conveniently visualized as a table whose entries are all of the same type. Note carefully that the first index of the array identifies the row of such a table, and the second identifies the column. This corresponds to the mathematical notation for a matrix, whose elements are identified by their subscripts (for example, $temp_{03}$).

Comparing Figures 13–1 and 13–4, we can see that our array has gained another dimension—the columns—identified by the second index.

Likewise, a three-dimensional array is sometimes employed. The following example illustrates such arrays.

EXAMPLE 13–7

The experiment of Examples 13–1 and 13–6 is further modified to measure the room temperature every hour, in triplicate, by measuring both at the floor and at the ceiling.

    The results are stored in a three-dimensional array that may be represented graphically as a cuboid (as in Fig. 13–5).

Hence, a three-dimensional array may be visualized as a cuboid, or a book of tables. The third dimension is the "depth."

To declare the array of Example 13–7, we may use these definitions and declaration:

type
    hour = *0 . . 23;*
    replica = *1 . . 3;*
    place = *(floor, ceiling);*
var
    temp: **array** [*hour, replica, place*] **of** *real;*

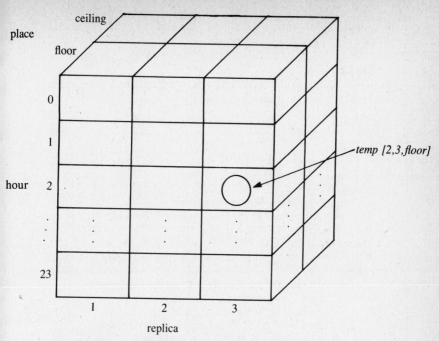

FIGURE 13–5. A three-dimensional array.

Note the use of the enumerated data type *place*. Such usage is preferable to coding, for example, *floor* as 1, and *ceiling* as 2 and using an integer subrange, since the meaning of the classification would become hidden.

> The use of enumerated data types as index types permits the programmer to explain the meaning of data and thus renders programs more self-explanatory.

In some cases (however infrequently) the need arises for arrays of more dimensions than three.

The number of components in an array equals the product of the possible values of its index types. Thus, in our case, the three-dimensional array *temp* has

$$24 \times 3 \times 2 = 144 \text{ components.}$$

Note again how easy it is to specify a large amount of space for an array; for example, the array

> *stuff*: **array** [*1 . . 100, 1 . . 100*] **of** *integer;*

would require 10,000 memory locations[5] and perhaps could not even be accommodated in your computer system.

EXAMPLE 13–8

These are other examples of definitions and declarations specifying multidimensional arrays. Study them carefully.

(a)

```
type
    row = 'A' .. 'K';
    seat = 1 .. 40;
var
    seatPrice: array [row, seat] of real;
    seatOccupancy: array [row, seat] of Boolean;  {is the seat
                                                    taken?}
```

(b)

```
type
    borough = (Bronx, Brooklyn, Manhattan, Queens,
                StatenIsland);
    sex = (female, male);
    registration = (Democrat, Republican, independent);
    phobia = (aero, claustro, cyber, demo, xeno);
    citizens = array [borough, sex, registration] of integer;
var
    voters, constituents: citizens;
    patientCount: array [phobia, borough] of integer;
```

A multidimensional array may also be considered an array of arrays, and declared as such. This is so since, as discussed in Section B, the component type of an array may be structured, in particular also as an array.

Thus, for example, given these constant definitions:

```
const
    lines = 200;
    columns = 240;
```

the same two-dimensional array *screen* may be declared in the following ways:

(a) **var**
```
    screen: array [1 .. lines, 1 .. columns] of Boolean;
```
(b) **var**
```
    screen: array [1 .. lines] of array [1 .. columns] of Boolean;
```

---

5. Or more in some machines.

(c) **type**
    singleLine = **array** [*1 . . columns*] **of** *Boolean;*
   var
    screen: **array** [*1 . . lines*] **of** *singleLine;*

Note that in the last case a one-dimensional array type *singleLine* has also been defined; thus *screen*[*i*] refers to the i-th such array.

Such groupings of array components into subarrays, as it were, are sometimes employed to stress the meaning of data. However, the resulting multidimensional arrays are entirely equivalent. Moreover, an individual component of such an array may be referred to as

$$screen\ [i][j] \qquad or \qquad screen\ [i, j]$$

equivalently. The abbreviated second form is used customarily.

Like one-dimensional arrays, multidimensional arrays are in general manipulated through their components. To identify an individual component, all of its index values need to be provided.

EXAMPLE 13–9

This code fragment identifies a primitive component in the array *voters* of Example 13–8b:

```
var
    region: borough;
    ⋮
begin
    ⋮
    region := Manhattan;
    writeln (voters[region, female, independent]);
    ⋮
```

Note the fashion of index specification.

To process multidimensional arrays, typically nested **for** loops are used. To ensure program correctness, we have to remember (see Chapter 7–C) that an inner loop is fully executed for each iteration of the immediately surrounding one.

A typical pseudocode segment for processing every component of a two-dimensional array is:

for every row **do**
   for every column **do**
      process the array component [row index, column index];

EXAMPLE 13–10

(a) Let us assume that the variable *screen* describes the screen of our video terminal. To set each of the screen dots (pixels) to the off position, we may use this code segment (see the declaration of *screen* above):

```
for i := 1 to lines do
    for j := 1 to columns do
        screen [i, j] := false;
```

Note the order in which the action of the nested loops is carried out: the first line is cleared by the inner loop traversing the columns from 1 to 240, then the second line, and so on until line 200. This order was immaterial in the above example, but often it does matter, as in the following case.

(b) We need to read the voter count into the array *voters* declared in Example 13–8b and to obtain the total count of voters in the city of New York, borough by borough. We will need these additional declarations:

```
var
    region: borough;
    gender: sex;
    affiliation: registration;
```

The following code segment will accomplish the task:

```
{read in the voter count for further processing and obtain total}
voterCount := 0;
for region := Bronx to StatenIsland do
    for gender := female to male do
        for affiliation := Democrat to independent do
            begin
                readln (voters[region, gender, affiliation]);
                voterCount := voterCount +
                              voters[region, gender, affiliation])
            end;
```

In this case, it is necessary to ensure that the input data are presented in the order in which they will be used. Thus, the first three data items presented must be the counts of Bronx female voters, from Democrats to independents; then the three counts for Bronx male voters, then Brooklyn females and so on. Study this carefully!

A program manipulating a two-dimensional array is included in the following section.

F. WHOLE–ARRAY OPERATIONS

As we have seen, general processing of arrays is done by reading in, processing, and writing out the values of their individual components, that is, indexed variables. The only operations possible on arrays as a whole are:

(1) assignment of one array to another,
(2) passing of an array as a parameter.

The value of one array may be assigned to another if the two arrays are of identical type; the same has to be true for corresponding actual and formal parameters. That is, both arrays must have been declared with the same type identifier, or with two type identifiers T1 and T2 defined as equivalent (T1 = T2) through a type definition. Alternatively, both arrays could be declared together in the same variable declaration.

> **EXAMPLE 13–11**
> With this definition and declaration:
>
> **type**
>   *assigned* = **array** *['A' . . 'P', 1 . . 25]* **of** *Boolean;*
> **var**
>   *reservations, seatPlan: assigned;*
>
> we may have this assignment:
>
> *seatPlan := reservations;*

Such an assignment of a whole array is equivalent to component-by-component assignment with the use of a loop, but is preferable because of code brevity and, generally, greater execution efficiency.

Like other variables, an array may be specified as an actual parameter to be passed to a procedure or function. Since structured types are all programmer-defined, the array type has to be defined in the block enclosing both the activation and the procedure or the function itself (see Chapter 10). Subsequently, this type identifier may be used in the procedure or function heading to specify the type of the formal parameter.

The following example combines passing of whole arrays as parameters with component-by-component processing.

EXAMPLE 13-12

Add two square matrices of integers.

```
program readAddMatrices (input, output);
       {add two square matrices of integer values}

const
   limit = 5;    {order of the matrices}
type
   matrix = array [1 .. limit, 1 .. limit] of integer;
var
   a, b,          {matrices to be added}
   c:   matrix;   {resulting matrix}

procedure readEcho (var x: matrix);
          {read in and echo a square matrix}
   var
      i, j: integer;
   begin {readEcho}
      for i := 1 to limit do
         begin
            for j := 1 to limit do    {read in and echo a row}
               begin
                  read (x[i, j]);
                  write (x[i, j]: 7)
               end;
            readln; writeln
         end
   end; {readEcho}

procedure addMatrices (x, y: matrix;      {matrices to be added}
                       var z: matrix);   {resulting matrix}
          {add two square matrices}
   var
      i, j: integer;
   begin {addMatrices}
      for i := 1 to limit do
         for j := 1 to limit do
            z[i, j] := x[i, j] + y[i, j]
   end; {addMatrices}

procedure writeMatrix (x: matrix);
          {write out a square matrix}
   var
      i, j: integer;
   begin {writeMatrix}
      for i := 1 to limit do
         begin
            for j := 1 to limit do
               write (x[i, j]: 7);
            writeln
         end
   end; {writeMatrix}
```

```
begin {readAddMatrices}
    writeln ('The matrices to be added:'); writeln;
    readEcho (a); writeln;
    readEcho (b); writeln; writeln;
    addMatrices (a, b, c);
    writeln ('The resulting matrix:'); writeln;
    writeMatrix (c)
end. {readAddMatrices}
```

Sample Output

The matrices to be added:

1	3	-5	7	11
-20	4	0	-5	8
10	7	17	-21	59
33	101	-15	20	0
10	29	40	150	7

200	-315	21	22	45
411	90	-91	125	-17
7	11	18	-10	-3
-5	85	14	140	141
31	35	12	14	0

The resulting matrix:

201	-312	16	29	56
391	94	-91	120	-9
17	18	35	-31	56
28	186	-1	160	141
41	64	52	164	7

Remembering that the passing of an array as a value parameter causes the copying of the entire array into the data area of the activated subprogram, many programmers pass arrays exclusively as variable parameters to save both execution time and memory space. Such a practice is laudable when these savings are important. It is necessary to consider, however, that in such a case the protection offered by value parameters is sacrificed.

Note that in Pascal the index type (or types) is a part of the type of an array variable. Thus, the requirement that the types of actual and formal array parameters be identical would appear to require, for example, that two different subprograms be written to compute the average value of a 50-component array of integers and that of another array of 55 integer components if both are needed during a single program execution. The waste implied in such a handling of the problem may be circumvented by specifying an array large enough to hold the largest one to be passed, and including a parameter (or parameters) specifying the extent of the array actually passed. Naturally, this complicates the program. In order to avoid this inconvenience, conformant array parameters (see Section H) are allowed in Level 1 of Standard Pascal.

G. PACKED ARRAYS

When economy of memory space devoted to array storage is required, such space may be saved in the case of arrays of certain component types by designating these arrays **packed.** Such a designation does not in general change the meaning of the program.

Pascal offers two transfer procedures, *pack* and *unpack,* which may be employed to transfer arrays from an unpacked form into a packed one, and vice versa.[6]

Packed arrays of *char-*type components, known as strings, are discussed in Chapter 14.

1. WHAT A PACKED ARRAY IS

Frequently, arrays consist of many components, posing considerable demands on main memory space. In some cases it would even prove impossible to accommodate an array in the available space; certain programs require several large arrays.

In order to specify to a Pascal processor that memory space has to be conserved in placing an array in memory, the given array specification may be prefixed with the word symbol **packed.** For example,

asserted: **packed array** [*1 . . 1000*] **of** *Boolean;*

The Pascal processor attempts in such cases to place several array components into a single memory location, thus "packing" the array into a limited space. Considerable savings of memory may be expected if the packed array is of Boolean, *char,* an enumerated, or a subrange type. Depending on the component type and the size of the memory locations of the given computer, a 2- to 32-fold savings in memory space may be expected in these cases.

Packing of arrays (or other data structures) does not change the meaning of the program. However, components of packed data structures cannot be passed to subprograms as actual variable parameters.

Otherwise, components of a packed array are indexed and manipulated in the same fashion as those of arrays which have not been packed. The manipulation of packed array components (as opposed to whole-array operations that involve copying) is less efficient, though. If efficient access to multiple individ-

---

6. Although any of the four structured types of Pascal may be designated **packed,** this feature is used mostly in array processing. Hence, the two transfer procedures apply to arrays only.

ual array components is desired, either the array should not be packed or transfer procedures, discussed next in this section, may be employed.

Note that a packed array cannot be assigned to a nonpacked one, and vice versa, since the two types are never identical.

Of particular importance in Pascal are packed one-dimensional arrays with components of *char* type. These are known as strings and possess certain additional properties (see Chapter 14).

2. TRANSFER PROCEDURES[7]

If in a certain part of a program multiple accesses are made to the individual components of a packed array, the program execution speed could be rather low. Two standard Pascal procedures are provided to help in such a case. The procedure *unpack* serves to transfer a packed array into a local nonpacked array, whose components may be processed efficiently. Following this processing, the *pack* procedure may be employed to pack the components back from the nonpacked into the packed array.

Thus, two arrays, a packed and a nonpacked one, are needed; we will employ these definitions and declarations:

```
const
    a = . . . ; b = . . . ; x = . . . ; y = . . . ;              {integers}
type
    componentType = . . . ;
var
    nonpackedArray: array [a . . b] of componentType;
    packedArray: packed array [x . . y] of componentType;
```

Since the transfer procedures allow for a packed array to be unpacked into a part of a larger nonpacked array, the following must be true:

$$b - a \geq y - x$$

The two procedures act as follows.

(1) The standard procedure *unpack* assigns the entire contents of a packed array to a nonpacked array, starting with the specified *startingIndex* in the latter (see Fig. 13–6). The procedure call has this format in our example:

> *unpack (packedArray, nonpackedArray, startingIndex);*

The nonpacked array has to have enough components, beginning with the one identified by the starting index, to accept all the components of the packed array; otherwise an error results.

7. This section may be omitted on first reading.

The *startingIndex* is an expression whose value is assignment-compatible with the index type of the nonpacked array.

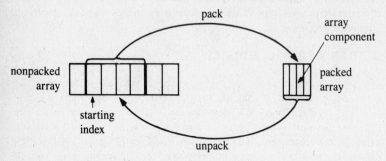

Figure 13–6. Actions of *pack* and *unpack* procedures.

(2) The standard procedure *pack* transfers a part of the components of the nonpacked array, beginning with the one identified by the starting index, into the packed array.
    The procedure call has this form:

$$pack\ (nonpackedArray,\ startingIndex,\ packedArray);$$

The nonpacked array has to have enough components, beginning with the starting index, to fill the packed array; otherwise an error results.
This procedure is an inverse of *unpack*.

H. CONFORMANT ARRAY PARAMETERS[8]

As discussed in Section F, when an array is passed as a parameter to a procedure or a function, the types of the actual and formal parameters must be identical. This means that the index types of the two have to be the same. In consequence, a procedure or a function written, for example, to process this array:

$$line:\ \textbf{array}\ [1\ .\ .\ 120]\ \textbf{of}\ real;$$

will not be fit to process the following array

$$line:\ \textbf{array}\ [1\ .\ .\ 60]\ \textbf{of}\ real;$$

8. This section may be omitted on first reading.

even though the only difference between the two is the length of the array.

Such a limitation makes subprograms quite inflexible in array processing, requiring that multiple subprograms be written to process similar arrays of a different size or that the subprograms be complicated by introducing additional parameters and, possibly, statements.

Conformant array parameters are designed to remove this limitation. They are allowed in Level 1 of the ISO Pascal standard, and are available in several implementations.

A *conformant* (or *dynamic*) *array parameter* is an array parameter specified with flexible lower and upper index bounds (in one or more dimensions) in its formal parameter section. According to the standard, it may be either a value parameter or a variable parameter.[9]

The general form of such a bound specification is:

lower-bound identifier . . upper-bound identifier: ordinal-type identifier

This specification defines the two bound identifiers to be of the specified ordinal type and to be stand-ins for the bounds of the array passed as the actual parameter.

A conformant array parameter is specified in a formal parameter section as follows:

array [bound specification; . . . ; bound specification] **of** type identifier

optional
(for multidimensional arrays)

This is an example of a procedure heading with such a specification:

procedure *calculate* (**var** *spread: array* [*first . . last: integer*] **of** *real*);

Here, the conformant array parameter *spread* is specified as a one-dimensional array of real components whose index is of integer type. The bounds of the array may be referred to in the procedure as *first* and *last;* the actual bounds will correspond to those declared for the array passed to the procedure as the actual parameter.

The bound identifiers may be used in the subprogram as any variable identifiers of the same type would be used. A conformant array is indexed like any other array.

In the subprogram activation, the actual conformant array parameter is specified in the regular fashion, by stating the identifier of that array. The declaration of the array will define the bounds of the conformant array.

---

9. However, various restrictions have been placed on the use of value parameters.

EXAMPLE 13-13

Using conformant array parameters, we will modify the procedure *add-Matrices* of Example 13-12 to add any two compatible square matrices (i.e., the number of rows and the number of columns in both matrices ought to be the same):

```
procedure addAnyMatrices
        (var x, y, z: array [start1 . . limit1: integer;
                             start2 . . limit2: integer] of integer);
{add any compatible square matrices}
    var
        i, j: integer;
    begin {addAnyMatrices}
        for i := start1 to limit1 do
            for j := start2 to limit2 do
                z[i, j] := x[i, j] + y[i, j]
    end; {addAnyMatrices}
```

Note:

(1) since the bounds have to be identifiers, a lower bound specified as 1 would not be allowed;
(2) since the procedure heading defines these identifiers, all of them have to be distinct;
(3) the procedure may be used to add compatible rectangular matrices as well.

The above procedure may be called by the following program:

```
program test (input, output);
const
    top1 = 10;
    top2 = 20;
type
    smallMatrix = array [1 . . top1, 1 . . top1] of integer;
    largeMatrix = array [1 . . top2, 1 . . top2] of integer;
var
    a, b, c: smallMatrix;
    m, n, p: largeMatrix;
procedure addAnyMatrices ( . . . );
    ⋮
begin {test}
    ⋮
    addAnyMatrices (a, b, c);
    addAnyMatrices (m, n, p);
    ⋮
end. {test}
```

The following apply:

(1) A packed conformant array is allowed to have only one dimension.
(2) If several conformant array parameters are defined in the same formal parameter section, mutual assignment of such arrays is possible as a whole-array operation. Thus, in the procedure *addAnyMatrices* of Example 13–13, we could specify, if needed:

$x := y;$

> The use of conformant array parameters requires significant care and should be considered only when a subprogram needs to manipulate similar arrays of different sizes during a single program execution. The details of the implementation are to be studied carefully.

14
STRINGS

Character strings are represented in Pascal as packed one-dimensional arrays of characters, with integer subscripts starting at 1. Thus, a Pascal string is of fixed length. While in general they are manipulated like other one-dimensional arrays, special consideration is afforded them, particularly in whole-string output and comparison operations.

A. STRING VARIABLES AND CONSTANTS

In Pascal, character strings must be represented as packed one-dimensional arrays of *char*-type components. That is, by definition in this programming language the following is the general form of a string-type specification:

packed array [1 . . integer constant] **of** *char*

where the integer constant specifies the number of characters (components) in the string of this type.

String variables are named entities of this type. For example,

var
    profession: **packed array** [*1 . . 12*] **of** *char;*

The important consequence is that, while a string variable may assume different values of the *char* type, its length remains fixed as specified for its type. The index of the first string component is always 1.

Since a string is an array, everything said in Chapter 13 about that data type applies to strings. They also possess certain additional properties, discussed in this chapter.

▷   In UCSD Pascal, a predefined data type **string** of 80 characters is available; thus variables may be declared directly of **string** type, possibly with an override of the default length of 80, if desired. The actual length of a string value may then vary up to this limit. A complement of built-in string-manipulation procedures and functions is also provided. ◁

Character strings enclosed in apostrophes (single quotes), introduced in Chapter 2–E, are considered constants of the string type of the same length.

EXAMPLE 14–1

Given this string declaration:

var
    name: **packed array** [*1 . . 4*] **of** *char;*

this constant:

'John'

is of type *name* (since its length is 4), but these constant character strings are not:

'Joe'
'Jimmy'

B. STRING OPERATIONS

The discussion of one-dimensional arrays offered in Chapter 13 applies to strings as well. The following review of operations includes certain special considerations valid for strings.

1. ASSIGNMENT

A string value, that is, the value of a string variable or constant, may be assigned to a string variable with the same declared number of components (but not necessarily of the same type).

EXAMPLE 14–2

Given these definitions and declarations:

const
    capital = *'Washington';*
type
    locality = **packed array** [*1 . . 10*] **of** *char;*
    politician = **packed array** [*1 . . 10*] **of** *char;*
var
    city, town: locality;
    president: politician;

these assignment statements are valid:

city := town;
city := capital;
town := 'Washington';
president := town;

Since the strings on the two sides of the assignment operator have to be of the same length, it is sometimes necessary to pad (complete) a string with blanks in order to perform the assignment. Usually, such a string is left-justified (that is, the actual value begins on the left side of the string), with the needed blanks added on the right.

EXAMPLE 14–3
Given the conditions of Example 14–2, this is a valid assignment:

city := 'Chicago___';

                      3 blanks

The following assignment would have been incorrect:

city := 'Chicago';

since the two sides are of different types.

2. INPUT

The value of a string variable has to be read in character-by-character with the *read* procedure, as any array would be, for example:

for *i := 1* **to** *10* **do**
   read (city[i]);

3. OUTPUT

Strings are given special consideration among Pascal arrays, in that a string may be written out in its entirety with a single *write* or *writeln* statement. For example,

        writeln ('The city is ', city, '.');

will write out the values of the string constant and variable:

        The city is Washington.

4. COMPARISON

The essential operations on strings are placing them in a desired order (sorting) and searching for a certain string or part of a string. The basic tool for these operations is the comparison of two strings with the use of relational operators.

Two string operands of the same length may be compared using the six relational operators introduced in Chapter 4–A–2:

$$=, <>, <=, <, >=, >$$

Thus, we may have:

if *city* $<>$ *'Washington'* **then**
   . . .

or

while *city* $>$ *town* **do**
   ⋮

The relative order of any two strings is called *lexicographical ordering;* it is the extension of the notion of alphabetical ordering to a broader domain, including all printing characters of the computer character set. The relative order of a pair of strings is the order of the first pair of characters, going from left to right, in which the two strings differ.

As discussed in Chapter 4–B, the character ordering (called the collating sequence) of the two major character sets, ASCII and EBCDIC, shown in Appendix C, differs in certain respects. However, in any Pascal implementation, the following relations are true:

'ABCD' $<$ 'BBCD'
'abcd' $<$ 'bbcd'
'ABCD' $<$ 'ABXD'
'1999' $<$ '9999'

The following are the lexicographical orderings of identical strings in the two predominant character sets (compare with Appendix C):

ASCII: '$100' $<$ '1000' $<$ 'AXLE' $<$ 'acid'
EBCDIC: '$100' $<$ 'acid' $<$ 'AXLE' $<$ '1000'

Since a single character set is employed by a given Pascal processor, sorting will be consistent if the data are represented in a consistent manner.

To maintain a sorted collection of character strings in a consistent order, it is necessary to use the same capitalization scheme for all its strings.

EXAMPLE 14-4

An ordered collection of character strings may be conveniently held in a table, that is, a two-dimensional array whose rows are strings.

Such a table of strings may be specified as follows:

```
type
    string = packed array [1 . . 10] of char;
    table = array [1 . . 50] of string;
var
    glossary: table;
```

These are examples of how such a table may be manipulated:

(1) writeln (glossary[7]); {write out the seventh entry in the glossary}
(2) glossary[7, 10] := ' '; {the tenth character of the seventh entry
                                          changed to a blank}
(3) {write out the capitalized entries beginning with 'A'}

```
        for i := 1 to 50 do
            if glossary[i, 1] = 'A' then
                writeln (glossary[i]);
```

The following program illustrates text processing.

EXAMPLE 14-5

Problem

Edit names for storage and sorting. Thus, convert a name from these input formats:

	first name	middle name	last name

or

	first initial.	middle initial.	last name

or

	first name	middle initial.	last name

to this output format:

last name, first initial. middle initial.

For example, "John Jay Adams" will be transformed to "Adams, J.J."

Analysis

The input string:

- may include any number of leading or separator blanks between the names;
- is terminated by the end-of-line marker.

The program may be converted to a procedure and included in a more extensive program reading in a series of names as part of a larger application.

Design

```
program editName;
    begin
        readString; {procedure to read in the name in input format}
        for first and second initial do
            begin
                get nextNonBlank as the initial; {function nextNonBlank
                                needed}
                move to nextBlank past the rest of the name; {function
                                nextBlank needed}
            end;
        move to nextNonBlank;
        copy the last name with comma into output;
        write out the two initials with periods
    end.
```

Implementation

```
program editName (input, output);
        {full name is edited into a sorting format, with initials only;
         full name consists of two first names and the last name,
         separated by arbitrary number of blanks}

const
    maxLength = 30;   {of the full name}
    blank = ' ';
type
    string = packed array [1 .. maxLength] of char;
    whichInitial = (firstInitial, secondInitial);
var
    name: string;
    lengthOfName,          {actual length of full name}
    cursor: integer;       {current position in the scan of full name}
    index: whichInitial;   {the initial being processed}
    initial: array [whichInitial] of char;
```

```
procedure readString (maximum: integer;        {allowed length}
                      var theString: string;
                      var length: integer);    {actual length}
         {read in a string of length limited by maximum and
          terminated by end-of-line, and determine the
          actual length of this string}
   begin {readString}
      length := 0;
      while not eoln and (length < maximum) do
         begin
            length := length + 1;
            read (theString[length])
         end;
   end; {readString}

function nextNonBlank (position: integer): integer;
         {returns the position of the non-blank character
          closest to the current position in the name}
   begin {nextNonBlank}
      while name[position] = blank do
         position := position + 1;
      nextNonBlank := position;
   end; {nextNonBlank}

function nextBlank (position: integer): integer;
         {returns the position of the closest blank character
          following the current position in the name}
   begin {nextBlank}
      position := position + 1;
      while name[position] <> blank do
         position := position + 1;
      nextBlank := position
   end; {nextBlank}


begin {editName}
   readString (maxLength, name, lengthOfName);
   writeln ('The full name is: ', name); writeln;
             {obtain the initials}
   cursor := 1;
   for index := firstInitial to secondInitial do
      begin
         cursor := nextNonBlank (cursor);      {move to next non-blank}
         initial[index] := name[cursor];
         cursor := nextBlank (cursor)          {move to next blank}
      end;
             {present the last name}
   write ('The edited name is: ');
   for cursor := nextNonBlank (cursor) to lengthOfName do
      write (name[cursor]);
             {present the initials}
   write (', ');
   for index := firstInitial to secondInitial do
      write (initial[index], '.')
end. {editName}
```

Two output printouts, with alternative forms of input:

(1)

```
The full name is:    Johann    Sebastian    Bach

The edited name is: Bach, J.S.
```

(2)

    The full name is: J.   S.   Bach

    The edited name is: Bach, J.S.

15
RECORDS

A record structure is used to represent relevant data concerning a certain object or event. These data may be of different types, and are stored in the individual components of a record, called fields. Fields have their own names and may themselves be of a structured type, in particular, arrays (often strings) or lower-level records. An array of records serves to represent tables containing components of differing types. A hierarchy of nested records may represent a complex interdependence of the object attributes.

A record type is specified in a **type** definition or, less frequently, directly in the declaration of a variable of this type.

In general, individual fields rather than complete records are subject to manipulation. To specify (select) a field, its identifier has to be qualified with the use of "dot notation" by the identifier of the record variable to which the field belongs. To simplify references to multiple fields of the same record variable, the **with** statement may be employed.

As a complete entity, a record may be assigned to another one of the identical type, or passed as an actual parameter.

If memory space has to be economized, a record may be specified as **packed.**

When records concerning similar objects have to differ in a certain aspect depending on the object being described, variant records may be used. The variant part of such a record type specifies the alternatives of its structure, corresponding to different classes of objects.

A. WHAT A RECORD IS

When the need arises to store and manipulate assorted data about a certain object or event (say, a car model or an airline flight), this information may be conveniently maintained as a record. Thus, a *record* contains data about an object or event, relevant to the given program.

EXAMPLE 15-1

(a) A child's birth record may consist of:

- last name;
- first name;
- middle name;
- date of birth;
- sex;
- names of parents;
- place of birth.

(b) A record of a calendar day may consist of:

- date;
- temperature;
- humidity;
- atmospheric pressure;
- list of activities.

The components of a record are called *fields;* each field has its own name and describes a certain aspect of the record's object. The relative position of fields within a record is not relevant to its processing; a field is identified by the record to which it belongs combined with its own name.

Let us compare records with arrays. An array is a collection of similar data items classified by their indices, while a record is a collection of various data about a single object. These distinctions follow:

- Arrays are homogeneous, that is, they consist of components of the same type. Records may be heterogeneous: each field has its own type, reflecting the nature of the data stored in it.
- Array components are identified by their indices, which classify them among other components; record fields have their individual names.

In many applications, a number of records describing a collection of objects of the same kind are maintained. They may be stored in main memory as arrays of records or, for larger volumes, in secondary storage as files of records (see Chapter 17). In such a collection of records, the value of one of the fields identifies the individual record since this field has a different value in every possible record of the collection; such a field is called a *key.* For example, Social Security number may be used as the key for a collection of personnel records.

B. DECLARATION OF RECORDS

As in the case of any variable of a structured type, in order to declare a record we have to specify its type either in a type definition or directly in the variable declaration.

The record type specification for a record with fixed structure has the following general form:

record
    identifier list: type denoter; ⎤
       ⋮   ⎬ optional ⎫ field list
    identifier list: type denoter ⎦   ⎭
end

The identifiers included in the lists are the names of the record fields, and are often called field identifiers. Thus, a record type specification consists of a field list enclosed in **record-end** brackets. Each field of a record is specified in the same way as a program variable. For example, the following record comprises six fields:

```
{sales record}
record
    month: 1 . . 12;
    day: 1 . . 31;
    year: 1970 . . 2100;
    price, tax, total: real
end;
```

Note the following:

1. The order of the listed fields is of no processing consequence.

> To make the program easier to understand, record fields should be specified in a logical order, reflecting their significance.

2. A type denoter for a field may specify any Pascal type. This may be one of the standard types, a type defined above the record type specification, or the type denoter itself may provide this specification. In particular, fields may be of a structured type themselves.

3. It is stylistically desirable to provide type definitions for record types. Such definitions are necessary, in particular, if a record of the given type is to be passed as an actual parameter to a subprogram.

4. The general form of record specification shown above does not include the so-called variant part, which provides for records of variable structure and is discussed in Section D.
5. All field identifiers listed in the specification of the given record type must be distinct. However, their scope[1] is limited to this record type. Hence, the same identifier may be used to name other program variables or fields of other records (including a record that is a field of the given one).

The following are some examples of record variable declarations:

EXAMPLE 15–2
(a)

```
type {ready for sorting}
    date = record
                year: 1900 . . 2100;
                month: 1 . . 12;
                day: 1 . . 31
            end;
var
    birthday, dateHired: date;
```

(b)
Assuming that the *date* type is defined as above, we may have:

```
type
    date = . . . ;      {as in 15–2a}
    string = packed array [1 . . 15] of char;
var
    birth: record
                lastName, firstName, middleName: string;
                birthDate: date;
                sex: (female, male);
                fathersName, mothersName: string;
                birthPlace: string
            end;
```

Note that six of the fields are arrays, and *birthDate* is a record in its own right.

---

1. Note that this adds to the scope rules discussed in Chapter 9–B.

(c)

```
type
    natural = 1 .. maxint;
    address = record
                  houseNumber: natural;
                  street, city: packed array [1 .. 12] of char;
                  state: packed array [1 .. 2] of char;
                  zipcode: natural
              end;
var
    businessAddress, homeAddress: address;
```

As can be seen from Example 15–2, record fields are often structured data items themselves, in particular, arrays (most often packed *char* arrays interpreted as strings) or other records. Some of these fields, or the entire record, may be declared **packed** in order to conserve memory space. A certain decline in execution time efficiency results, as discussed in Chapter 13–G; the meaning of the program is not altered, however.

Since a record may contain fields that are records themselves, several levels of structuring may be employed to describe a given object. A tree-like hierarchical data structure is then obtained (see Fig. 15–1).

EXAMPLE 15–3

Let us consider the employee record illustrated in Fig. 15–1.

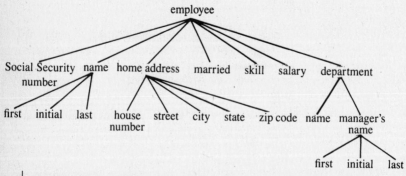

FIGURE 15–1. A hierarchical record.

This record type may be specified as follows:

type
    natural = 1 . . maxint;
    string = **packed array** *[1 . . 15]* **of** *char;*
    personName = **record**
                 first: string;
                 initial: char;
                 last: string
          end;
    address = . . . ;   *{as in Example 15–2c}*
    employee = **record**
                 SSnumber: **packed array** *[1 . . 9]* **of** *char;*
                 name: personName;
                 homeAddress: address;
                 married: Boolean;
                 skill: string;
                 salary: real;
                 department: **record**
                           name: (production, marketing,
                                   accounting);
                           manager: personName
                   end
       end;

Using the above type specification, we may have these variables:

var
    fullTime, partTime: employee;

Hierarchical structuring of record types makes it possible to group fields that describe related attributes of the object of the record into a lower-level record. This makes the program easier to understand and facilitates record processing, since such a structured field may be manipulated as a single entity. Namely, fields that are themselves records may be handled like other record-type variables with whole-record operations (see Section C–3 of this chapter).

The scope rules for field identifiers permit us to use the same identifier for the field of a record and, should the record contain fields which are records themselves, for a field of such a subrecord (see the use of the identifier *name* in Example 15–3). In the case of such nested record definitions, the rule of the smallest scope applies: the field identified belongs to the immediately enclosing record.

C. MANIPULATION OF RECORDS

Records are generally manipulated through the selection and manipulation of their fields. A special control statement, the **with** statement, is available to simplify such field processing. As is the case with the other structured types, only such whole-record operations as assignment and the passing of a record as a parameter are available (for records of identical type).

1. SELECTION AND MANIPULATION OF FIELDS

Generally, the data contained in a record is processed field by field. To select an individual field of a record, a *field designator* of the following general form is used:

record variable.field identifier

The meaning of a field designator is "the x field of the y record." For example, considering the definitions and declarations of Example 15–2c, we may have:

businessAddress.street

which refers to the "street of the business address."

Thus, the field identifier has to be qualified by the record variable to which it belongs. Note that the record variable rather than its type identifier is specified in the field designator (anyhow, several variables of the same type may be declared in the program).

> A field identifier may not appear unqualified in the program statements except under the control of **with** statements (see below).

A field designator (like an indexed variable specifying an array component) may appear anywhere in the program statements where a regular variable of the same type may appear. Records are manipulated by selecting their fields with a field designator and using them in Pascal statements.

EXAMPLE 15–4

Assuming that the program contains these definitions and declarations:

```
type
    course = record
                    name: packed array [1 . . 20] of char;
                    id: packed array [1 . . 5] of char;
                    credits: 0 . . 4;
                    grade: (A, B, C, D, F)
             end;
var
    required, elective: course;
```

we may have these mutually independent statements in our program:

```
elective.id := 'CS505';
required.name := elective.name;
if required.credits < 4 then
    required.credits := required.credits + 1;
read (required.name, required.id);
writeln (pass (required.grade)); {pass is a declared Boolean function}
```

If a record itself is a field of a larger one, the field designator has to specify with the "dot notation" all the records it is a component of, from the outermost in ("top-down"). The components of arrays which are fields are specified as indexed variables (see Chapter 13–C).

EXAMPLE 15–5
Assuming the definitions and declarations of Example 15–3, these are valid field designators:

- (a) *fullTime.salary*
  is treated as a real variable;
- (b) *fullTime.name*
  is a record of type *personName* and may, for example, participate in an assignment statement with another record of the same type (see Section C–3 of this chapter);
- (c) *fullTime.skill[13]*
  is the thirteenth component (character) of this field;
- (d) *partTime.name.first*
  is a one-dimensional packed array of *char*-type components (i.e., a string variable) of length 15;
- (e) *partTime.department.name*
  is treated as a variable of the specified enumerated type.

Records are frequently aggregated into arrays to provide information about a collection of objects. A one-dimensional array of records is more general as a data structure than a two-dimensional array with components of a simple type since records may contain data of different types (see the following example and Example 15–11 below).

EXAMPLE 15–6
A collection of employee-type records of Example 15–3 may be kept in the following array:

```
var
    personnel: array [1 . . 50] of employee;
```

An individual i-th record is then specified as *personnel[i]*. We may have the following program statements:

(a) assuming *key* is a variable of the same type as *SSnumber*,

```
if personnel[i].SSnumber = key then
    writeln ('The employee's salary is ', personnel[i].salary: 9: 2);
```

(b)

```
{ give 5% salary raise to the personnel of the marketing department}
for i := 1 to 50 do
    if personnel[i].department.name = marketing then
        personnel[i].salary := (round (personnel[i].salary * 105))
                                / 100;
```

Note that the salary has to be expressed in dollars and cents, hence its processing.

2. FIELD MANIPULATION USING WITH STATEMENT

Often the processing of various fields of a record is done in a limited program fragment. It is then possible to avoid the tedium of qualifying the field identifiers with the same record variable name by using the **with** statement.

As one of the Pascal control statements, the **with** statement specifies a record variable name so that the field identifiers of that variable may appear unqualified within the statement (simple or compound) controlled by the **with** statement. A **with** statement may also specify several record variable names.

The general form of the **with** statement is:

optional
with record variable, . . . , record variable **do**
    statement

Assuming for the moment a single record variable in the **with** statement, we may have, for example (taking the definitions and declarations of Example 15–3):

```
with fullTime do
    begin
        married := true;
        salary := 500.55;
        skill := 'electrician
    end;
```

Thus, since the record variable *fullTime* is specified in the **with** statement, within its enclosed compound statement the fields of that variable appear unqualified.

A **with** statement functions as a block (see Chapter 9) in which the field identifiers of the specified record variable(s) may be considered declared as regular variables.

EXAMPLE 15–7

Given these definitions and declarations:

```
type
    memo = record
                celebration: packed array [1 . . 15] of char;
                date: record
                            month: (June, July, August);
                            day: 1 . . 31
                        end;
                day: (Mon, Tue, Wed, Thu, Fri, Sat, Sun);
                hour: 1 . . 12;
                dayTime: (am, pm)
            end;
var
    birthday, anniversary: memo;
    date: integer;
```

we may have these statements, which assign values to all the record fields:

```
with birthday do
    begin
        celebration := 'garden party    ';
        date.month := July;
        date.day := 16;
        day := Tue;
        hour := 1;
        dayTime := pm
    end;
```

Note that due to the scope rules there is no ambiguity concerning the *day* field present in the outer and inner records.

A **with** statement specifying several record variables may be considered to open their scopes in a nested fashion. Thus:

```
with v₁, v₂, . . . , vₙ do
    statement
```

is equivalent to:

with v_1 **do**
  with v_2 **do**
     ⋮
    with v_n **do**
       statement

Hence, all the identifiers which are field names within the scope opened by the **with** statement are considered qualified by the listed record variables.

EXAMPLE 15–8

Considering the definition and declarations of Example 15–7, this statement:

with *birthday, date* **do**
  day := day + 2;

refers to the field:

$$birthday.date.day$$

and *not* to the field *birthday.day*. Had we wanted to refer to the latter field within the above **with** statement, we would need to write it out fully!

The scope determined by the **with** statement obeys the general rules of scope (see Chapter 9–B). Thus, if there are program variables whose identifiers coincide with field identifiers used free within a **with** statement, these program variables cannot be accessed there.

EXAMPLE 15–9

The program variable *date* (integer) declared in Example 15–7 cannot be accessed in this statement:

with *birthday* **do**
  ⋮

Only the field *birthday.date* (a record in its own right) may be accessed there.

The record variable to which a **with** statement refers is determined once the statement is entered and cannot be changed during execution of the statement controlled by it.

EXAMPLE 15-10

The following statements illustrate this fact:

```
i := 3;
with personnel[i] do      {see declaration of Example 15-6}
   begin
      ⋮
      {no assignment to the variable i made here can
      change the fact that the record variable is
      personnel[3]}
      ⋮
   end;
```

A **with** statement may list several record variables which are not nested within one another. Such usage, however, leads to confusion and is error-prone. It is preferable to use a **with** statement for accessing a single record in an abbreviated form.

In general, the use of **with** statements makes it possible to write more readable programs and in many cases contributes to the efficiency of program execution.

3. WHOLE-RECORD OPERATIONS

The following two operations on complete records are defined:

(a) Two records of the same type (that is, declared with the same or equivalent type identifiers, or in the same declaration) may appear on the two sides of an assignment statement. Thus, in Example 15-3 we may have:

fullTime := partTime;

Such an assignment is more terse and usually more efficient than multiple assignments of the respective field values. Of course, all the field values of the record variable on the right-hand side must have been defined.

(b) A record may be passed as an actual value or variable parameter to a subprogram specifying a formal parameter of identical type in the corresponding position. As usual, the type definition must include within its scope both the subprogram declaration and the activation(s).

This program illustrates the manipulation of records.

EXAMPLE 15–11

The records of our subscriptions are maintained as the table shown in Fig. 15–2, which can conveniently be implemented as an array of records.

Magazines (journals)

Name	Year	Expiration Month	Day	Price	Renewal
New Yorker	1990	2	3	56.90	true
American Scientist	2000	3	7	67.00	false
JACM	1995	11	30	32.50	true
⋮	⋮	⋮	⋮	⋮	⋮

FIGURE 15–2. An array of records.

It is typical that a relatively large data structure such as *magazines* is declared as global to several procedures (and functions) which collectively manage (access and update) it. We assume that here.

Our objective is to design typical procedures for management of a table of records (such as that of Fig. 15–2) for their subsequent incorporation into one or more programs.

The following procedures are designed to manage *magazines*.

(1) Procedure *searchForRecord* accesses and prints out the record of the subscription with the given *title* (name).

Since the records are not sorted (i.e., they are not ordered on any key), there is no alternative to *sequential search*. During sequential search, we compare the key *(title)* of the record sought with the consecutive records in the *magazines* table, starting with the first one. The search terminates with success when the record is found (and, in our case, displayed), or with failure if the end of the table is reached without the record having been found.

This is the pseudocode of the sequential search procedure:

```
procedure searchForRecord (key); {key specifies the record sought}
    begin
        while there are more records in the table and
                the record not found yet do
            begin
                if the key of the current record equals the sought key then
                    begin
                        writeRecord;        {procedure to display
                                             record needed}
                        indicate record found
                    end
                else
                    move to the next record
            end;
        if record not found then
            display message indicating that the record is not in the
                    table
    end;
```

Sequential search is inherently slow: a successful search requires on the average n/2 comparisons in a table holding n records. If a table has been sorted on the key to be used in the search, the much faster binary search may be employed (see Example 15–12 below).

(2) Procedure *readTable* reads in the table of magazine subscriptions.

(3) Procedure *displayTable* displays the table of subscriptions.

In order to test the three table-management procedures, a driver program was written implementing this pseudocode:

```
program lookForJournal;
    begin
        readTable;
        displayTable;
        enter name of journal sought;
        searchForRecord (of the journal)
    end.
```

In the complete program below, note in particular the definitions and declarations of the array of records presented in Fig. 15–2.

```
program lookForJournal (input, output);
        {drive sequential search for specified magazine or journal}

const
   total = 5;              {number of journals}
   nameLength = 25;   {maximum length of journal name}
type
   string = packed array [1 .. nameLength] of char;
   subscription = record
                        name: string;
                        expiration: record
                                         year: 1990 .. 2100;
                                         month: 1 .. 12;
                                         day: 1 .. 31
                                     end;
                        price: real;
                        renewal: Boolean    {decision to renew}
                   end;
   table = array [1 .. total] of subscription;
var
   magazines: table;
   keyName: string;
   i: integer;

procedure readTable;
        {read in the table of magazine subscriptions}
   var
      decision, i, j: integer;
   begin {readTable}
      for i := 1 to total do
          with magazines[i], expiration do
             begin
                for j := 1 to nameLength do
                    read (name[j]);
                readln (year, month, day, price, decision);
                if decision = 0 then
                    renewal := false
                else
                    renewal := true
             end
   end; {readTable}

procedure displayTable;
        {display the table of magazine subscriptions}
   var
      i: integer;
   begin {displayTable}
      writeln ('Expiration': 41);
      writeln ('   Name', ' ': 20, 'Year  Month  Day  Price  Renewal');
      for i := 1 to total do
          with magazines[i], expiration do
             begin
                write (name: 25, year: 6, month: 6, day: 7, price: 9: 2);
                if renewal then
                    writeln ('      yes')
                else
                    writeln ('       no')
             end
   end; {displayTable}
```

```
procedure searchForRecord (title: string);
         {retrieve a record using sequential search;
          title is the key of the record sought}
   var
      count: integer;     {count of records reviewed so far}
      found: Boolean;          {was the record found?}

   procedure writeRecord (index: integer);
            {display the record identified by the index}
      begin {writeRecord}
         with magazines[index], expiration do
            begin
               writeln ('Subscription expires on ', month: 1, '/',
                        day: 1, '/', year: 1);
               write ('Subscription price is $', price: 3: 2);
               if renewal then
                  writeln('; decided to renew.')
               else
                  writeln('; decided not to renew.')
            end
      end; {writeRecord}

   begin {searchForRecord}
      count := 1;
      found := false;
      writeln;
      writeln (title);
      while (count <= total) and (not found) do
         if magazines[count].name = title then
            begin
               writeRecord (count);
               found := true
            end
         else
            count := count + 1;
      if count > total then
         writeln ('No subscription record exists for this journal.')
   end; {searchForRecord}

begin {lookForJournal}
   readTable;
   displayTable;
   for i := 1 to nameLength do
      read (keyName[i]);
   readln;
   searchForRecord (keyName)
end. {lookForJournal}
```

This is the table presented by *displayTable:*

| | | Expiration | | | |
Name	Year	Month	Day	Price	Renewal
New Yorker	1990	2	3	56.90	yes
American Scientist	2000	3	7	67.00	no
JACM	1995	11	30	32.50	yes
Computer	1993	3	15	25.00	no
Vanity Fair	1991	10	1	27.50	yes

This is the result of a successful look-up:

```
Computer
Subscription expires on 3/15/1993
Subscription price is $25.00; decided not to renew.
```

The following record was not found:

```
Cricket
No subscription record exists for this journal.
```

The following example shows a much faster searching method, applicable to a sorted collection of records.

EXAMPLE 15–12

Problem

We have a table of records, sorted in ascending order on a field called *key*. We need to find a record with a specified *key* value.

Solution via Binary Search

The *binary search* algorithm, applicable to a sorted table of records, resembles a procedure we could use to look up a word in an unfamiliar dictionary. First, we check the middle of the table of records: if our look-up key is smaller than that in the middle of the table, the search will continue in the first half of the table; if our key is larger than the middle one, the search will be confined to the second half of the table. We then search the selected half in the same way, by checking its middle record, and so on. The search is completed with success when the record with the desired key is found, or with failure if no such record is found and no further halving of the table segment is possible.

Binary search requires, on the average, about $\log_2 n$ comparisons to find a record in a table of n records.

Binary Search Algorithm

The following presentation illustrates the incorporation of parameters into a pseudocode specification. Note that the **out**-parameters will be coded as variable parameters in Pascal. In the present case, a detailed pseudocode is required; it is very close to the statement part of the Pascal procedure included below.

```
procedure binarySearch (in: list, {to be searched}
                            length, {of the list}
                            key; {of the record sought}
                       out: index, {position of the found record}
                            found); {was the record found?}
   begin
      low := 1; {index of first item in sublist to be searched}
      high := length; {index of last item in sublist to be searched}
      found := false;
      while low ≤ high and record not found yet do
         begin
            determine middle of the sublist;
            if key = key of the list entry in the middle then
               begin
                  index := middle;
                  found := true
               end
            else if key < key of the list entry in the middle then
               high := middle − 1 {look in the lower sublist}
            else
               low := middle + 1 {look in the upper sublist}
         end
      end;
```

The use of the procedure is illustrated on the following table of integers,
with *length* of 9 and *key* of 300:

Before First Comparison	Before Second Comparison	Before Third Comparison
5 low	5	5
21	21	21
73	73	73
124	124	124
middle → 241	241	241
300	300	→ 300
450	→ 450	450
701	701	701
715 high	715	715

low = 1	low = 6	low = 6
high = 9	high = 9	high = 6
middle = $\lfloor \frac{1 + 9}{2} \rfloor = 5$	middle = $\lfloor \frac{6 + 9}{2} \rfloor = 7$	middle = $\lfloor \frac{6 + 6}{2} \rfloor = 6$
↑ integer part of		

Application

The following program drives the procedure *binarySearch:* we have to find the name of a product with the given unique integer code, which serves as the key. To test the routine, several product names (some of nonexistent records) will be sought.

```
program findName (input, output);
      {find the name of a product (testing binary search routine)}

const
   limit = 5;        {number of records}
   nameLength = 10;  {the length of product name}
type
   product = record
               keyField: integer;   {product code}
               name: packed array [1 .. nameLength] of char
            end;
   table = array [1 .. limit] of product;
var
   productTable: table;
   codeWanted,                        {code of the record sought}
   position,                          {of this record in the table}
   i, j: integer;
   isThere: Boolean;                  {is the product in the table?}

procedure binarySearch (list: table;    {the list to be searched}
                        length,          {of the list}
                        key: integer;    {of the record sought}
                        var index: integer;   {of the record found}
                        var found: Boolean);  {true if the record found}
        {identifies the index of a record with the given key in
         a sorted table of records}
   var
      low,   {index of the first item in the sublist currently searched}
      high,  {index of the last item in the sublist currently searched}
      middle: integer; {midpoint of the sublist currently searched}
   begin {binarySearch}
      low := 1;
      high := length;
      found := false;
      while (low <= high) and not found do
         begin
            middle := (low + high) div 2;
            if key = list[middle].keyField then
               begin
                  index := middle;
                  found := true      {record found}
               end
               {select lower or upper sublist for further search}
            else if key < list[middle].keyField then
               high := middle - 1    {look in the lower sublist}
            else
               low := middle + 1     {look in the upper sublist}
         end
   end; {binarySearch}
```

```
begin {findName}
                {read in and echo the table}
    for i := 1 to limit do
        with productTable[i] do
            begin
                read (keyField);
                for j := 1 to nameLength do
                    read (name[j]);
                readln;
                writeln (keyField, ' ', name);
            end;
                    {test the binary search routine with several product
                     codes; terminate with negative code}
    readln (codeWanted);
    while codeWanted > 0 do
        begin
            binarySearch (productTable, limit, codeWanted, position, isThere);
            if isThere then
                writeln ('The name of the product with code ',
                        codeWanted: 1, ' is ', productTable[position].name)
            else
                writeln ('The product with code ', codeWanted: 1,
                        ' is not in the table.');
            readln (codeWanted)
        end
end. {findName}
```

This is the echoed table of products:

```
   10    GADGET
   77    WIDGET
   82    KLUDGE
  121    GIZMO
10011    PLOUGH
```

Here are the results of several look-ups:

```
The name of the product with code 77 is WIDGET
The product with code 91 is not in the table.
The name of the product with code 121 is GIZMO
The name of the product with code 10011 is PLOUGH
```

D. VARIANT RECORDS[2]

In some applications the records describing various objects or events of a certain class must contain somewhat different data. The nature of the data contained in a record depends on the object described by it. In other words, records of the same kind differ with respect to the presence and/ or type of certain fields. For example, the nature of the data in a personnel record may partially differ depending on whether the employee is active or retired.

2. May be omitted on first reading.

To provide this flexibility in the record type definition, Pascal makes it possible to include along with its fixed part, discussed in Section B, a variant part. (A record type may also consist entirely of a variant part.) The *variant part* of a record specifies an assortment of *variants:* alternative field lists. The variant actually stored in a given record depends on the value of its so-called tag field,[3] which allows the programmer to distinguish between records of alternative structure.

Records containing a variant part (only one variant part may be contained in a record type) are often called *variant records.*

The variant part of a record must follow its fixed part (if any). The general form of the variant part with a tag field is:

case tag field: type identifier **of**
    case constant list: (field list); ⎫
        ⋮   ⎬ optional
    case constant list: (field list) ⎭ ← a variant

Hence, the variant part of a record consists of several variants. Each variant specifies fields in the same general form as the fields of the fixed part of the record are specified (see the field list in the record specification of Section B). However, each field list of the variant part is enclosed in parentheses.

The identifier and the type identifier of the tag field are specified by the **case** line. The value of the tag field acts as a variant selector: the variant actually stored in the given record is determined by this value. Every possible value of the tag field is listed in one and only one case constant list. The given record contains the variant corresponding to the value of its tag field.

Assuming this type definition:

type
    status = (active, retired, disabled);

this is an example of a variant part of a record (the fixed part is not shown):

case *activity: status* **of**
    active: (*department: 1 . . 12;*
             position: **packed array** *[1 . . 15]* **of** *char;*
             salary: real);
    retired, disabled: (pension: real)

---

3. We will see below that tag fields are actually optional (but recommended).

Note carefully the following:

(1) The single variant part of a record is always placed immediately before the record's closing **end** bracket; this is the reason the variant part does not have its own **end.**

(2) The tag field is one of the fields actually contained in the record; in addition, it serves to determine the variant included in it. Thus, we have the field *activity.*

(3) The tag field must be of an ordinal type; since the **case** structure must specify the type identifier of this field, the type of the tag field must be previously defined.

(4) A case constant may appear in one case constant list only.

(5) A variant has to be specified for every possible value of the tag field. If no fields are to be contained in the variant part of the record for a certain value of the tag field, an empty field list is specified.

For example, if our type definition above were:

type
    status = (active, retired, disabled, onLeave);

then our variant part could include this variant:

onLeave: ( )

(6) No processing importance is attached to the order of the variants.

(7) While the general form of the variant part resembles the **case** statement of Pascal (discussed in Chapter 7–A), the meaning of the two is of course entirely different. The **case** statement is, however, a fine tool for processing records with a variant part, as can be seen below.

(8) The field identifiers in each variant must be unique throughout the record. This makes it possible to use them without qualifying them with the value of the tag field. Therefore, they are selected in the same way as the fields of the fixed part of the record. The example below presents a complete variant record.

EXAMPLE 15–13
We will define a record type to represent references for a term paper. Since a reference may be to a book, a journal publication, or a paper in a collected work, the structure of records will partially differ.

```
const
    limit = 100;
type
    natural = 1 . . maxint;
    shortString = packed array [1 . . 15] of char;
    longString = packed array [1 . . 25] of char;
    kind = (book, journal, collection);
    reference = record
                    firstAuthor: shortString;
                    title: longString;
                    year: 1455 . . 2200;
                    case work: kind of
                        book:       (edition: 1 . . 10;
                                     publisher, city: shortString);
                        journal:    (issue, volume, startPage,
                                                endPage: natural);
                        collection: (editionNo: 1 . . 10;
                                     collectionTitle: longString;
                                     editor: shortString;
                                     publishedBy, cityOf:
                                                shortString;
                                     beginPage, lastPage: natural)
                end;
var
    bibliography: array [1 . . limit] of reference;
```

Note that we had to introduce different identifiers for fields with the same meaning in different variants; for example: *edition* and *editionNo* in the first and third variants, respectively.

Thus, assuming that the current value of the tag field *work* is *collection*, this is a correct program statement:

$$writeln\ (bibliography[i].editionNo);$$

(9) As we said, a record may contain only a single variant part. However, any variant may in turn contain a fixed part followed by a variant part, in the same fashion as the entire record. Such nesting of variants may lead to a great variety of record structures (and ought to be employed with great care).

EXAMPLE 15–14

If in the *reference* record type defined in Example 15–13 we wanted to include the listing of the last names of authors other than the first one in the case of books only, that variant would be modified as follows:

```
book: (edition: 1 . . 10;
      publisher, city: shortString;
      case names: authors of
          multiple: (otherNames: longString);
          single:  ( )); {semicolon is necessary!}
journal: . . .
```

provided that the type definition

authors = (multiple, single);

is included among the definitions of Example 15–13, before that of *refer-ence.*

It is crucial to realize that by the very nature of variant records, the number and type of their fields changes during the execution of statements going through a collection of such records. Until a value is assigned to a tag field, no variant fields can be accessed, since it is not clear which variant is the current one. When a value associated with a different variant is assigned to the tag field, a change of variant occurs.

It is an error to attempt to access a field of a variant different than the current one. However, in most implementations this error will not be detected by the Pascal system and subtle execution errors will result.

> It is thus a good programming practice to test the tag field value before accessing a variant part. In particular, the **case** statement with the tag field acting as the case index is a handy tool for this task.

EXAMPLE 15–15

The following procedure serves to write out a reference as defined in Example 15–13. The procedure will be activated by this statement:

writeReference (bibliography[i]);

DATA STRUCTURES IN PROGRAMMING   253

Here is the procedure:

```
procedure writeReference (item: reference);
    {a bibliographical reference is written out}
    begin {writeReference}
        with item do
            begin
                writeln (firstAuthor, ', ', title, ',');
                case work of
                    book:        begin
                                     if edition > 1 then
                                         write (edition: 1, ' edition, ');
                                     writeln (publisher, ', ', city, ', ',
                                                 year: 1)
                                 end;
                    journal:     writeln (volume: 1, '(', issue: 1, '), ', year:
                                             1, ', pp. ', startPage: 1,
                                             '-', endPage: 1);
                    collection:  begin
                                     writeln (' in ', collectionTitle, ', ed. ',
                                         editor);
                                     if editionNo > 1 then
                                         write (editionNo: 1, ' edition, ');
                                     writeln (publishedBy, ', ', cityOf, ', ',
                                         year: 1, ', pp. ', beginPage: 1, '-',
                                         lastPage: 1)
                                 end
            end
        end
    end; {writeReference}
```

Note that, naturally, record fields may be accessed in any order.

Variant records are also employed in the more elaborate Example 17–6, illustrating processing of files of records.

Actually, the inclusion of the tag field in a variant record and thus in the **case** construct is optional. The type identifier of the tag field, however, always needs to be stated in the **case** construct. If no tag field is necessary and it is not included, a certain amount of space is saved in record storage. The value of the case constants for the variant selection is then supplied from elsewhere in the program or is implicit in the program context.

For a record without a tag field, a change of variant is implied by an assignment to a field within a new variant. Hence, the correctness of a reference to a variant field is more difficult to ascertain.

> It is good programming practice to include, whenever possible, the tag field in variant records in order to prevent erroneous reference to a field which does not exist in the current variant.

16

SETS

Sets have been adapted as a Pascal structured type from the set theory of mathematics. A Pascal set contains a limited collection of unordered distinct values belonging to the so-called base type of the set. Only ordinal values may be elements of a Pascal set.

A set type is defined by specifying its base type (the number of values in the base type is limited by the implementation). A variable of a set type may assume any, all, or none of the values of the base type at any time during program execution.

A set value is specified with the use of a set constructor. Such values, along with set variables, appear in set expressions, which may include the operators denoting set union, difference, and intersection. Five relational operators are also defined on set values, including the operator **in,** which tests for the presence of an element in a set.

General manipulation of sets is accomplished via assignment statements. Input and output of set values is performed element by element, as appropriate for the values of the base type.

A. SETS IN PASCAL

In certain programming situations, it is convenient to have a variable which may contain simultaneously several distinct values, without any meaning being attached to their order. The number of values held by such a variable may change within prescribed limits during program execution. Such a collection of distinct elements (values here) into a whole is called a *set*.

EXAMPLE 16–1
These are some examples of sets that may occur in programming:

(a) the computer science courses being taken by a student;
(b) different coin denominations on hand;
(c) distinct letters in a line of text.

Set theory is a branch of mathematics; Pascal sets have been adapted from it as a structured data type by introducing certain limitations for the sake of greater efficiency of the language implementation and program execution.

Specifically, a Pascal set may draw its values from a limited universe: the so-called *base type* of the set. A base type must be ordinal, so no real, structured, or pointer-type[1] set elements are allowed. Moreover, the number of values in a base type is limited in every implementation. Hence, the number of values in a set variable is also limited.

In certain applications, sets provide a more natural form of programming than equivalent arrays which could be used to simulate them. Operations for set manipulation are also offered by Pascal.

EXAMPLE 16–2
Having the sets of computer science courses currently being taken by every student (this entire data structure can be represented as an array of sets), we may determine, for example:

- the enrollment in all the courses;
- the most frequent pairings of courses taken by the students;
- the best time schedule for the courses.

Like any Pascal structured data type, sets may be designated **packed.**

B. DECLARATION OF SETS AND PROPERTIES OF PASCAL SETS

In order to declare a set, we need to specify its type either in a type definition (usually preferable stylistically) or directly in the variable declaration.

A set type specification has the following general form:

set of base type

where base type is an ordinal type.

This specification means that a variable of the given set type may contain all, some, or none of the distinct values of the specified base type (but no other

---

1. Discussed in Chapter 18.

values!). The number of values in the variable may change during program execution.

The value of a set-type variable is enclosed in Pascal in square brackets.[2]

EXAMPLE 16–3

Let us consider these type definitions and variable declarations:

type
> *CScourses = (CS201, CS205, CS217, CS243, CS273);*
> *coursesTaken = set of CScourses;*

var
> *myCourses, yourCourses: coursesTaken;*

Here, the set type *coursesTaken* is defined on the enumerated type *CScourses*. Hence, the variables of this set type, *myCourses* and *your-Courses*, may assume any of these values, for example:

[*CS205, CS243*]
[*CS273, CS205, CS243*]
[*CS243, CS201, CS205, CS217, CS273*]

The order of elements is irrelevant; thus, these are identical sets:

$$[CS201, \; CS205]$$

and

$$[CS205, \; CS201]$$

Using the terminology of set theory, we may say that the value of a set variable may be any of the subsets of its base type.[3] The *empty set* [ ], containing no elements (and analogous to 0 in arithmetic) is included in every Pascal set.

EXAMPLE 16–4

Given these definitions and declarations:

type
> *someScales = (do, re, mi);*
> *scales = set of someScales;*

var
> *played: scales;*

the variable *played* may assume any of these 8 values:

---

2. Curly braces, the customary enclosure for sets in mathematics, are used in Pascal for comments.

3. Thus, if the base type contains n distinct values (we remember that the number of distinct values in a data type is called its cardinality), the cardinality of a set type defined on it is 2^n. In set theory, this collection of all subsets of a set is called its powerset.

[ ], [*do*], [*re*], [*mi*], [*do, re*], [*re, mi*], [*do, mi*], [*do, re, mi*].

As we said, the order of elements in multielement sets is immaterial, and the number of elements in a variable's value may vary during program execution.

Let us summarize the properties of Pascal sets.
Like any set in mathematics, a Pascal set has these characteristics:

(a) It must contain only distinct elements.
(b) No significance is attached to the order of elements (in other words, the only relationship between the set elements is that of belonging to the set).

In addition the following things are true for a Pascal set:

(c) Its elements must be drawn from a defined universe, called the base type, and hence all are of the same ordinal type.
(d) The number of elements that may be contained in a Pascal set is limited by the implementation. Typically, a base type (and hence sets of the type defined on it) may contain no more than 60 to 1024 elements, although in certain implementations set membership is limited even further. Likewise, implementations specify the smallest and largest ordinal values of a set's elements, for example, 0 to 255 for a certain implementation allowing up to 256 set elements.

Therefore, a Pascal set of integers has to be defined on an integer subrange rather than the integer base type. Certain implementations with severe set membership limitations make even this definition prohibited:

set of *char* {check whether this is possible in your Pascal!}

In these cases, subranges of characters that are consecutive in the given character set must be employed as base types.

EXAMPLE 16–5
These are more examples of set type definitions and variable declarations:

(a)

    type
        coin = *(penny, nickel, dime, quarter, halfdollar, dollar);*
        coinKind = **set of** *coin;*
    var
        purseChange, pocketChange: coinKind;

(b)

    var
        characters: **set of** *'a' . . 'z';*

(c)

    type
        scoreValues = 0 . . 12;
        scores = set of scoreValues;
    var *{students have different numbers of scores}*
        studentScores: **array** *[1 . . 25]* **of** *scores;*

In some programming situations, arrays are built of sets (as in Example 16–5c) or records contain fields which are sets.

C. CONSTRUCTION OF SET VALUES

Once declared, a variable of a given set type may asume any value consisting of distinct elements of its base type. Such a set value is specified as a *set constructor*, with the following general form:

[element designator, . . . , element designator]

        optional

where an element designator may:

- specify a single set element through an expression of the base type; or
- specify a range of set elements with the subrange notation (through and including):

$$\text{expression-1 . . expression-2,}$$

where both expressions are of the base type. For example, 3 . . 5 specifies the following set elements: 3, 4, 5.

EXAMPLE 16–6
Given the definitions and declarations of Example 16–5, these are valid set constructors:

[dime, quarter] as a value of *pocketChange;*
['a' . . 'c', 'f', 'x' . . 'z'] as a value of *characters;*
[10, 3, 5 . . 8] as a value of *studentScores[15];*
[ ] as a value of any of the variables;
[pred (dollar)] as a value of *purseChange.*

Note that square brackets do not surround a set-type variable, but must always be included around a set value.

Assuming that *original* and *final* are variables of the type *scoreValues* and the values of the expressions are within the allowed subrange, we may have:

$$[(final - original) \bmod 5 . . 10, final + 2]$$

as the value of, say,

$$studentScores[17].$$

Note that set constructors are often one of the alternative ways a set may be specified.

EXAMPLE 16-7

Assuming that the value of a *char*-type variable *initial* is "x," the value of the one-element set *characters* containing it may be specified as any of these:

characters
[*initial*]
['x']

Set constructors are most frequently employed to initialize set variables or to update their values, as discussed in detail in Section E.

The following hold for set constructors:

(a) It is an error if the value of a set element is specified outside the limits defined for the given Pascal implementation.

(b) Since set elements are always distinct, in the case that a set element is specified more than once in a set constructor, only one element of this value is included.

(c) An element designator

$$x . . y \qquad where \qquad x > y$$

specifies no elements.

D. SET OPERATIONS

For the manipulation of set values, Pascal provides:

- five relational operators, serving to test membership in a set and to compare the membership of two sets;

- three operations for set arithmetic, which combine two operand sets to produce a resulting set.

1. RELATIONAL OPERATORS

A relational operator joins two operands to assert a certain relation between them; the value of a relation is thus Boolean: *true* or *false,* as discussed in Chapter 4–A–2.

Five relational operators are defined for sets. Four of these join two sets of the same type[4] (and both are either packed or not). These operators act as follows:

$x = y$ tests the equality of sets x and y;
$x <> y$ tests the inequality of sets x and y;
$x <= y$ tests whether the set x is included in the set y;
$x >= y$ tests whether the set y is included in the set x.

A set s is **included in** another set t if every element of s is also an element of t (but t may contain other elements as well).

The fifth relational operator, **in,** tests the presence of a given set element in a set. Thus,

$$a \text{ in } x$$

tests whether the element (not a set!) a is present in the set x. The element a must belong to the base type of the set x.

Note the following:

(1) The two operators for strict inclusion ($<$ and $>$) are not defined for Pascal sets, but can easily be programmed with Boolean expressions and other relational operators.
(2) All relational operators in Pascal (including **in**) have the same precedence, namely, the lowest in the operator hierarchy (see Chapter 4–A–2). Thus, in Boolean expressions parentheses are commonly used around the relations to enforce the desired order of evaluation.
(3) If the value of a in the relation

$$a \text{ in } x$$

is outside the limits specified for sets in the given implementation, the value of the relation is *false.*
(4) The empty set [ ] is included in every set.

---

4. Actually, the set types may be only compatible, that is, they may have the same base type, or the base types may be subranges of the same type, or one of the base types may be a subrange of the other.

EXAMPLE 16–8

(a) Note the values of the following relations between sets of the type *coinKind* of Example 16–5a:

> [*dime, quarter*] = [*quarter, dime*] gives the value *true;*
> [*dime*] < > [*quarter*] gives the value *true;*
> [*quarter, halfdollar, dollar*] < = [*dollar, halfdollar*] gives the
> value *false;*
> [*nickel, dime, quarter*] > = [*quarter, nickel*] gives the value *true;*
> *dime* **in** [*nickel, dime*] gives the value *true;*
> *quarter* **in** [*nickel, dime*] gives the value *false;*

(b) Provided that *contained* is a Boolean variable, we may have this program statement:

> *contained* := *dollar* **in** *purseChange;*

(c) Note that as opposed to the relations in arithmetic, both

> [*quarter, dime*] > = [*dime, nickel*]

and

> [*quarter, dime*] < = [*dime, nickel*]

give the value *false.*

The **in** operator serves in certain situations to simplify the form in which conditions are expressed, as illustrated in the following example.

EXAMPLE 16–9

(a) Assuming these definitions and declaration:

type
    fallWinter = *(September, October, November, December,
                    January, February);*
var
    month: fallWinter;

we may write:

if *month* **in** [*September, December . . February*] **then**
    ⋮

in preference to the less readable:

if *(month* = *September)* **or** *(month* = *December)* **or**
    (month = *January)* **or** *(month* = *February)* **then**
    ⋮

(b) Assuming that *i* is an integer variable, instead of writing:

if [*i*] < = [*1 . . 10, 15 . . 25*] **then**
⋮

it is preferable to use the more readable form:

if *i* **in** [*1 . . 10, 15 . . 25*] **then**
⋮

(c) This test checks for correct input from the terminal:

if not *(response* **in** [*'y', 'Y', 'n', 'N'*]) **then**
    writeln ('The response is incorrect. Please answer yes or no.'):

2. SET ARITHMETIC

Three operations, analogous to arithmetic addition, subtraction, and multiplication, are defined for sets. They are sometimes referred to as the operations of set arithmetic. These operations are performed on two sets of the same type, and produce as a result a set of this type (actually, this is a useful simplification).

The operations are:

- *union,* denoted by +,

  x + *y* produces the set of elements belonging to *x* or *y,* or both;

- *difference,* denoted by −,

  x − *y* produces the set of all elements of *x* which are **not** elements of *y;*

- *intersection,* denoted by *,

  x * *y* produces the set of elements which belong to both *x* and *y*.

Set intersection takes precedence over set union and difference, both of which are of equal precedence.

Note that the following operations have no effect:

(1) adding (via the union operation) to a set an element already contained there;
(2) subtracting (via the difference operation) from a set a value which is not an element of the set.

EXAMPLE 16–10
This application of set operators to set constructors illustrates the effect of the operators:

[nickel, dime] + [quarter] gives [nickel, dime, quarter];
[nickel, dime] + [quarter, dime] gives [nickel, dime, quarter];
[nickel, dime] − [quarter, dime] gives [nickel];
[nickel, dime] * [quarter, dime] gives [dime];
[nickel, dime] + [nickel, dollar] * [dollar] gives [nickel, dime, dollar].

Note that in the last example the intersection operation, having the higher precedence, is carried out first.

Set union may serve to build up a set. Such a set may be initialized to the empty-set value, with singleton (single-element) sets repeatedly added to it.

Conversely, set difference may serve to remove elements from a set in a regular fashion.

Set intersection may serve to identify common elements of several sets if several operators are employed combining the sets pairwise.

E. MANIPULATION OF SETS

The principal tool for manipulating sets is the assignment statement. Any of the subsets of the base type are assignable to a set variable defined on that type. In general, a set expression, possibly including the three operators for set arithmetic discussed in Section D–2, may be assigned to a set variable, provided that the two are compatible and that the base type of the variable includes all the elements of the value being assigned. Note that a value of the base type may *not* be assigned to a set variable.

> Remember to initialize set variables appropriately in the statement part of your program!

EXAMPLE 16–11

(a) Assuming these definitions and declarations:

type
    books = (mystery, thriller, scifi, novel, romance);
    bookSelection = **set of** books;
var
    beach, bedroom, omnibus: bookSelection;

we may initialize two of the set variables as follows:

> beach := [scifi . . romance];
> bedroom := [ ];

and subsequently employ these assignment statements as needed:

> beach := beach + [mystery]; {has no effect if the element already there}
> beach := beach − [novel]; {has no effect if the element not there}
> bedroom := beach − [scifi];
> omnibus := beach * bedroom; {identifies common elements}

Note again that set values are enclosed in square brackets, while variable identifiers are not.

(b) Provided these definitions and declarations have been made:

> **type**
> > systemOption = (commInterface, videoAdapter, drive, graphics);
> > options = **set of** systemOption;
> **var**
> > vendor, mailOrder, store, common: options;

this statement identifies the common options:

> common := vendor * mailOrder * store;

Sets may appear as subprogram parameters, but may not be returned as values of functions.

To read in or write out a set, we have to deal with individual elements. Thus, to read in the current value of a set variable, input has to proceed element by element, as in the following procedure.

EXAMPLE 16–12

This common method is employed to read in the elements of a set: the set variable is initialized to the empty set, and the elements are added to its value one-by-one with the set union operation.

These global definitions are assumed:

> **const**
> > first = 10;
> > last = 25;
> **type**
> > member = first . . last;
> > setOfElements = **set of** member;

The following procedure may be employed within the scope of these definitions.

```
procedure readSet (var inputSet: setOfElements);
        {read in the value of set variable}
    var
        element: member;
    begin {readSet}
        inputSet := [ ];
        while not eof do {elements are read in from the input file}
            begin
                readln (element);
                inputSet := inputSet + [element]
            end
    end; {readSet}
```

Similarly, a set cannot be written out with a single *write* or *writeln* statement; each of its elements must be written out individually, as in the following procedure.

EXAMPLE 16–13

In order to write out the elements of a set, we commonly step through all the values of its base type and test their membership in the set being written out.

Assuming the definitions of Example 16–12, we have this procedure:

```
procedure writeSet (outputSet: setOfElements);
        {write out the value of set variable}
    var
        element: member;
    begin {writeSet}
        for element := first to last do
            if element in outputSet then
                writeln (element)
    end; {writeSet}
```

The following program illustrates the use of sets.

EXAMPLE 16–14

Sieve of Eratosthenes

Problem

Generate all prime numbers[5] in a selected range:

$$1 < \text{prime} \leq n, \text{ where } n > 1$$

5. A positive integer is prime if it is divisible evenly only by 1 and by itself (for example, 17, 23, etc.).

Solution

Several algorithms exist. The one chosen here is called Eratosthenes' sieve after its inventor, a Greek mathematician of the third century B.C.

The algorithm first places in "the sieve" (which actually is an ordered list of integers) all integers between 2 and n. All multiples of the first prime (i.e., of 2) "fall through" the sieve, that is, are removed from further consideration as being nonprime. The next prime is the smallest integer still "in the sieve"; it and its multiples are in turn eliminated. The process continues until all primes are selected from the sieve.

Pseudocode of the Algorithm

program *findPrimes;*
begin
    read the bound of the interval desired;
    place in the sieve all integers between 2 and the bound;
    while there are numbers in the sieve **do**
        begin
            write the smallest number still in the sieve as prime;
            delete this number and all its multiples from the sieve
        end
end.

Implementation (interactive)

```
program findPrimes (input, output);
        {all primes larger than 1 and not larger than a given
         positive integer are generated}

const
    sieveLimit = 200;    {the limit of the program}
var
    bound,                 {the limit selected by the program user}
    multiple, candidate,
    onLine: integer;     {number of primes displayed on current line}
    primes: set of 2 .. sieveLimit;

begin
    primes := [2 .. sieveLimit];
    writeln ('Enter the limit desired, no larger than ', sieveLimit: 1, ': ');
    readln (bound);
    writeln ('The primes not larger than ', bound: 1, ' are:');
    onLine := 0;
    for candidate := 2 to bound do {consider next integer in the set}
        if candidate in primes then
            begin
                write (candidate: 5);
                onLine := onLine + 1;
                if onLine > 10 then
                    begin
                        writeln;
                        onLine := 0
                    end;
                    {delete this prime and all its multiples}
                for multiple := 1 to (bound div candidate) do
                    primes := primes - [multiple * candidate]
            end
end.
```

A sample run (user's input underlined):

```
Enter the limit desired, no larger than 200:
175
The primes not larger than 175 are:
    2    3    5    7   11   13   17   19   23   29   31
   37   41   43   47   53   59   61   67   71   73   79
   83   89   97  101  103  107  109  113  127  131  137
  139  149  151  157  163  167  173
```

17
FILES

Almost arbitrarily large data collections may be stored as files in the secondary storage of a computer system. The existence of a file, once it has been created, may be made independent of individual programs. Thus a file may be used over a long period of time by several programs of a certain application whenever the need arises to run these programs.[1]

As the only structured data type stored in relatively plentiful secondary storage, a file may consist of an unspecified number of components of the same type (most often records). A special kind of file, declared to be of the standard type *text,* is a textfile.

Files of Standard Pascal are exclusively sequential. Once generated (written), such a file can be read only without any updates, in the same order it was created.

A number of standard procedures and functions are available for file processing. Some of them we already know, since we have used them for the processing of the two standard files, *input* and *output.* These two are actually textfiles, and like any textfile, they may be processed as a sequence of characters, as a sequence of values of certain standard data types, or as a sequence of text lines.

A. INTRODUCTION TO PASCAL FILES

More complex computer applications are usually served by systems of programs rather than by a single program. Such a software system is a collection of programs devoted to the same task; each program in the system has a subtask allotted to it. The unifying element is a permanent collection of data;

---

1. Such a data file becomes a member of the general collection of files stored in the system as discussed in Chapter 1.

some of the programs use (access) these data, some update the data. Thus the need arises to keep collections of data in a computer system independently of the programs which use the data. These collections are stored in relatively plentiful secondary memory and are made available to the programs requesting them. Such named organized collections of data stored in secondary memory (usually on a magnetic disk, sometimes on tape) are called *files*. The programs comprising an application system are able to communicate by exchanging data through these files.

EXAMPLE 17–1a

Consider a payroll system. It may be built around a personnel file containing data about every employee. One of the system's programs will maintain this file by producing its new version to reflect hirings and separations, as well as changes in status of current employees. Another program will be responsible for periodic printing of paychecks. A third program will handle tax reporting, et cetera.

In some cases, the need for a file arises from the requirements of a single program for a large collection of data, which would be impractical to keep fully in main memory. These data may be kept in a file stored in secondary storage, with only some of its components brought into main memory when they are needed. It may or may not be desired to keep such a data file in the computer system for future use.

In conclusion, the need arises for the programmer to be able to create and use two kinds of files. *External files*, once created, exist in the system independently of the currently executing program. *Internal files* are created by the currently executing program and cease to exist when its execution stops.

The components of a file (other than a textfile, discussed below) are most often records, since such a component can provide all the needed data about a single real-world entity or event. A file of records usually holds a collection of data about a certain class of entities or events.

The relevant attributes of an entity are generally described by data of different types; record fields serve well to describe these attributes. One of the fields usually uniquely identifies a record within a file; this is the *key* of the file. Frequently, files are ordered (sorted) on the key.

EXAMPLE 17–1b

A single record of our personnel file may contain fields of these types:

Social Security number—string
name—string
weekly salary—real

number of dependents—integer subrange

department—integer subrange

This file has the structure shown in Fig. 17–1.

Social Security Number	Name	Salary	Dependents	Department
211223712	Joseph Smith	500.00	3	7
422317918	James Jones	410.50	1	3
718992131	Peter Wiles	825.25	4	7

FIGURE 17–1. A file.

Note that the Social Security number may serve as the key to the file.

As can be seen from Fig. 17–1, a file superficially resembles an array of records. However, because it is stored in secondary memory the size of a file is not declared and can far surpass a practically possible array size.

Also, Pascal files are exclusively *sequential* (or, more exactly, serial); their components may be accessed only in consecutive order, from the first to the last. At any given time, a Pascal file may be available either for reading or writing but not both. Only a single file component is accessible in main memory at any time. (We may observe that Pascal files are an abstraction of a prevalent type of magnetic-tape storage.) Later in this chapter, the term *file* stands as an abbreviation for such a sequential file.

Some nonstandard Pascal implementations also provide far more versatile *random access files*, where it is possible to access an individual component directly, by specifying the key or at least the position of the needed component.

For the manipulation of text, Pascal provides textfiles. These are structured as sequences of lines consisting of characters. We have been using two standard files of this type, *input* and *output,* all along.

B. DECLARATION OF FILES

A Pascal file is a sequence of components of the same type. The number of components is not specified and a file may grow to a great length during program execution.

A file type specification has this general form:

file of component type

where the component type is presented as a type denoter. For example:

type
　　counts = **file of** *integer;*

or

　　var *{invoice is a previously defined record type}*
　　　　sales: **file of** *invoice;*

A defined file type may, as usual, serve to declare file variables, for example,

var
　　itemsSold, itemsPaid: counts;

The components of a file may be of any simple, structured, or pointer (see Chapter 18) type, with the exception of other files or structures including files as their components. Most frequently, file components are of a record type. The standard files *input* and *output* must not be declared.

External files, existing independently of the program where they are used, must be:

- declared in the main program block; and
- listed in the **program** heading as program parameters (other such parameters are the standard files *input* and *output,* where required), in an arbitrary order.

▷
Make sure that the lengths of identifiers of your external files do not exceed the limit allowed in your system for file names (this limit may be lower than the allowed length of Pascal identifiers). ◁

Internal files are local variables like any others.

EXAMPLE 17–2
Our program will employ:

- an external file *personnel,*
- an internal file *temporary,*

both consisting of *employee* records.
　The following shows the distinction in their specification:

```
program maintain (input, output, personnel);
type
    employee = record
                    SSnumber: packed array [1 . . 9] of char;
                    name: packed array [1 . . 25] of char;
                    salary: real;
                    dependents: 0 . . 20;
                    department: 1 . . 10
               end;
var
    personnel, temporary: file of employee;
    hired: employee;
```

C. FILE PROCESSING

A Pascal file is originally generated by consecutive writing of individual component values into an empty file. Such a file may later be inspected (read) as many times as desired, but always in the order it was written. The end-of-file condition may be tested.

Every file has associated with it a *buffer variable,* whose value is that of the file component currently accessible in main memory. The direct use of this variable, which will be discussed later in this section, makes for simpler programs in certain cases.

Processing of a special type of file, the textfile, is discussed in the next section.

1. GENERAL FEATURES OF PASCAL FILE PROCESSING

Standard Pascal offers only sequential files. Such a file is produced (generated) by:

(a) always starting with an empty file;
(b) consecutively appending file components to the file's end by writing into the file.

A Pascal file is used (inspected) by:

(a) always starting at the beginning of a previously generated file;
(b) consecutively accessing (reading) file components in the order they have been placed in the file until the end of the file is reached. If the currently accessed component is not needed by the program, it is

simply ignored. A file component, once read, is processed as any variable of its type would be.

The following are impossible with a file of Standard Pascal:

- We cannot access a file component (by specifying its position number or key) without having to read in all the components separating it from the beginning of the file.
- We cannot have a file available both for inspection (reading) and generation (writing) at the same time.
- We cannot update (change) an individual file component or add a component in the middle of a non-empty file. If such results are desired, we have to copy the current file into another one (initially empty), updating the appropriate component(s) as we are doing so.

Files may be passed as parameters to procedures and functions. However, a parameter of a file type must be a variable parameter, even if its value is not updated by the subprogram. (This is because passing a file as a value parameter would require making a copy of it, which, given the length of some files, would take an unreasonable amount of time.)

In conclusion, these are the only operations applicable to file variables:

- generation (write), one component at a time;
- inspection (read), one component at a time;
- passing as a variable parameter.

As an exception, more than one component at a time may be read from or written into a textfile (see Section D).

In particular, no assignment can be made between two variables of a file type. Only component-by-component transfer of values is possible.

A test for the end-of-file condition is possible using the *eof* function, introduced in Chapter 5–E–2. Thus,

$$eof\ (f)$$

returns the value *true* if the current position in the file f is past the last file component; otherwise it returns the value *false*.

The specific fashion in which files are processed is due to their residence in secondary storage rather than in main memory where other data structures are placed. Only a single component of a file is accessible to the program in main memory at any time. This component constitutes the value of the so-called buffer variable that is automatically associated with every file.

We may assume that a declaration of a file f also "declares" a *buffer variable,* whose general form is

$$f\char`\^$$

(in some standard implementations, instead of the circumflex "^" the upward arrow "↑" is used).

It is convenient to think of a file and its buffer variable as shown in Fig. 17-2. The contents of the buffer variable depend on the current position in the file during its reading or writing.

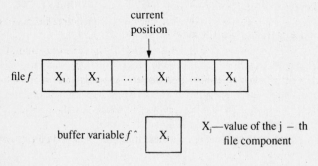

FIGURE 17-2. A file and its buffer variable (before reading component i)

The buffer variable of a file is of the same type as the file components; thus, the operations applicable to them are also applicable to this buffer variable.

EXAMPLE 17-3

Assuming the definition and declarations of Example 17-2, we have:

personnel^—the buffer variable of the file *personnel;* of the record type *employee;*

personnel^.*salary*—the real-type field of the current record in the buffer variable;

personnel^.*name*[7]—the seventh character in the string-type field *name* currently in the buffer variable.

The following uses are correct:

hired.SSnumber := personnel^.*SSnumber;*
writeln (personnel^.*name);*
with *personnel*^ **do**

> Make sure that you use the file identifier and not the component-type identifier to refer to a field of a buffer variable of a record type.

It is possible to process a Pascal file without reference to its buffer variable. A declared variable serving such a buffering (i.e., holding temporarily) purpose is then required, though. Understanding of buffer variables also enhances our understanding of file processing in Pascal.

We may conclude that at all times the processing of a Pascal file is determined by:

- the type of the file component;
- the current position in the file (reflected at appropriate instances in the value of the buffer variable);
- the mode of access: generation (writing) or inspection (reading).

▷ Certain nonstandard implementations of Pascal also afford the following facilities:

(1) Random-access files.
   Located on a magnetic disk, such a file allows for direct access to a specified component as follows:

   seek (file, component number)

   where the component number is an integer expression with positive value indicating the component which is to be read next from the file.
(2) Association of a system name for a file with a program name.
   Files present in the computer system are catalogued in a system directory under system-wide names. The following nonstandard statement:

   open (file—program name, file—system name, attributes)

   makes the catalogued file with a certain system name known to the program under the program name; file attributes (such as sequential or direct access, etc.) may also be specified. If the file does not exist, it is created with the listed attributes.

   Following use of the file, the following statement makes it further inaccessible to the program (and deletes it, if it is an internal file):

   close (file—program name) ◁

2. GENERATION OF A FILE

In order to generate (write into) a file we have to:

(a) prepare for writing by creating an empty file;

(b) consecutively append to the current end of the file as many components as needed.

An empty file is created by invoking the standard procedure *rewrite*. The call to this procedure, of the following general form,

$$rewrite \ (f)$$

makes the declared file f ready for writing into by establishing the current writing position at its beginning. If the file f contained any components, they are automatically erased.

There are two techniques for writing into a file: using the procedure *write* or using the procedure *put*. These are explained and compared below.

To append new components to a file f, the standard procedure *write* may be called as follows:

$$write \ (f, \underbrace{e_1, \ldots, e_n})$$ (*)
$$\text{optional}$$

where $e_1, \ldots, e_n$ are expressions whose values are assignment-compatible with the component type of the file f. These values will be appended, in the given sequence, to the file f. For example, in reference to Example 17–2, these statements:

rewrite (personnel);
write (personnel, hired);

will write the contents of the record *hired* as the first component of the file *personnel*. The statement (*) is equivalent to:

begin *write* $(f, e_1); \ldots ;$ *write* (f, e_n) **end**

Note:

(1) Before any *write* into a file is executed, the file must be made ready by executing *rewrite* with the file identifier as a parameter. The exception is the standard file *output*, which is made ready automatically; the programmer does not need to specify a *rewrite* for this file.

(2) Following a *rewrite* of a file, the component written into it must be the first one in the file; thus, it is impossible to append components to a file that was not empty to begin with.

Since the component being written into a file is always the last one, while the file f is being generated the function *eof* (f) gives the value *true* (though in general no need for such a test arises during file generation).

The following partially pseudocoded sequence is usually employed for generating a file:

rewrite (outfile);
while generation needed **do**
    begin   (**)
        obtain *nextout;*
        write (outfile, nextout)
    end;

where *nextout* is a variable that is assignment-compatible with the component type of the file *outfile.*

The mechanism for writing into a file actually consists of two steps, illustrated in Fig. 17–3, where x_i is the value of the expression e_i in the statement (*) above.

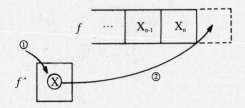

FIGURE 17–3. File generation (writing) mechanism in Pascal.

These two steps are:

(1) The value to be written is assigned to the file's buffer variable.
(2) A new component with the value contained in the buffer variable is appended to the file as its last component.

This mechanism may be used directly in programming instead of generating the file with the procedure *write.* Thus,

$$write\ (f,\ e)$$

is equivalent to

begin
    $f\hat{}\ := e;$
    put (f)
end

The standard procedure *put,* invoked as shown above, has the following effects:

(a) The current value of the buffer variable $f^\wedge$ is assigned to the component appended to the end of the file f.

(b) The value of the buffer variable $f^\wedge$ becomes undefined (it is "emptied" by the procedure).

Thus, the sequence (**) above may also be written as follows:

rewrite (outfile);
while generation needed **do**
    begin
        obtain *nextout;*
        outfile $^\wedge$ *:= nextout; {a value may be assigned by other means as well}*
        put (outfile)
    end;

The convenience of this usage rests on the fact that the value of the next file component may be placed directly in the buffer variable. Thus, a record may be built up, field by field, in the file buffer, without the need for an intermediate variable.

3. INSPECTION OF A FILE

A file generated by a program or available to it as an external file may be inspected (read) sequentially. In order to inspect a file we must:

(a) prepare the file for reading;

(b) consecutively read the file's components, starting with the first one, in the order they were written into it.

A file is prepared for reading by invoking the standard procedure *reset*. The call to this procedure, of the following general form,

$$reset\ (f)$$

has several possible effects. If the file f is not empty, then

(a) the value of its first component becomes assigned to the buffer variable $f^\wedge$, and

(b) the value of *eof* (f) becomes *false*, since there remains at least one component (the one whose value is currently in the buffer variable) to be read.

Otherwise, if the file f is empty,

(a) the value of the buffer variable $f\hat{}$ is undefined,
(b) the value of *eof (f)* is *true*.

There are two techniques for reading a file: using the procedure *read* or using the procedure *get*. These are explained and compared below.

In order to read the contents of a non-empty file f, the standard procedure *read* may be called as follows:

$$read\ (f,\ \underbrace{v_1,\ \ldots,\ v_n}_{\text{optional}})\qquad\qquad(*)$$

where $v_1, \ldots, v_n$ are variables (more precisely, each of them can be a variable-access) with which the component type of the file f is assignment-compatible. The values of consecutive file components will be assigned to these variables.

For example, in Example 17–2, assuming that the file *personnel* has been previously generated, these statements:

reset (personnel);
read (personnel, hired);

will read the value of the first component of the file *personnel* into the record variable *hired*.

The statement (*) above is equivalent to:

begin *read (f, v_1); . . . ; read (f, v_n)* **end**

Note:

(1) Before any read from a file is executed, the file has to be made ready by executing *reset* with this file as a parameter. The exception is the standard file *input* which is reset automatically; the programmer does not have to specify a *reset* for this file.
(2) In order to read again a file component that has already been read, we need to *reset* the file once again and reach this component by accessing all others intervening between the file's beginning and the needed component.
(3) An attempt to read from an empty file or from a file whose last component has already been read will fail. Thus, before any read on a file is performed, a check for the end-of-file condition is necessary.

The following partially pseudocoded sequence is usually employed for inspecting an entire file (it is, of course, possible to inspect a part of a file by providing additional loop conditions):

```
reset (infile);
while not eof (infile) do
    begin                           (**)
        read (infile, nextin);
        process nextin
    end;
```

where *nextin* is a variable that is assignment-compatible with the component type of the file *infile*.

The mechanism of reading from a file actually consists of two steps, involving a look-ahead: when the current component is being read, the next one is placed in the buffer variable, as shown in Fig. 17–4.

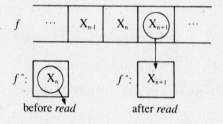

FIGURE 17–4.   File inspection (reading) mechanism in Pascal.

Thus, the following occur when *read (f, v)* is executed, assuming that *eof (f)* has the value *false:*

(1) the value of the buffer variable $f^\wedge$ is copied into the variable *v;*
(2) the value of the next component of *f,* if there is such a component, is placed in the buffer variable (this is the look-ahead); if there are no more components, the value of *eof (f)* becomes *true*.

Note that, consistent with this sequence, the value of the file's first component is placed in the buffer variable by the *reset* procedure.

The above mechanism may be used directly in programming instead of file inspection with the procedure *read*. Thus, the action of

read (f, v)

is equivalent to

```
begin
    v := f^;
    get (f)
end
```

The standard procedure *get,* invoked as shown above, has the following effects:

- if there is another component to be read in the file *f,* its value is assigned to *f^,*
- otherwise (the end of file has been reached), the value of *eof (f)* becomes *true,* and the value of *f^* is undefined.

Note that *eof (f)* becomes true only *after* an attempt is made to get the nonexistent component following the last component of the file. After the first, legitimate, such attempt (which is necessary to establish that the file has been completely inspected), another *get* will fail as a programming error.

The sequence (**) above may then also be written as follows:

```
reset (infile);
while not eof (infile) do
    begin
        process infile^;
        get (infile)
    end;
```

Such a separation of the two parts of *read* is desirable, for example, when we are sequentially searching for a specific file component. We could examine the current component right in the buffer variable and overwrite it, if so desired, by the next one without copying it out of this buffer.

EXAMPLE 17–4
The definition and declarations of Example 17–2 are assumed. We want to print out of the *personnel* file the names of the employees of the merchandising department, whose department code is 7. We also want to spin off a separate file of merchandising department employees declared as:

```
var
    merchandising: file of employee;
```

This sequence will accomplish the above tasks:

```
begin
    writeln ('The employees of merchandising department are: ');
    reset (personnel);
    rewrite (merchandising);
    while not eof (personnel) do
        begin
            if personnel^.department = 7 then
                begin
                    writeln (personnel^.name);
                    merchandising^ := personnel^;
                    put (merchandising)
                end;
            get (personnel)
        end
    end;
```

Note that the first component of *personnel* is immediately available for inspection in the buffer variable due to the *reset* procedure.

Observe how the direct use of the buffer variables of both the inspected and generated files saves us the need for intermediate variables and for transfer of data into them.

The following example illustrates another typical use of buffer variables.

EXAMPLE 17–5

To "peek ahead" into the next component of a file *f* in order, for example, to compare its key with that of the component previously read into a record variable *present*, we may use this statement:

```
if f^.key > present.key then
    ⋮
```

This is a typical example of a file-processing application.

EXAMPLE 17–6

File Update

Problem

Update a master file of personnel records by processing against it a transaction file which contains amendments to the master file collected over a period of time.

File update is a classical business batch application; its general block-diagram is shown in Fig. 17–5.

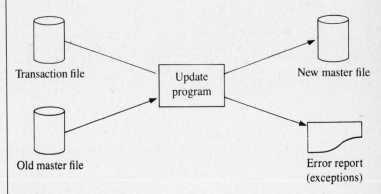

FIGURE 17-5. Batch file update.

Both the current (soon to become old) master file and the transaction file have been sorted on the same key; the update program creates a new master file, also sorted on this key. Any errors discovered in updating (that is, erroneous transactions) are written into an error report.

The key to our files will be the Social Security number of an employee. The transaction file will contain three kinds of transactions:

- insert a new record (fully included in the transaction itself) into the master file;
- delete a record (identified by its key) from the master file;
- modify the record with the given key (full new contents are included in the transaction record).

The transaction file has been preprocessed: it is sorted and includes at most a single record with a given key.

Design

This is the pseudocode of our program:

```
program updateFile;
begin
            {list both input files for testing purposes}
      listStaff (oldStaff);                {list oldStaff file}
      listTransactions;                    {list transaction file}
            {general update}
      while there are records in both oldStaff file and transaction file do
         begin
            if key of transaction record > key of oldStaff record then
               copyRecord                  {copy oldStaff record into
                                                        newStaff file}
            else if key of transaction record = key of oldStaff record then
               if transaction is "modify" then
                  modifyRecord             {modify oldStaff record
                                               according to transaction}
               else if transaction is "delete" then
                  deleteRecord             {delete this oldStaff record}
               else
                  processError             {write an exception}
            else
               if transaction is "insert" then
                  insertRecord             {insert transaction record
                                                     into newStaff file}
               else
                  processError
         end;
            {append the appropriate records remaining in one of the
            files to newStaff file}
      while there remain records in transaction file (only) do
         if transaction is "insert" then
            insertRecord
         else
            processError;
      while there remain records in oldStaff file (only) do
         copyRecord;
            {list the new master file for testing purposes}
      listStaff (newStaff)
end.
```

Each of the five identified updating (rather than listing for testing
purposes) procedures will read the next record of the appropriate
file.

The structure chart of the program is shown in Fig. 17–6.

Note that we have incorporated into the structure chart the parameters used to communicate with the subprograms. Every parameter is shown as a named arrow directed

- either down to the module, for an in-parameter (as in our case),
- or up from the module, for an out-parameter.

Thus, the interfaces between the modules of the program may be specified on the structure chart itself. If for a particular design the chart would get crowded, an interface table may be created, listing every module with its in- and out-parameters in two columns.

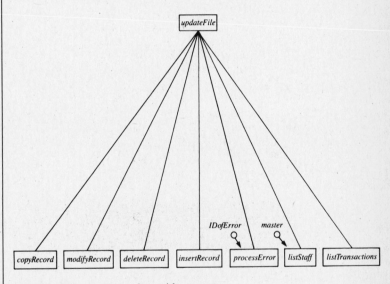

FIGURE 17–6. Structure chart with parameters.

Implementation

(1)

The following program, *createFiles,* was written to populate the test files *oldStaff* and *transact* (note that the identifier of this file has been shortened) in order to test the program *updateFile*. Note in particular the communication between the two programs via external files.

```pascal
program createFiles (input, oldStaff, transact);
       {populate test files}

const
   nameLength = 15;
   SSlength = 9;
type
   SStype = packed array [1 .. SSlength] of char;
   staffInfo = record
                   name: packed array [1 .. nameLength] of char;
                   salary: real;
                   dependents: 0 .. 20;
                   department: 1 .. 10
               end;
   memberOfStaff = record
                       SSnumber: SStype;    {the key}
                       info: staffInfo
                   end;
   personnelFile = file of memberOfStaff;
   transKind = (I, D, M); {I to insert, D to delete, M to modify}
   staffTransaction = record
                          SSnumber: SStype; {the key}
                          case kind: transKind of
                              I, M: (employee: staffInfo);
                              D  : ()
                      end;
var
   oldStaff: personnelFile;
   transact: file of staffTransaction;

procedure createMaster;
       {create master file of staff}
   var
       staffRecord: memberOfStaff;
       countOfMaster: integer;              {number of records in master file}
       j, k: integer;
   begin {createMaster}
       rewrite (oldStaff);
       readln (countOfMaster);
       for k := 1 to countOfMaster do
           begin
               with staffRecord, info do
                   begin
                       for j := 1 to SSlength do
                           read (SSnumber[j]);
                       for j := 1 to nameLength do
                           read (name[j]);
                       readln (salary, dependents, department)
                   end;
               write (oldStaff, staffRecord)
           end
   end; {createMaster}
```

```
procedure createTransactions;
        {create transaction file}
    var
        transRecord: staffTransaction;
        countOfTrans: integer;    {number of records in transaction file}
        kindLetter : char;        {printable form of kind}
        j, k: integer;
    begin {createTransactions}
        rewrite (transact);
        readln (countOfTrans);
        for k := 1 to countOfTrans do
            begin
                with transRecord do
                    begin
                        read (SSnumber, kindLetter);
                        case kindLetter of
                            'I': kind := I;
                            'M': kind := M;
                            'D': kind := D
                        end;
                        case kind of
                            I, M: with employee do
                                        begin
                                            for j := 1 to nameLength do
                                                read (name[j]);
                                            readln (salary, dependents, department)
                                        end;
                            D   : readln
                        end
                    end;
                write (transact, transRecord)
            end
    end; {createTransactions}

begin {createFiles}
    createMaster;
    createTransactions
end. {createFiles}
```

(2)

This is the listing of the program *updateFile*, whose pseudocode was
shown above:

```
program updateFile (output, oldStaff, transact, newStaff);
        {oldStaff file is updated from transaction file to create
         newStaff file; all files in ascending order}

const
    nameLength = 15;
    SSlength = 9;
type
    SStype = packed array [1 .. SSlength] of char;
    staffInfo = record
                    name: packed array [1 .. nameLength] of char;
                    salary: real;
                    dependents: 0 .. 20;
                    department: 1 .. 10
                end;
```

```
    memberOfStaff = record
                       SSnumber: SStype;    {the key}
                       info: staffInfo
                    end;
    personnelFile = file of memberOfStaff;
    transKind = (I, D, M); {I to insert, D to delete, M to modify}
    staffTransaction = record
                          SSnumber: SStype; {the key}
                          case kind: transKind of
                             I, M: (employee: staffInfo);
                             D  : ()
                          end;
    error = (modDelete, insert, leftover);
var
    oldStaff, newStaff: personnelFile;
    transact: file of staffTransaction;

procedure copyRecord;
         {copy a record from oldStaff to newStaff file}
    begin {copyRecord}
       newStaff^ := oldStaff^;
       put (newStaff);
       get (oldStaff)
    end; {copyRecord}

procedure modifyRecord;
         {modify oldStaff record by transferring its new values
          from transaction file to newStaff file}
    begin {modifyRecord}
       newStaff^.info := transact^.employee;
       newStaff^.SSnumber := transact^.SSnumber;
       put (newStaff);
       get (oldStaff);
       get (transact)
    end; {modifyRecord}

procedure deleteRecord;
         {delete an oldStaff record}
    begin {deleteRecord}
       get (oldStaff);
       get (transact)
    end; {deleteRecord}

procedure insertRecord;
         {insert a record from transaction file into newStaff file}
    begin {insertRecord}
       newStaff^.SSnumber := transact^.SSnumber;
       newStaff^.info := transact^.employee;
       put (newStaff);
       get (transact)
    end; {insertRecord}

procedure processError (IDofError: error);
         {write error message and discard transaction}
    begin {processError}
       with transact^ do
          case IDofError of
             modDelete: writeln (SSnumber, ' improper transaction:',
                                 ' attempt to insert existing record.');
             insert   : writeln (SSnumber, ' improper transaction:',
                                  ' attempt to delete or modify ',
                                  'nonexistent record.');
             leftover : writeln (SSnumber, ' transaction other than insert',
                                  ' encountered past the end of master.')
          end;
          get (transact)
    end; {processError}
```

```
procedure listStaff (var master: personnelFile);
         {list the current staff file}
   begin {listStaff}
      writeln ('Social Security Number', 'Name': 12, 'Salary': 18,
               ' Dependents  Department');
      reset (master);
      while not eof (master) do
         begin
            with master^, info do
               writeln (SSnumber: 15, name: 25, salary: 12: 2,
                        dependents: 7, department: 12);
            get (master)
         end
   end; {listStaff}


procedure listTransactions;
         {list the transaction file}
   var
      kindLetter: char;  {printable form of kind}
   begin {listTransactions}
      writeln (' ': 20, 'Transaction File');
      writeln;
      writeln ('Social Security Number  Type', 'Name': 9, 'Salary': 19,
               ' Dependents  Department');
      reset (transact);
      while not eof (transact) do
         begin
            with transact^ do
               begin
                  case kind of
                     I: kindLetter := 'I';
                     M: kindLetter := 'M';
                     D: kindLetter := 'D'
                  end;
                  write (SSnumber: 15, kindLetter: 11);
                  case kind of
                     I, M: with employee do
                                 writeln (name: 18, salary: 12:2,
                                          dependents: 7,    department: 12);
                     D    : writeln
                  end
               end;
            get (transact)
         end
   end; {listTransactions}

begin {updateFile}
                  {list oldStaff and transaction files}
   writeln (' ': 20, 'Old Staff File');
   writeln;
   listStaff (oldStaff);
   writeln; writeln;
   listTransactions;
   writeln; writeln;
```

```
                    {process transactions}
reset (oldStaff);
reset (transact);
rewrite (newStaff);
writeln (' ': 20, 'Error Report');
writeln;
while not (eof (oldStaff) or eof (transact)) do
    begin
        if transact^.SSnumber > oldStaff^.SSnumber then
            copyRecord
        else if transact^.SSnumber = oldStaff^.SSnumber then
            if transact^.kind = M then
                modifyRecord
            else if transact^.kind = D then
                deleteRecord
            else
                processError (modDelete)
        else        {transact^.SSnumber < oldStaff^.SSnumber}
            if transact^.kind = I then
                insertRecord
            else
                processError (insert)
    end;
while not eof (transact) do
    if transact^.kind = I then
        insertRecord
    else
        processError (leftover);
while not eof (oldStaff) do
    copyRecord;
                                {list newStaff file}
writeln; writeln;
writeln (' ': 20, 'New Staff File');
writeln;
listStaff (newStaff)
end. {updateFile}
```

This batch input was submitted to the program *createFiles:*

```
4
237122145Sam Spade              550.50 3 7
241015789Jane Marple            820.00 1 7
242010000Hercule Poirot        1250.75 12 4
410155555Philip Trent           350.50 1 2
7
200000000IAlbert Campion        900.00 1 4
241015789D
242010000IPeter Wimsey          750.25 2 1
300000000D
410155555MPhilip Trent         1600.00 2 2
500000000IKate Fansler         2500.00 2 7
700000000D
```

From it, these files were created by the program *createFiles* and listed by the program *updateFile:*

Social Security Number	Name	Salary	Dependents	Department
237122145	Sam Spade	550.50	3	7
241015789	Jane Marple	820.00	1	7
242010000	Hercule Poirot	1250.75	12	4
410155555	Philip Trent	350.50	1	2

Transaction File

Social Security Number	Type	Name	Salary	Dependents	Department
200000000	I	Albert Campion	900.00	1	4
241015789	D				
242010000	I	Peter Wimsey	750.25	2	1
300000000	D				
410155555	M	Philip Trent	1600.00	2	2
500000000	I	Kate Fansler	2500.00	2	7
700000000	D				

This is the result of file update by the program *updateFile:*

Error Report

```
242010000 improper transaction: attempt to insert existing record.
300000000 improper transaction: attempt to delete or modify nonexistent record.
700000000 transaction other than insert encountered past the end of master.
```

New Staff File

Social Security Number	Name	Salary	Dependents	Department
200000000	Albert Campion	900.00	1	4
237122145	Sam Spade	550.50	3	7
242010000	Hercule Poirot	1250.75	12	4
410155555	Philip Trent	1600.00	2	2
500000000	Kate Fansler	2500.00	2	7

D. TEXTFILES

In support of text processing, Pascal provides the standard file type *text*. A file declared to be of this type is known as a *textfile* and consists of characters structured into lines. Used, for example, in such applications as text editing, textfiles may be processed either as a sequence of characters or a sequence of lines (consisting of characters). It is also possible to write into a textfile or read directly from it values of several standard types.

To declare a textfile *t,* it is sufficient to specify:

var
    t: text;

It will be easier to understand the processing of textfiles if we consider that the standard files *input* and *output* are automatically declared by the Pascal system as textfiles. Indeed, the input to a program, or an output from it, is a text.

All the procedures and functions applicable to files in general, namely, *rewrite, reset, write, read, put, get, eof,* are applicable to a textfile *t,* as if it were declared as follows:

t: **file of** *char;*

In addition, when *read* from a textfile or *write* into it is specified, automatic type conversion is possible, as further discussed below.

The special standard procedures *writeln* and *readln* and the standard function *eoln* (discussed as applied to the standard files *input* and *output* in Chapters 3–E and 5–E–2) are applicable exclusively to textfiles for line-by-line processing. Also, the procedure *page* (introduced in Chapter 3–H) is available for pagination of text presented on an appropriate output device.

A line of characters in a textfile is terminated by a special symbol, the end-of-line marker. Its file image depends on the Pascal processor; its value, however, is always read in as a space (blank). This marker is generated only by the procedure *writeln,* recognized only by *readln,* and tested by *eoln.*

The following is a discussion of the standard file-processing procedures and functions applicable to textfiles.

1. *REWRITE* AND *RESET*

These procedures must be invoked before accessing a textfile for writing or reading. They need not be applied to the standard files *input* and *output.*

2. *WRITE* AND *READ*

For writing or reading a character at a time, these procedures are defined for textfiles in the same fashion as for general files discussed in the preceding section. An end-of-line marker will be read as a space.

It is also possible to invoke these procedures (following the parameter specifying the textfile) with parameters other than those of the component type (that is, other than of the type *char*), as discussed below. Automatic conversions will be performed in such a case.

Thus, in a manner similar to the processing of the *input* and *output* files, we may specify:

write (t, e);

where the expression *e* may be of *char,* integer, real, Boolean, or string type; and

read (t, v);

where the variable *v* may be of *char,* integer, or real type. In both cases, *char* and integer subrange types are also acceptable.

As with general files, several such parameters may be listed following the parameter specifying the textfile. If no textfile parameter is specified, *output* is assumed for *write*, and *input* for *read*.

The effect of the execution of these procedures is the same as previously discussed for the standard files *output* and *input*. Thus:

(a) For *write* parameters, field widths may be specified as discussed in Chapter 3–H.
(b) For *read* parameters of integer or real type, leading spaces and end-of-line markers are skipped, and the value is read in as the value of the variable *v* (with the first character following this value then placed into the buffer variable $t^\wedge$). An error results if a value of the proper type does not directly follow the skipped blanks, in particular, if *eof (t)* becomes *true* before the value is found.

3. *WRITELN, READLN,* AND *EOLN*

The procedures *writeln* and *readln* have the same effect on the value being written out or read in as *write* and *read*, respectively. In addition, *writeln* writes the end-of-line marker into the textfile following the last value written out. The procedure *readln* is able to recognize this marker and, following the input of the last value specified, it advances the reading position in the textfile past the current line.

The function *eoln (t)* returns the value *true* if the current character in the textfile *t* is the end-of-line marker; otherwise its value is *false*. When used without a parameter, *eoln* refers to the file *input*.

A procedure call of this form:

writeln (t)

where *t* is a textfile, serves to write the end-of-line marker. A procedure call of this form:

readln (t)

serves to advance past the closest end-of-line marker in the textfile *t*. Thus,

$$writeln\ (t,\ e_1,\ \ldots,\ e_n)$$

is equivalent to:

begin *write (t, e_1);* . . . ; *write (t, e_n); writeln (t)* **end**

Similarly,

$$readln\ (t,\ v_1,\ \ldots,\ v_n)$$

is equivalent to:

$$\textbf{begin}\ read\ (t,\ v_1);\ \ldots;\ read\ (t,\ v_n);\ readln\ (t)\ \textbf{end}$$

Also,

readln (t)

is equivalent to:

```
begin
    while not eoln (t) do
        get (t);
    get (t)
end
```

4. GET, PUT, AND EOF

The usage is the same as for general files. If used without a file parameter, *get* and *eof* refer to the standard file *input*, and *put* refers to the standard file *output*.

5. PAGE

A call

page (t)

may be applied only to a file *t* in output mode. If the output is directed to a device suitable for pagination (e.g., a line printer), subsequent output will appear on a new page.

When used without a parameter, *page* refers to the standard file *output*.

The following example illustrates the specific nature of textfiles (among other advantages is the possibility of skipping entire lines when reading them with the *readln* procedure).

EXAMPLE 17-7

The following program skips every other line while copying one file into another.

```
program copyAlternates (master, spinoff);
        {copy of every other line is made from master into spinoff file}

var
    master, spinoff: text;
    c: char;

begin
    reset (master);
    rewrite (spinoff);
    while not eof (master) do
        begin
            while not eoln (master) do
                begin
                    read (master, c);
                    write (spinoff, c)
                end;
            writeln (spinoff);
            readln (master);
            if not eof (master) then     {skip a line}
                readln (master)
        end
end.
```

Compare this program with the one presented in Example 5–13, where
the standard file *input* was copied (fully) into the standard *output* file.

18
POINTERS AND DYNAMIC DATA STRUCTURES

The pointer data type makes it possible to implement dynamic data structures, which are created and modified as needed during program execution. Such data structures, which are very flexible, lead to algorithms of considerable elegance. These structures consist of dynamic variables, which may be created or destroyed by program statements.

As entities unknown (other than as to their type) when the program is being written, dynamic variables do not have their own identifiers. These variables are called into existence, manipulated, and (if unwanted) released by referring to them indirectly through pointers. Two built-in procedures, *new* and *dispose,* are provided for allocation and deallocation of these variables. In manipulation, these so-called referenced (by a pointer) variables are treated as static variables of the same type would be.

As components (nodes) of dynamic data structures, dynamic variables of a record type are ordinarily employed. One or more fields of such a record are pointers, linking the node into the overall data structure and thus establishing its logical relationship with other nodes.

Important classes of dynamic (linked) data structures are the linear list (and particularly its restricted forms, such as stacks and queues) and the nonlinear structures trees and graphs.

A. IMPORTANCE OF DYNAMIC DATA STRUCTURES

All the data structures provided directly in Pascal as its structured types—arrays, records, sets, and files—are static. This means that a variable of any of these types must be declared in the program block where it is wanted, and this variable exists throughout the execution of the block.

Since the number of static variables has to be known before program execution begins, such variables are not flexible enough for certain applications where the composition of the data structure (and not only the values of its components) will change significantly during execution. Structures that may be expanded or contracted during program execution are known as *dynamic data structures*. Components of such a structure are *dynamic variables;* they are created (and may be deleted, if desired) during program execution.

EXAMPLE 18–1

Our program has to reverse a sequence of integers of unknown length. Thus, for example,

this input:	5	12	3	2	1	0	777
must result in this output:	777	0	1	2	3	12	5

Assuming that the number of integers may vary widely and it is difficult to estimate its upper limit, it is best to create variables to hold the integers as they are read in, until the input is exhausted. The number of dynamic variables needed will equal the number of integers read in. Then, using the dynamic data structure so created, we can present the integers on output in reverse order. We will discuss this algorithm in more detail below.

Since before execution begins, the very existence of dynamic variables is unknown, they cannot be declared. Instead, their type is defined to serve as a template for the variables to be created during execution, and one or more pointers are declared in order to access these variables. A *pointer* is a variable of a pointer type: the value of such a variable is the memory address of a dynamic variable. Hence, through a pointer to it, a nameless dynamic variable may be accessed (referenced) indirectly.

A pointer type is always defined as referencing a specific type of dynamic variable, and pointer variables are then declared. Through these pointer variables, dynamic variables of the appropriate type can be created, manipulated, and, if so desired, released (destroyed when no longer needed).

With the use of pointers, dynamic variables may also be organized into dynamic data structures. The pointers serve as links between the variables; since these links may be changed through the execution of program statements, the composition of the dynamic data structure may change also.

The variables which compose dynamic data structures are most often records (these components are often called nodes). With links, the components may be organized into such linear structures as stacks and queues, or such nonlinear ones as trees and graphs. The structuring method itself may be modified during execution to reflect a changed relationship among the components.

EXAMPLE 18–2

Let us assume that the task of Example 18–1 is changed: we now want to have the second half of the sequence of integers precede the first one.

Such a structural change is quite simple to accomplish with a change of a few pointers in a dynamic data structure. On the other hand, if this task needed to be done in a static data structure, such as an array of integers, all the values of its components would have to be changed (the values would have to be moved around).

In general, dynamic data structures are more flexible than static ones, since by changing the values of pointers, components may easily be dropped, new components incorporated, and desired structural changes made. This is accomplished at the cost of maintaining the pointers and the facility for dynamic allocation and deallocation of variables referenced by them.

B. DEFINITION OF DYNAMIC VARIABLES AND DECLARATION OF POINTERS

Pointer types are the third kind of Pascal data type, alongside the simple and structured types.

The definition of a pointer type has this general form:

$$\text{pointer type} = \hat{\ }\text{domain type}$$

where both the pointer type and the domain type (note this!) are type identifiers. For example,

type
     position = *^component;*

The above definition specifies that variables of the pointer type *position* will point to (reference) variables of the domain type *component* (defined elsewhere in the same type definition). Hence, it may be read as follows: "*position* points to *component*."

Subsequently, variables of a pointer type (called, for short, pointers) may be declared in a **var** declaration. Pointers are static ("ordinary") variables, as opposed to the dynamic variables they point to. As we may conclude, a pointer of a given type may point only to variables of its domain type. It is often said that the pointer type is bound to its specified domain type.

In some standard implementations, the symbol "^" (circumflex) used in the pointer definition above is replaced by an upward arrow "↑."

What then, actually are the values of pointers? As illustrated in Fig. 18–1, they are the memory addresses (see Chapter 1–B–3) of variables of the domain type.[1] These values are used to access the appropriate variables, but we cannot "see" the addresses: they cannot be presented on output. Addresses should not be confused with integers. Thus, the values of a pointer variable cannot be read in or written out; they also cannot participate in arithmetic expressions (no computation is possible on them).

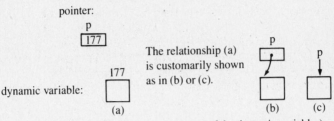

pointer:

p

177

The relationship (a) is customarily shown as in (b) or (c).

177

dynamic variable:

(a)   (b)   (c)

(Here 177 is the memory location (address) of the dynamic variable.)

FIGURE 18-1. A pointer p and the dynamic variable it references.

Variables of the domain type are dynamic variables; as such, they are not declared. These variables have no identifiers—they are anonymous. A dynamic variable is accessed indirectly through a pointer to it, since as shown in Fig. 18-1 the pointer specifies where in memory this variable is. As discussed below, when a dynamic variable is created during program execution, its address is assigned simultaneously to the specified pointer.

Pointers are used to organize dynamic variables into dynamic (linked) data structures, reflecting the relationship between these variables, such as, for example, a sequence. Typically, the components of such structures (i.e., the dynamic variables) are records (see Chapter 15). In order to link these components into structures, each component must contain a pointer as at least one of its fields. The following discussion illustrates this.

Let us consider these definitions of a pointer type and its domain type, together with pointer declarations:

```
type
    listPointer = ^student;
    student = record
                  name: packed array [1 . . 20] of char;
                  grade: 0 . . 5;
                  next: listPointer
              end;
var
    first, another: listPointer;
```

1. Since a variable of the domain type usually occupies more than one memory location, the pointer actually points to the first of these locations.

During execution of the program containing these definitions and declarations, the dynamic structure of Fig. 18–2 can be created, for example. This structure is not created by the definitions and declarations; they only make it possible to create the structure with the use of the program statements discussed in the next section.

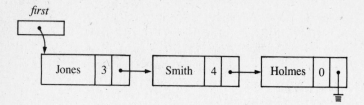

FIGURE 18–2. A linear list.

When manipulating dynamic data structures, it is very helpful to visualize them in a graphic form such as that of Fig. 18–2.

In the example of Fig. 18–2, the pointer field (called also a *link,* for reasons obvious from the figure) organizes the anonymous variables into a data structure, in this case a linear list (further discussed in Section E below). Each of the components (records) of this structure contains the prescribed information about its subject (a student), that is, a name and grade, as well as the pointer *(next)* to the next component of the list. The beginning of the list is indicated by the pointer *first.* The last component has no follower; a special symbol is required to indicate this (as in Fig. 18–2, often the electrical "ground" symbol is used to show this graphically).

Pascal provides a word symbol **nil** indicating that a pointer does not point to any location (but the value of the pointer is defined). Such a pointer value may be employed as a terminator.

Note that in the above example the identifier of the domain type *student* was used to define the pointer type *listPointer* before having been defined itself. Note also that reversing the two type definitions would not make them conform to the general "define before use" principle. Since this is a typical usage of pointers, Pascal makes a single exception from this rule for it.

The domain type T of a pointer type ^T may be defined anywhere in the type definition where the pointer type is defined.

Some implementations require that the pointer type definition precede the domain type definition (as in the above example).

C. DYNAMIC ALLOCATION PROCEDURES

As we said, dynamic variables are not declared. Their template only is provided as their type definition, but not a single instance of such a variable is created before program execution begins.

A dynamic variable is created explicitly during program execution with the use of the standard procedure *new,* supplied with a pointer to the variable as the actual parameter. This procedure allocates memory space for the variable which is being created and sets the pointer to point to it.

The general form[2] of the procedure call is:

new (p)

where *p* is a variable of a pointer type.

This procedure call results in:

(1) the creation of a variable of the domain type of the pointer *p* with all the values of this dynamic variable being undefined, and
(2) the pointer *p* acquiring a value pointing to this variable.

Thus, graphically, the situation of Fig. 18–1 is established. Referring to the example of the previous section,

new (first);

creates a record (whose values are undefined) of the type pointed to by *first,* and thus a record of the type *student.* The pointer *first* contains its address. As we will see in the next section, this enables us to reference the newly created variable and its individual fields.

A dynamic variable, created with the use of the procedure *new,* exists throughout the execution of the program[3] (not just during the execution of the block containing the call to *new*) unless and until it is explicitly destroyed with the use of the other dynamic allocation procedure, *dispose.*

The procedure *dispose,* which is actually a dynamic deallocation procedure, is called as follows:

dispose (p)

where *p* is a variable of a pointer type with a defined value other than **nil** (i.e., there has to be a dynamic variable to be disposed of). The results of this procedure call are:

---

2. Specifics of space allocation and deallocation for variant records are discussed in Section F.

3. Space for dynamic variables is allocated during program execution in the so-called **heap,** an area in memory which is different from the memory stack (do not confuse it with programmed stacks discussed in this chapter) provided for static variables according to the scope rules.

(1) the dynamic variable pointed to by pointer p ceases to exist (the memory space occupied by it is released for further use);

(2) the value of the pointer p becomes undefined (not **nil!**) and the values of any other pointers pointing to this variable also become undefined.

The procedure *dispose* is employed by the programmer to save memory space (rather than to further the principal goals of the program). In using this procedure, care should be exercised in order not to delete any dynamic variables that are still being pointed to by other active pointers (see Section E).

It is an error to specify

dispose (p)

if the variable pointed to by p is currently:

(a) an actual variable parameter, or
(b) specified as a record variable of a **with** statement.

D. MANIPULATION OF REFERENCED VARIABLES AND POINTERS

As described in the previous section, dynamic variables are created by calling the standard procedure *new*. Such variables are also known as *referenced variables*[4] because they can be accessed (referenced) only through pointers, since they do not have identifiers of their own.

A referenced variable is denoted as follows:

pointer variable^

where the pointer variable points to the required referenced variable.

Thus, in our example of Section B,

first ^

will denote a variable of type *student*.

In Pascal implementations where the upward arrow "↑" is employed in pointer-type definitions, referenced variables are denoted as follows: pointer variable ↑.

A specification of a referenced variable is valid only if the pointer employed in it has a defined value other than **nil.** Accessing the variable referenced by a pointer is often called *dereferencing* the pointer.

4. Also called identified variables.

Do not forget that:

(1) The declaration of a pointer does not provide it with a value. Thus, until the pointer is assigned a value during program execution, its value is undefined.
(2) The execution of *new (p)* defines the value of the pointer *p,* but does *not* define the value of its referenced variable.

It is crucial in programming with pointers to appreciate the difference between them and referenced variables. A referenced variable is of the type defined for it, and is manipulated as a static variable of the same type would be. A pointer has its own pointer type, bound to the type of variables it may reference. The main goal of a program is usually the manipulation of referenced variables; pointers are manipulated to further this goal.

A component of a referenced variable is specified as fitting to the type of this variable. If, as most often happens, the referenced variable is of a record type, its components (fields) are specified with the dot notation (see Chapter 15–C–1). Thus, again referring to the example of Section B, we may have:

first ˆ.name   —denotes the string-type field of the record *first ˆ;*
first ˆ.grade   —denotes the variable of the integer subrange type specified as a field of *first ˆ;*
first ˆ.next   —denotes the pointer-type field of *first ˆ;*
first ˆ.name[3]   —denotes the third character of the string *name.*

A referenced variable, or any of its components as appropriate for its type, may be included in an expression, assigned a value, or have its value read in or written out, all in accordance with the general type rules of Pascal.

EXAMPLE 18–3
We may employ these statements involving the above referenced variables conforming to the definitions and declarations provided in Section B:

(a)
    first ˆ.grade := 2;

    assigns the value 2 to the field *grade* of the record variable referenced by *first;*

(b) following the execution of the statement:

new (another);

and statements assigning values to all of the fields of *first ˆ,* we may have

another ˆ := first ˆ;

which assigns the field values of *first ˆ* to the corresponding fields of *another ˆ;*

(c)

readln (first ˆ.grade);

will read in an integer in the range from 0 to 5;

(d)

writeln (first ˆ.name);

writes out a 20-character string;

(e) the following statement makes it possible to use the field identifiers of the referenced variable *first ˆ* in unqualified fashion (see Chapter 15–C–2):

with *first ˆ* **do**
⋮

Referenced variables may be accessed only through the pointers to them; hence the need arises to manipulate the pointers themselves. It is this ability to manipulate pointers that makes dynamic data structures so flexible.

Values of pointers may be:

(1) assigned to other pointer-type variables of the same type;
(2) compared using one of two relational operators, those for equality ($=$) and inequality ($<>$);
(3) passed as parameters or provided as the result of a function;
(4) changed to **nil** as the result of an assignment;
(5) redefined using *new (p);*
(6) undefined by *dispose (p).*

No other manipulation of pointers is possible.

EXAMPLE 18–4

These are correct independent statements, manipulating the pointers declared in the example of Section B:

```
    another := nil;
    first := another;
    while first = another do
        ⋮
    if first <> nil then
        ⋮
    procedure find (var location: listPointer);
        ⋮
```

It is very important to distinguish the effect of a pointer-type assignment from that of an assignment of referenced variables.

EXAMPLE 18–5

Let us assume these definitions and declarations:

```
type
    link = ^node;
    node = record
                key: integer;
                next: link
            end;
var
    this, that, first: link;
    selected: integer;
```

Let us further assume that these statements were executed:

```
new (this); this^.key := 3; this^.next := nil;
new (that); that^.key := 7; that^.next := nil;
```

This results in the situation of Fig. 18–3a.

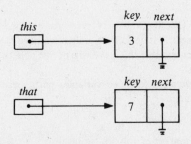

FIGURE 18–3a.

(1) Let us now consider two different assignment statements:

(a) The pointer-type assignment:

   this := that;

   produces the situation of Fig. 18–3b.

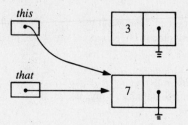

FIGURE 18–3b.

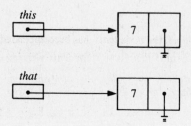

FIGURE 18–3c.

Note that the values of the referenced variables remain unchanged. Note also that, unless we have other pointers to the
former variable *this^*, we will not be able to access this record
again.

(b) If, instead, referenced variables participate in an assignment
statement:

   this^ := that^;

   the situation of Fig. 18–3c results.

   Note that the values of the pointers *this* and *that* remain
unchanged.

(2) The following two assignments are also syntactically correct (note their effect):

this^.key := that^.key;
selected := this^.key;

(3) Study carefully the effect of this assignment statement:

this^.next := that;

The result is illustrated in Fig. 18–4 (we assume the starting situation of Fig. 18–3a).

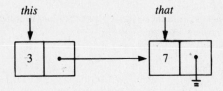

FIGURE 18–4.

As we can see, the node *that^* has been appended to the node *this^*. This is a typical use for the pointers included in dynamic variables.

If we now execute this statement:

this := this^. next;

we will delete the first node, with the effect shown in Fig. 18–5. (Note that the former first node can no longer be reached.)

FIGURE 18–5.

(Obviously, in the above situation

this := that;

would have had the same effect.)

> Great care should be exercised when programming with pointers to avoid confusing them with the variables referenced by them.

EXAMPLE 18-6

All the statements of this example, involving referenced variables and pointers as defined and declared in Example 18–5, are incorrect; they represent typical programming errors.

   (a) inadmissible (and meaningless) combinations of different data types in an assignment statement, as in:

this^ := that;
this := that^; } wrong!

   (b) the same kind of error in a different form:

*this^ := **nil**; {error—nil can be assigned only to a pointer variable}*
that := 77; {error—an integer value cannot be assigned to a pointer}

   (c)

writeln (this); {error—pointer values cannot be written out}

   (d)

this := this + that; {error—no arithmetic is allowed on pointers}

To summarize, a pointer may be given a value in one of these ways:

(1) by using the pointer as the parameter of the procedure *new;*
(2) by assigning to the pointer the value of another pointer of the same type;
(3) by assigning to the pointer the value **nil;**
(4) by the pointer acquiring a value on return from a procedure for which it serves as an actual variable parameter, or from a function for which it is the result.

A pointer loses its value (i.e., the value becomes undefined) if the variable referenced by it has been released by the procedure *dispose.* This may occur if the pointer itself was used as the actual parameter for this procedure. However, it will also happen if another pointer pointing to the same variable was used to dispose of it.

It is common in the manipulation of dynamic data structures for more than one pointer to reference the same node, thus providing alternative access paths to it. All such pointers become undefined if the node is deleted through any one of them.

> A "dangling" pointer, whose value is undefined, may not be used to reference a variable. Such an occurrence is a frequent programming error. No node should be disposed of unless we make certain that a reference to it will not occur again in the program.

The following examples are typical simple tasks in managing dynamic data structures. They also illustrate important aspects of the care that should be taken in manipulating pointers and referenced variables.

In Examples 18–7 and 18–8, the definitions and declarations of Example 18–5 are assumed.

EXAMPLE 18–7

We will delete the first component of the linked list (this structure is further discussed in the next section) shown in Fig. 18–6a, thus obtaining the list of Fig. 18–6b:

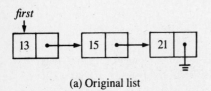

(a) Original list

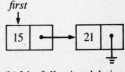

(b) List following deletion

FIGURE 18–6.

This sequence of statements accomplishes the task:

this := first; {replicate the pointer}
first := first^.next; {delete the first node}
dispose (this); {dispose of the deleted node}

Note that if instead of this sequence, we tried to accomplish this task with:

dispose (first);

we would have lost our list, since the value of *first* would have become undefined! So, do not dispose of a node if a pointer whose value you will need is pointing to it; employ auxiliary pointers as needed.

EXAMPLE 18-8

We will insert a node referenced by the pointer *that* as the second component of the linked list of Fig. 18–7a transforming it into the list of Fig. 18–7b.

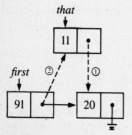 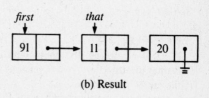

(a) Effects of assignments are shown with dotted lines.

(b) Result

FIGURE 18–7.

We will need this sequence:

that^.next := first^.next; {pointer 1 assigned new value}
first^.next := that; {pointer 2 assigned new value}

Try to reverse these statements to convince yourself that it would lead to an error: the list would become irretrievably broken. Thus we see that the order in which pointer values are assigned is often crucial.

E. DYNAMIC DATA STRUCTURES

Dynamic variables, usually of a record type, can be organized with pointers into data structures serving important classes of applications. The choice of data structures best representing the relationship among the data used by the program is as important as the selection of the algorithm: the better the organization of data, the clearer and more elegant is the algorithm for their processing.

Data structures built of dynamic variables allow for easy insertions and deletions of nodes, and can be dynamically reorganized to match the current needs of the running program. This reorganization is done by manipulation of pointers (since pointers are also called links, dynamic data structures are also known as linked data structures).

Dynamic data structures are organized either as linear chains or as more complex nonlinear structures, such as trees and graphs. The nodes are most frequently records.

The most general linear data structure is the *linear list*. The nodes of the structure form a sequence, with every node, except for the first and the last, having a single predecessor and a single successor; a pointer is always provided to the first node (see Fig. 18–2) but auxiliary pointers may be employed as well. Such a structure thus represents a sequential ordering of data.

In processing a linear list, insertions of additional nodes or deletions of existing ones may occur anywhere, according to the needs of the running program (see Examples 18–7 and 18–8). Such a list is often ordered on one of the fields, which uniquely identifies every record; this field is the key of the list.

Two restricted types of linear lists have important applications; these are stacks and queues. The restrictions concern the nature of the operations applicable to these special lists.

A *stack* (customarily shown as in Fig. 18–8) is a linear list where both insertions and deletions occur at a single end, called the top of the stack. Additional components are said to be pushed onto the stack; existing components can be popped off the stack (i.e., deleted from it).

Stacks are employed in computing where reversals are needed: as events occur, data representing them are pushed onto the stack, so that these data may be subsequently processed in last-in-first-out (LIFO) order. Important applications include the compilation of programming languages and the representation of procedure calls during program execution (see Chapter 12–A and Fig. 12–1 in particular).

The following example provides a complete set of routines for stack management; they should be studied as typical routines of linked-list processing. This example provides at the same time a solution to the problem offered in Example 18–1.

EXAMPLE 18–9

Problem

Reverse a sequence of integers of unknown length.

Solution

We will use a stack, such as in Fig. 18–8, to store the incoming integers.

top

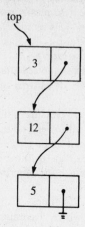

FIGURE 18–8 A stack.

The following program accomplishes the task.

```
program reverse (input, output);
      {reverse a sequence of integers}

type
   pointer = ^node;
   node = record
             entry: integer;
             link: pointer
          end;
var
   top: pointer;
   number: integer;

procedure push (info: integer);
      {push a new entry onto the stack}
   var
      p: pointer;
   begin {push}                  {programming notes:}
      new (p);                   {get an empty node}
      with p^ do
         begin
            entry := info;    {place information in this node}
            link := top       {link it in above the former top node}
         end;
      top := p                   {make the top pointer point to this nod
   end; {push}
```

```
procedure pop (var info: integer);
          {pop an entry off the stack}
   var
      p: pointer;
   begin {pop}
      p := top;                {duplicate the pointer}
      with p^ do
         begin
             info := entry;   {get the information needed}
             top := link       {delete the top node from the stack}
         end;
      dispose (p)
   end; {pop}

begin {reverse}
   top := nil;                 {initialize the stack}
        {place the incoming sequence on stack}
   writeln ('The original sequence is:');
   while not eof do
      begin
          readln (number);
          writeln (number);
          push (number)
      end;
   writeln;
        {remove the reversed sequence from the stack}
   writeln ('The reversed sequence is:');
   while top <> nil do
      begin
          pop (number);
          writeln (number)
      end
end. {reverse}
```

A Sample Output

```
            The original sequence is:
                    17
                    33
                    -2
                    18
                     0
                    -3
                    11

            The reversed sequence is:
                    11
                    -3
                     0
                    18
                    -2
                    33
                    17
```

Note, in particular, how through the repeated execution of the *push* procedure the stack is originally created. This is a typical technique for creating a linked structure.

A *queue*, like its correspondent in the vernacular, is a linear list where insertions are allowed at one end (called its rear), and deletions occur at the other (called its front). Thus, a queue implements a first-in-first-out (FIFO) regimen, and is used to represent events that are to be considered by the program in the order they occur. A queue may, for example, be used to simulate a service system where the events are job arrivals, or one may be used in the operating system of the computer itself to enqueue requests for computer resources. The customary structure of a queue is shown in Fig. 18–9.

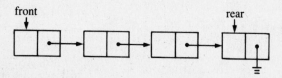

FIGURE 18-9. A queue.

The following example presents an insertion into a queue.

EXAMPLE 18-10
We will assume these definitions and declarations:

```
type
    pointer = ^node;
    node = record
                entry: char;
                link: pointer
            end;
var
    front, rear: pointer;
```

The queue is initialized as follows:

front := **nil**; *rear* := **nil**;

The following procedure is used to insert a node into the queue:

```
procedure enqueue (letter: char);
    var
        p: pointer;
    begin
        new (p);
        with p^ do
            begin
                entry := letter;
                link := nil {this node will become the last one}
            end;
        if front = nil then
            front := p {if this is the first node in the queue}
        else
            rear^.link := p; {link it to the current last node}
        rear := p {make the new node the last one}
    end; {enqueue}
```

Care is necessary when processing linked structures. Thus:

(1) Do not hesitate to declare auxiliary pointers. In particular, the pointers indicating a special position in a structure, such as *top* of a stack, or *front* and *rear* of a queue, should never be used for any other purposes. If a roving pointer is needed to move through the structure, the *top* or the *front* pointer should be replicated and not moved itself.

(2) Always check for the presence of nodes in a structure before attempting a deletion from it.

(3) Confirm that your algorithm works for all special conditions, such as an empty structure or a single-component structure.

(4) Do not leave any dangling pointers.

(5) While the values of pointers cannot be written out, the data contained in other fields of a node can. These data may thus be used to test and debug your program.

In some applications, multilinked structures are used: each node of these may contain several pointers. For example, the nodes of a doubly linked list have two pointers each: one points to the node's predecessor in the list and the other one to the node's successor. This symmetry provides, at the cost of maintaining additional pointers, greater flexibility of manipulation.

Nonlinear structures, such as trees and graphs, are in general multilinked. Trees are employed to represent such relationships as a hierarchy of data or the branching of a decision process. Graphs (networks) may represent any relationship among their nodes.

An example of a nonlinear structure is the **binary tree.** A binary tree is a set of nodes that is either empty or contains a root node and two binary trees coming from it called the left and right subtrees of the tree. This recursive definition describes structures such as that of Fig. 18–10.

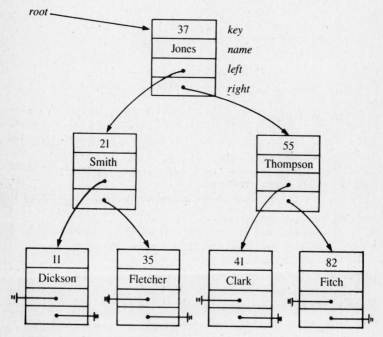

FIGURE 18–10. A binary tree.

The structure of Fig. 18–10 is a binary search tree, whose components are ordered (sorted) on the integer field *key*. Namely, for any node p, the key of every node in its left subtree is smaller than the key of p, and the key of every node in its right subtree is greater than the key of p. Once sorted into such a tree, records may be retrieved through a binary search (actually, binary tree search) much faster than by a sequential search of a linear list.

EXAMPLE 18–11

To define and declare the structure of Fig. 18–10, we may use these:

```
type
    treePointer =  ^treeNode;
    treeNode = record
                    key: integer;
                    name: packed array [1 .. 20] of char;
                    left, right: treePointer
               end;
var
    root: treePointer;
```

When processing a binary tree, a frequent operation is tree traversal: gaining access to every node once (for example, in order to print out the values stored there). Since a tree structure does not have an obvious sequential ordering of the nodes as a linear list does, several methods of such tree linearization exist. They are defined in a recursive fashion, which reflects the recursive nature of tree structures.

One of the traversal methods, *inorder* (symmetric order), is defined as follows:

(1) traverse the left subtree in inorder;
(2) access the root;
(3) traverse the right subtree in inorder.

This is further explicated by the following example.

EXAMPLE 18–12

Applying the inorder traversal algorithm recursively, we will find that we first access the leftmost node in the tree. If traversed in inorder, the tree of Fig. 18–10 will be linearized in this order of keys: 11, 21, 35, 37, 41, 55, 82. Note that this is the order in which the nodes have been sorted. The following recursive Pascal procedure implements the inorder traversal algorithm on the tree defined in Example 18–11. It is assumed that the purpose of the traversal is to write out the names stored in the nodes.

```
procedure inorder (current: treePointer);
        {traverse binary tree in inorder; current points to the root}
    begin {inorder}
        if current < > nil then
            with current ^ do
                begin
                    inorder (left);
                    writeln (name);
                    inorder (right)
                end
    end; {inorder}
```

F. VARIANT RECORDS AS REFERENCED VARIABLES[5]

The domain type of a pointer may be a record with a variant part (see Chapter 15–D). Different variants of such a record require, in general, different amounts of memory space.

If in order to create a new dynamic variable p ^, which is a variant record, we use a call

new (p);

then memory space will automatically be allocated for the largest variant of the record type.

In some programming situations, however, the variant to be created by the procedure new is known in advance and, moreover, it is known that the variant will remain fixed throughout the lifetime of the given dynamic variable. In such a case, the exact amount of memory needed can be allocated by using new with additional parameters.

The general form of such a call is:

new (p, c_1, . . . , c_n)
        $\underbrace{}$
        optional

where p is a pointer to a variant record; c_1, . . . , c_n are case constants specifying the desired variant of the record, as described later in this section.

If the variant part of the record is not nested, only c_1 needs to be specified. For nested variants, the selected case constants c_1, . . . , c_n are to be specified in order of increasing nesting of the variant parts, that is, from the outermost to the innermost. Specifications of the innermost (only!) variants may be left out, thus allowing for their variation.

---

5. May be omitted on first reading.

EXAMPLE 18–13

Let us assume we need to allocate dynamically a record of the type *reference,* as defined in Example 15–13 and extended in Example 15–14.

We will need these definitions and declaration:

type
    link = ^*reference;*
    reference = **record**
                     : }as in Examples 15–13 and 15–14
           end;
var
    first: link;

Then:

    new (first) creates a record which may be any of the variants;
    new (first, book) creates a record which must be that of a *book;*
    new (first, book, multiple) creates a record for a *book* of *multiple*
                              authors.

The specification of the desired variant in the call to *new* leads to significant memory savings in certain applications.

The following hold:

(1) The variant specified in the call of *new* may not be changed later in the program.
(2) The tag field value must be explicitly assigned in the program.
(3) A referenced variable created with the variant-specifying form of *new* may not be used in its entirety as an operand in an expression, assigned a value by an assignment statement, or serve as an actual parameter.

A variant record created through a call to *new* with variant specification may be deleted only by a call to *dispose* specifying the same number of case constants as parameters. The general form of such a call is:

dispose (p, $c_1, \ldots, c_m$)
             optional

The variable referenced by the pointer *p* must contain the variant specified by $c_1, \ldots, c_m$.

APPENDIX A.
PROGRAM/SUBPROGRAM
OUTLINE

Every program and subprogram of Pascal has the following general form:

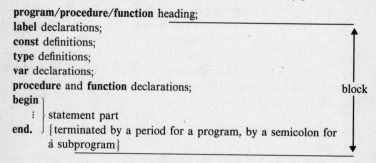

program/procedure/function heading;
label declarations;
const definitions;
type definitions;
var declarations;
procedure and **function** declarations;   block
begin
⋮   } statement part
end. } {terminated by a period for a program, by a semicolon for
          a subprogram}

APPENDIX B. RESERVED WORDS OF PASCAL

These are the reserved words of Pascal, which cannot be used as identifiers:

1. Word Symbols

and	do	function	nil	program	type
array	downto	goto	not	record	until
begin	else	if	of	repeat	var
case	end	in	or	set	while
const	file	label	packed	then	with
div	for	mod	procedure	to	

2. Directive

forward

APPENDIX C. CHARACTER CODES

Two character codes are commonly employed: the American Standard Code for Information Interchange (ASCII) and the Extended Binary Coded Decimal Interchange Code (EBCDIC).

In Tables C–1 and C–2, the characters that can be printed (displayed) are shown as represented in these binary codes.

TABLE C–1. Printable Characters in ASCII Code

	0	1	2	3	4	5	6	7	8	9	10	11	12	13	14	15
0																
16																
32	ƀ	!	″	#	$	%	&	′	(	)	*	+	,	–	.	/
48	0	1	2	3	4	5	6	7	8	9	:	;	<	=	>	?
64	@	A	B	C	D	E	F	G	H	I	J	K	L	M	N	O
80	P	Q	R	S	T	U	V	W	X	Y	Z	[	\	]	^	—
96	`	a	b	c	d	e	f	g	h	i	j	k	l	m	n	o
112	p	q	r	s	t	u	v	w	x	y	z	{	|	}	~	

TABLE C–2. Printable Characters in EBCDIC Code

	0	1	2	3	4	5	6	7	8	9	10	11	12	13	14	15
0																
16																
32																
48																
64	ƀ										¢	.	<	(	+	|
80	&										!	$	*	)	;	¬
96	−	/										,	%	_	>	?
112											:	#	@	'	=	"
128		a	b	c	d	e	f	g	h	i						
144		j	k	l	m	n	o	p	q	r						
160			s	t	u	v	w	x	y	z						
176																
192		A	B	C	D	E	F	G	H	I						
208		J	K	L	M	N	O	P	Q	R						
224			S	T	U	V	W	X	Y	Z						
240	0	1	2	3	4	5	6	7	8	9						

The ordinal number of a character in a given set is obtained by adding its row and column numbers. Thus, for example, in ASCII, "A" is represented by the binary equivalent of 64 + 1 = 65; in EBCDIC, "A" is represented by the binary equivalent of 192 + 1 = 193. In both tables, ƀ stands for the blank space.

SUGGESTIONS FOR FURTHER READING

To broaden your understanding of programming, software engineering, and programming languages, you may study:

Dijkstra, Edsger: **A Discipline of Programming,** Prentice-Hall, Englewood Cliffs, N.J., 1976.

Horowitz, Ellis: **Fundamentals of Programming Languages,** Computer Science Press, Rockville, Md., 1983.

Horowitz, Ellis, and Sahni, Sartaj: **Fundamentals of Computer Algorithms,** Computer Science Press, Rockville, Md., 1978.

Kernighan, Brian, and Ritchie, Dennis: **Software Tools in Pascal,** Addison-Wesley, Reading, Mass., 1981.

Knuth, Donald: **The Art of Computer Programming, Vol. 1: Fundamental Algorithms,** 2nd ed., Addison-Wesley, Reading, Mass., 1975.

Shneiderman, Ben: **Software Psychology,** Winthrop, Cambridge, Mass., 1980.

Shooman, Martin: **Software Engineering,** McGraw-Hill, New York, 1983.

Tenenbaum, Aaron, and Augenstein, Moshe: **Data Structures Using Pascal,** Prentice-Hall, Englewood Cliffs, N.J., 1981.

Weinberg, Gerald: **The Psychology of Computer Programming,** Van Nostrand Reinhold, New York, 1971.

Wirth, Niklaus, **Algorithms + Data Structures = Programs,** Prentice-Hall, Englewood Cliffs, N.J., 1976.

Yourdon, Edward, and Constantine, Larry: **Structured Design,** Prentice-Hall, Englewood Cliffs, N.J., 1979.

Zelkowitz, Marvin, Shaw, Alan, and Gannon, John: **Principles of Software Engineering and Design,** Prentice-Hall, Englewood Cliffs, N.J., 1979.

As a general introduction to computer systems and computer science, you may consider:

Zwass, Vladimir, **Introduction to Computer Science,** Barnes & Noble, New York, 1981.

The following book may serve as a source of a great variety of programming problems:

Maurer, H.A., and Williams, M.R., **A Collection of Programming Problems and Techniques,** Prentice-Hall, Englewood Cliffs, N.J., 1972.

INDEX

File, in systems, 5, 10, 271
  creation of, 10
  editing, 10
File update system, 285–286
for statement, 114
forward, 183
Function, 130, 162
  designator, 49, 164
  heading, 163
  ordinal, 71–73, 102
  purpose of, 162–163, 166
  required, *see* Function, standard
  standard, 48, 62, 72–73
  transfer, 50

get, 283
Global entities, 132
goto statement, 121

Hardware, 2
Heap, 303
Hiding of information, 148, 190
Higher-level languages, 7
Host type, 103

Identifier, 16–17
  scope, *see* Scope rules
if statement, 78
Implementation, 8–9
Indentation of programs, 55, 77,
  79, 132
Indexed variable, 200–201, 208
  see also **array**
Index of array, 194, 208
Indirect recursion, 182
in operator, 262
Inorder traversal, 319
Input, 33–37, 91–95, 103
input file, 16
Input/output devices, 5
Input termination
  with count, 92, 116
  with *eof, see eof*
  with sentinel, *see* Sentinel
Instruction, 2
Integer data, 28–29, 52–53

Interactive mode, 9–11, 39–40, 47,
  56
Interpreter, 7
Iteration, 85
  see also Repetition

Key, 231, 271, 285, 319

Label, 121–122
Library (of subprograms), 184
LIFO structure, *see* Stack
Linear list, 313, 317
Link, 302
  see also Pointer
Linked data structures, 301, 317
ln, 49
Loader, 8, 10
Local entities, 132
Localization of entities, 148–149
Location, in memory, 4
Loop structures
  for, 114
  repeat, 112
  while, 84–86
  see also Repetition
Loop body, 85

Machine language, 4, 6, 7
Main program, 127
maxint, 29
Memory, 3–5
  main, 3–5
  secondary, 3–5
mod, 43, 45
Modifiability of programs, 26, 127
  see also Readability of programs
Modular programming, 126–128,
  134–137, 160–161
Module, 126
  see also Function, Main
    program, Procedure

Nesting
  of blocks, *see* Scope rules
  of **if** statements, 80–83, 111
  of loops, 89, 117, 211
Network data structure, 313

new, 303, 320
nil, 302
Node, 299
   see also Dynamic variable
Nonlocal entities, 139
not, 64–66

Object program, 7
odd, 62
open, 277
Operating system, 6
Operators
   arithmetic, 43–45
   Boolean, 64–65
   relational, 63, 225, 262
   set, 264–265
   see also Precedence of operators
or, 64–66
ord, 73
Ordinal functions, *see* Function,
   ordinal
Ordinal number, 72, 102
Ordinal types, 71, 99
Output, 33, 52–55
   field, 52
output file, 16
Overflow, 48

pack, 217–218
packed, 193
   arrays, 216, 222, 234
   see also String
page, 54–55, 296
Parameter, 49, 151
   actual, 133, 152, 184
   formal, 131–132, 152, 184
   functional, 151, 185
   list, 151–153, 185
   procedural, 151, 184
   value, 151, 153–155
   variable, 151, 156–158
   see also Conformant array
   parameters, Program
   parameters
Parentheses, 45–46, 65

Pascal, XI, XII, 7–9
   see also Standard Pascal
Pascal, Blaise, XI
Pointer, 299–300, 306, 310
Portability, 7
Positional notation, 29–31, 53–54
Precedence of operators, 45, 65,
   262
Precision, 30, 48
pred, 72–73
Predicate, 62
Prime number generation, *see* Sieve
   of Eratosthenes
Procedure, 130
   heading, 131
   statement, 133
   see also Call, Parameter,
   Recursion
Production program, 26
Program, 2
   block, 15–16, 18
   clarity, 23
   heading, 15–16
   parameters, 16, 273
   template, 138, 322
program, 16, 273
Programming, XI, XII, 5, 14,
   22–26, 56–57
   see also Analysis of problems,
   Design of programs
Programming languages, 5
Prompting, 39
Pseudocode, 23, 56, 76
Pseudorandom numbers, *see*
   Random number generation
put, 279

Queue, 316

Random access, 203
Random number generation,
   167–168
Range of numeric values, 29, 30,
   48
read, 35–36, 91–95, 281–282

true, 60–61
trunc, 50
type, 100
  denoter, 197
  see also Assignment
    compatibility, Compatibility of
    operands, Data type

UCSD Pascal, 9, 222
unpack, 217–218
Utilities, 6

var, 33, 61, 69, 156
Variable, 32–33, 42

Variable *(cont.)*
  dynamic, 299, 304
  static, 298
Variable-access, 193
Variant record, 249, 320

while statement, 84–86
Wirth, Niklaus, XI
with statement, 238
Word, 4
Word processing, 68
Word symbol, 17, 323
write, 37–38, 278
writeln, 37–38, 295

About the author

Vladimir Zwass received his Ph.D. in computer science from Columbia University in 1975. He is currently professor of computer science and chairman of the Computer Science Committee at Fairleigh Dickinson University. He was previously a member of the professional staff of the International Atomic Energy Agency in Vienna, Austria. As a consultant, he has advised, among other companies, Citicorp, Metropolitan Life Insurance Company, and The Diebold Group.

Professor Zwass is the author of **Introduction to Computer Science** and **Programming in FORTRAN,** companion volumes in the Barnes & Noble Outline Series, and has contributed to professional journals. He is the editor-in-chief of the **Journal of Management Information Systems.** Professor Zwass is a member of the Association for Computing Machinery, IEEE, Sigma Xi and Eta Kappa Nu.